Praise for *Catalyzing Innovations for a Sustainable Future*

"The world's innovation landscape is rapidly changing. Singapore Airlines' new start-up-style internal incubator *KrisLab*, Tencent's multipurpose messaging, social media and mobile payment app *WeChat*, or Indonesia's technology unicorn *Gojek* underscore Asia's growing innovation potential. Beyond any doubt, innovation will be a major driver of future economic growth in the region. In a world marked by disruptive innovation and unsustainable business practices, there is an urgent need for corporate innovators to manage effectively sustainable value creation and value capture to seize the multiple opportunities associated with economic, environmental, and social developments. To meet these challenges, several innovation management capabilities are required — ranging from the development of new business ideas and models to mastering digital tools and successfully delivering one's unique value proposition to local and international customers. This new book by Thomas Menkhoff skilfully addresses key innovation challenges and outlines what business leaders can do to overcome them with regard to innovation strategy, people & organisational culture, innovation processes, knowledge & learning, as well as innovation governance. The book also features three interesting case studies: Singapore Airlines, National Library Board, and Qian Hu. They will help the reader to appreciate and comprehend how these budding innovation award winners managed to overcome innovation barriers in order to foster and sustain their competitiveness."

Arnoud DE MEYER

University Professor
Lee Kong Chian School of Business
Singapore Management University (SMU)

"The COVID-19 pandemic continues to disrupt both small and big businesses in unanticipated ways. The search is on for new and more sustainable business models aimed at creating, delivering, and capturing value. To effectively deal with contemporary VUCA (short for volatility, uncertainty, complexity, and ambiguity) challenges requires competent responses from business leaders such as asking questions that challenge common wisdom, risk taking, or active experimentation by testing new ideas via prototypes and launching pilots. What distinguishes innovation *leaders* from mediocre managers is the capability to recognize and exploit new entrepreneurial opportunities. Whether one categorises this competency as 'Entrepreneurial Leadership', 'Transformational Leadership', or 'Innovation Leadership' is for academics to debate. What matters in terms of successful innovation practice is that innovation leaders facilitate the entire innovation process from strategic ideation to bringing newly created products and services to market. This book competently demonstrates the full potential of effective innovation governance and outlines what Innovation Leaders need to know and do in order to make innovation work."

Howard THOMAS
Professor Emeritus of Strategic Management
and Management Education
Singapore Management University (SMU)

CATALYZING
INNOVATIONS
FOR A SUSTAINABLE FUTURE
Bite-Sized Commentaries
and Resource Materials

CATALYZING
INNOVATIONS
FOR A SUSTAINABLE FUTURE
Bite-Sized Commentaries
and Resource Materials

Thomas Menkhoff
Singapore Management University, Singapore

World Scientific

NEW JERSEY · LONDON · SINGAPORE · BEIJING · SHANGHAI · HONG KONG · TAIPEI · CHENNAI · TOKYO

Published by

World Scientific Publishing Co. Pte. Ltd.

5 Toh Tuck Link, Singapore 596224

USA office: 27 Warren Street, Suite 401-402, Hackensack, NJ 07601

UK office: 57 Shelton Street, Covent Garden, London WC2H 9HE

Library of Congress Control Number: 2021907611

British Library Cataloguing-in-Publication Data
A catalogue record for this book is available from the British Library.

CATALYZING INNOVATIONS FOR A SUSTAINABLE FUTURE:
BITE-SIZED COMMENTARIES AND RESOURCE MATERIALS

ISBN 978-981-123-891-8 (hardcover)
ISBN 978-981-123-892-5 (ebook for institutions)
ISBN 978-981-123-893-2 (ebook for individuals)

For any available supplementary material, please visit
https://www.worldscientific.com/worldscibooks/10.1142/12333#t=suppl

Desk Editors: Balamurugan Rajendran/Laul Bhakti/Sylvia Koh

Typeset by Stallion Press
Email: enquiries@stallionpress.com

Printed in Singapore

Foreword

For many businesses, the COVID-19 pandemic has turned out to be an enormous disruptor, challenging traditional organizational habits, working patterns, and ways of living. The pandemic has prompted the search for more sustainable business models and demonstrated the criticality of strong environmental, social, and corporate governance (ESG). It has also triggered greater concerns for sustained innovativeness aimed at continuous value creation and value capture in support of strategic transformation and new growth strategies.

Further, the COVID-19 disruption has shown the benefits of associational thinking, that is, connecting the dots between questions, problems, or ideas from unrelated fields and collaborative innovation to create more resilient and self-sustaining business models. In a way, this is not new: every crisis creates opportunities, and the survivors have been able to adapt and meet the market's need when such changes happen.

I have had the chance to live through several major crises in my working life. Starting with my first job, experiencing the oil crisis of the 1970s, and, during my time with Eu Yan Sang, seeing the Asian Financial crisis and the dot com boom and bust in the late 1990s, the SARS outbreak of the early 2000s, the Global Financial Crisis of 2008, and now COVID-19. It is astounding to think that we still have to learn new ways of dealing with disruption each time.

Of course, with passing time, we now have the benefit of technology and better knowledge. To seize new opportunities for growth arising from the current crisis requires several urgent actions such as corroborating the foundation of a firm's innovation management framework, rebalancing corporate innovation portfolios, digitizing go-to-market models such as digital direct-to-consumer channels, and so on.

This new book by Thomas Menkhoff shows how to make innovation work by creating and capturing new value to achieve a sustainable future. The bite-sized commentaries on innovation management and governance are structured with regards to Leadership & Strategy, People & Organisational Culture, Innovation Processes, Knowledge & Learning, and Innovation Governance. With the help of three illuminating case studies of innovation award winners, viz Singapore Airlines, National Library Board Singapore, and Qian Hu Corporation Ltd, this timely resource book demystifies leading innovators' building blocks and explains what it takes to stay innovative.

Richard Eu Yee Ming
Chairman of Eu Yan Sang International Ltd

About the Author

Thomas Menkhoff is Professor of Organisational Behaviour & Human Resources (Education) at the Lee Kong Chian School of Business, Singapore Management University (SMU), which he joined in 2001.

Between 2013 and 2018, he served as Academic Director of SMU's Master of Science in Innovation Programme.

An award-winning educator, Dr. Menkhoff has published numerous articles in scholarly journals and several books on the socio-cultural dimensions of managing knowledge transfer, innovation, and change in multi-cultural contexts and Asian entrepreneurship.

Three of his recent publications are as follows: (i) Thomas Menkhoff, Chay Yue Wah, Hans-Dieter Evers, and Hoon Chang Yau (eds.) 2014, *Catalyst for Change — Chinese Business in Asia*, New Jersey: World Scientific Publishing; (ii) Thomas Menkhoff, Kan Siew Ning, Hans-Dieter Evers, and Chay Yue Wah (eds.) 2018, *Living in Smart Cities: Innovation and Sustainability*, New Jersey: World Scientific Publishing; and (iii) Chay Yue Wah, Thomas Menkhoff, and Linda Low (eds.) 2020, *China's Belt and Road Initiative — Understanding the Dynamics of a Global Transformation*, New Jersey: World Scientific Publishing.

His current research interests centre on sustainable innovation at ("smart") city and corporate levels; technology-enhanced learning; and Industry 4.0 adoption by Asian SMEs.

Dr. Menkhoff has served (among others) as consultant to the German Agency of Technical Cooperation (GTZ/GIZ), the Government of Singapore, the Singapore University of Social Sciences (SUSS),

Design Singapore Council, Mahidol University (Bangkok/Thailand), the Commonwealth Secretariat, Arthur D. Little, Asian Productivity Organization (APO), the World Bank, the Asian Development Bank (ADB), the Government of Malaysia, and various small and big private sector firms.

He has formerly taught at the National University of Singapore (NUS), the University of Cologne, and the University of Bielefeld in Germany. In 2009, Dr. Menkhoff was the recipient of SMU's university-wide "Most Innovative Teacher Award". In 2017, he was awarded the SMU Faculty/Staff Contribution to Student Life Award (Individual).

About the Contributors

Chay Yue Wah is an Associate Professor, School of Human Development and Social Services, Singapore University of Social Sciences. He has held various faculty and administrative appointments at the National University of Singapore (NUS), Singapore Management University (SMU), Nanyang Technological University (NTU), and SIM University (UniSIM). A psychologist by training, Dr Chay has published in the areas of entrepreneurship, work commitment, citizenship behaviour and expatriation. His current research interests are focused on smart cities, knowledge systems, innovation and maritime ports. Email: ywchay@suss.edu.sg.

Jennifer Chong is an Entrepreneur and Designer behind Linjer, a brand selling high quality accessories without the luxury markup. She studied economics and design thinking at Dartmouth College. Website: www.linjer.co.

Mark Chong is Associate Professor of Communication Management (Practice) at Singapore Management University (SMU). An award-winning teacher, he is the co-author of the books *Living the Corporate Purpose: Insights from Companies in Asia* (World Scientific Publishing), *Brainfruit: Turning Creativity into Cash from East to West* (McGraw-Hill), and *Winning Corporate Reputation Strategies* (McGraw-Hill). Mark received his PhD from Cornell University. Prior to joining academia, Dr Chong worked for close to a decade in both corporate and consulting roles. Email: markchong@smu.edu.sg.

Benjamin Kok Siew Gan is an Associate Professor of Information System (Education) at the Singapore Management University (SMU). Dr Gan received his PhD degree in Computer Science from the University of Iowa. He has more than 24 years of teaching experience. His research interests include effective learning activities, project-based learning, capstone courses, interaction design, technopreneurship study missions, and supply chain analytics. He has published widely in education and learning-related journals. He is the recipient of the National Day Award Public Administration Bronze Medal and the SPRING Singapore Quality and Standards Merit Award, Singapore. Email: benjamingan@smu.edu.sg.

Loizos Heracleous is Professor of Strategy at the Warwick Business School, and Associate Fellow of Green Templeton College and the Said Business School at Oxford University. His work on strategic management, discourse conceptualisation and analysis as well as organisation change has been published in leading journals including the *Academy of Management Journal, Academy of Management Review, MIS Quarterly, Strategic Management Journal, Journal of Management Studies, Organization Studies, Human Relations, Harvard Business Review*, and *MIT Sloan Management Review*. More information about Dr Heracleous can be found on www.heracleous.org. His Twitter feed is @Strategizing. Email: Loizos.Heracleous@wbs.ac.uk.

Kan Siew Ning worked 27 years for the Singapore Government in various capacities; his last appointment was as Director, Police Technology Department from 2004 to 2011. He has taught part-time in various universities including SMU, NTU, NUS and SIT. He was a former President of iKMS (Information & Knowledge Management Society), has published a book, *Practical Knowledge Management* and is co-editor of two other books. Email: siewningkan@smu.edu.sg.

Alex Koh is a junior at Lee Kong Chian School of Business at SMU, majoring in Finance. He is a recipient of the Global Impact Scholarship Award, SMU's flagship scholarship award. In his free time, he likes to read, travel, and play sports. He is also active in community service, having led a 24-strong team to Jaipur, India, in 2019.

Natasha Lian is a second year undergraduate at the Lee Kong Chian School of business and a recipient of SMU's Global Impact Scholarship

Award. As a student, she explores her interests in emerging countries & the global economy through her time as a Research Associate at SMU Emerging Markets. She enjoys photography, swimming, and reading about anthropology, the history of Asia, and the future of the world around her.

Jacie Lim is a second-year law undergraduate at SMU and a recipient of SMU's Global Impact Scholarship Award. She finds significance in improving society and changing lives one step at a time. To this end, she loves serving the community and is widely engaged in many pro bono activities.

Neo Kin Kah is an Adjunct Lecturer at Singapore Management University (SMU), University of Stirling and University of Newcastle (AUS). He is also an entrepreneur and founder of two companies. Dr Neo has worked in management positions in various MNCs. His research interests are entrepreneurship and entrepreneurial leadership. Email: kkneo@smu.edu.sg.

Ong Geok Chwee is a Senior Executive in the telecommunications industry with extensive experience in managing the incubation, development and launch of new technologies and businesses in the enterprise sector. Dr Ong holds a Bachelor of Electrical Engineering from the National University of Singapore, a Master of Business Administration from the University of Bradford, United Kingdom and a Doctor of Innovation from Singapore Management University. Email: Geokchwee@Gmail.com.

Jonas Schorr is Co-Founder of Urban Impact, a Berlin-based agency that helps urban tech/smart city start-ups to grow their impact faster and better across Europe. Jonas spent the last ten years working on a variety of international projects in the field of sustainable cities, including the initial development and coordination of the USE platform (previously called Policy Transfer Platform). Email: jonas@urbanimpact.eu.

Seah Yi Shan is a sophomore pursuing degrees in Business and Social Sciences. She is a recipient of SMU's Global Impact Scholarship Award. Yi Shan enjoys being able to play a little part in creating social impact, and does so through engaging in pro bono consulting projects and on the ground volunteering.

Frank Siegfried is Director at Management Consulting firm Black Moon Pte. Ltd., specialised in conceptualizing and deploying sustainable strategies, complex transformations, data-driven business models and value propositions to accelerate growth, enhance efficiencies, convert ideas into opportunities and lead turnaround or post-M&A projects across industries. As a former early-stage Venture Capital investor, Dr Siegfried has deep expertise in commercializing emerging technologies, raising funds and mentoring start-ups/spin-off teams. Frank is an associate faculty at Singapore Management University, the National University of Singapore and Manchester Business School, teaching at Master/MBA level. Email: frank.siegfried@blackmoon.com.sg.

Eugene K. B. Tan is Associate Professor of Law and Lee Kong Chian Fellow at the School of Law, Singapore Management University. Dr Tan's inter-disciplinary research interests include constitutional and administrative law, law and public policy, the government and politics of Singapore, the regulation of ethnic conflict, business ethics and corporate responsibility, and the ethical and policy framework on artificial intelligence. Email: eugene@smu.edu.sg.

Alex Teo Hong Hak is a Business Improvement Specialist of the Office of Business Improvement at Singapore Management University. He works with schools and administration offices to identify and improve business processes. Alex has more than 12 years of experience in continuous improvement projects across the manufacturing and education industries. Majority of the projects involve multiple functions and the use of Lean, Six Sigma, and Design Thinking methods. Alex is a Certified Six Sigma Black Belt and Lean Practitioner. He graduated with honours from the National University of Singapore with a degree in Mechanical Engineering and also holds a Masters of Science in Mechanical Engineering from National University of Singapore and a Masters of Science in Finance from University College Dublin, Ireland. Email: alexteo@smu.edu.sg.

Sven Tuzovic is Senior Lecturer at the School of Advertising, Marketing and Public Relations, Queensland University of Technology, Brisbane, Australia. Prior to joining QUT, Dr Tuzovic was Associate Professor at the Business School of Pacific Lutheran University, Tacoma, WA, USA. He has been a Visiting Professor at Griffith University, Murray State

University, and the University of New Orleans. In 2014 he joined Leo Burnett in Chicago as a participant in the Advertising Educational Foundation's (AEF) Visiting Professor Program (VPP), a two-week fellowship to expose selected professors to the day-to-day operations of a global advertising agency. Dr Tuzovic is currently Associate Editor of the Journal of Services Marketing. Email: sven.tuzovic@qut.edu.au.

Jochen Wirtz is Vice Dean, Graduate Studies and Professor of Marketing at the NUS Business School, National University of Singapore. Dr. Wirtz has published over 200 academic articles, book chapters and industry reports, including 6 features in Harvard Business Review. His over 10 books include *Services Marketing: People, Technology, Strategy* (World Scientific, 8th edition, 2016), Essentials in Services Marketing (Pearson Education, 3rd edition, 2018, and *Winning in Service Markets* (World Scientific, 2017). For free downloads of his recent work and selected books see ResearchGate (https://www.researchgate.net/profile/Jochen_Wirtz) and follow his work on LinkedIn (https://www.linkedin.com/in/jochenwirtz). Email: jochen@nus.edu.sg.

Sarah Woon is a second-year SMU Information Systems student majoring in Cybersecurity and a recipient of SMU's Global Impact Scholarship Award. She is a strong proponent for the application of technology in humanitarian work and disaster response. Outside of school, Sarah enjoys reading, dancing and travelling.

Contents

Chapter 1

Introduction: Catalyzing Innovations for a Sustainable Future

Making Innovation Work is Critical in an Era of Climate Change

As a consequence of the Paris Agreement on Climate Change, ASEAN countries such as Singapore are rolling out new climate mitigation initiatives in order to curb CO_2 emissions. A recent example is the US$5 billion Coastal and Flood Protection fund to tackle the risk of rising sea levels as announced by DPM Heng during the 2020 budget speech. Singapore plans to build dykes and polders at low-lying coastal areas in anticipation of rising sea levels, a national challenge that is estimated to cost about US$100 billion or more over the next 100 years.

Singapore's Housing and Development Board (HDB) has initiated and showcased several "citizen-centric" solutions with regard to issues such as urban heat (planted rooftops), mobility (installation of cycling racks in void decks) or air pollutants emitted by fossil fuels (solar installations on rooftops). An example is the HDB Greenprint programme piloted at Yuhua estate in Jurong which was aimed at transforming 38 blocks of flats into a "Green Neighbourhood".

HDB's Greenprint Programme

"With increasing global warming and rising sea levels, it is important that everyone joins in to protect the environment. To ensure that Singapore can remain a great place for current and future generations to live in, we are bringing sustainable living into existing HDB estates with the HDB Greenprint, part of our 'Roadmap to Better Living in HDB Towns'. The HDB Greenprint is a comprehensive and integrated framework of goals and strategies to guide greener HDB town development, and create sustainable homes. In the Greenprint framework, we extend the concept of green and sustainable lifestyles beyond Punggol, to build Green Neighbourhoods, Green Flats, and Green Communities. The HDB Greenprint was first piloted at Yuhua estate in Jurong, where 38 blocks of flats have been transformed into a 'Green Neighbourhood'. Launched in 2012, the pilot HDB Greenprint programme in Yuhua aimed to bring energy-efficient, water management, and waste management features into this estate. It has since been completed …".[1]

While more can be done, such measures underscore the urgency of global climate change action as reflected in SDG (UN Sustainable Development Goal) 13 which calls for international cooperation "in building resilience and adaptive capacity to its adverse effects, developing sustainable low-carbon pathways to the future, and accelerating the reduction of global greenhouse gas emissions".

Examples of climate actions include: (i) stepped-up efforts to reduce greenhouse gas emissions; (ii) strengthening resilience and adaptive capacity to climate-induced impacts such as climate-related hazards; (iii) integrating climate change measures into national policies, strategies and planning; and (iv) improving education, awareness-raising and human and institutional capacity with respect to climate change mitigation, adaptation, impact reduction and early warning.

Climate change effects include: (i) the displacement of about 21 million people by climate or weather-related events each year since 2008 according to the UN High Commissioner for Refugees; (ii) shortfalls of agricultural yields due to poor harvests of maize, wheat and other major

---

[1] https://www.hdb.gov.sg/cs/infoweb/about-us/our-role/smart-and-sustainable-living/hdb-greenprint.

SDG Goal 13: Take Urgent Action to Combat Climate Change and its Impacts

Targets

- Strengthen resilience and adaptive capacity to climate-related hazards and natural disasters in all countries.
- Integrate climate change measures into national policies, strategies and planning.
- Improve education, awareness-raising and human and institutional capacity on climate change mitigation, adaptation, impact reduction and early warning.
- Implement the commitment undertaken by developed-country parties to the United Nations Framework Convention on Climate Change to a goal of mobilizing jointly US$100 billion annually by 2020 from all sources to address the needs of developing countries in the context of meaningful mitigation actions and transparency on implementation and fully operationalize the Green Climate Fund through its capitalization as soon as possible.
- Promote mechanisms for raising capacity for effective climate change-related planning and management in least developed countries and small island developing States, including focusing on women, youth and local and marginalized communities.[2]

---

staple crops; and (iii) substantial adaptation costs ranging between US$140–300 billion per year by 2030 based on estimates of the UN Environment's Adaptation Finance Gap Report (2016).[2]

While we could continue discussing the need for urgent climate action, it is important to note that this reader doesn't focus on climate change matters. One reason why we featured the climate crisis at the beginning of this reader is because the climate crisis shows how important it is to catalyze innovations.

A local example is PUB's "Sustainable Singapore Gallery"[3] which showcases both the issues pertaining to sustainability as well as the policy measures adopted by the Singapore Government to manage it, such as mitigating the effects of urban heat or managing e-waste. The meticulously curated exhibits and learning stations enable visitors to understand

---

[2] https://www.un.org/development/desa/disabilities/envision2030-goal13.html.
[3] https://www.pub.gov.sg/marinabarrage/ssg.

the importance of technology in dealing with urban challenges such as water scarcity, global warming, pollution or waste management. A major takeaway from the Sustainable Singapore Gallery visit complemented by a tour of the Marina Barrage (a dam built across the 350-metre wide Marina Channel to create a freshwater lake aimed at boosting Singapore's water supply and to prevent flooding in low-lying city areas) is the insight of how fragile Singapore actually is, e.g. in terms of water, climate, waste and energy sustainability, and that Singapore continues to come up with innovative solutions that can help to tackle urban problems ranging from smart flood control systems to smart energy grids.

Creating Value through Innovation

The term *innovation* refers to the implementation of a new or significantly improved product, service or process that meets/exceeds customers' needs at an affordable price. Examples include autonomous cars, predictive marketing methods (social media), cloud-based business practices, crowdsourcing etc. The term is derived from the Latin words *novus* ("new") and *innovatio* ("something newly created"). Innovation implies change and risks: innovations can range from small incremental improvements such as Nabisco's extension of the Oreo product line to radical breakthroughs such as the reusable SpaceX rockets. Invention forms part of the innovation process but the latter goes far beyond invention because it embraces successful commercialisation. Without value creation and value capture, innovations cannot be sustainable (see Table 1).

In 2010, communications expert Carmine Gallo published a book titled *The Innovation Secrets of Steve Jobs*, summarising the core

Table 1:   Forms and Types of Innovation

Forms of Innovation (Examples)	Types of Innovation (Examples)
Product innovations	**Radical innovation**
Dyson's bagless vacuum cleaner	Flat-screen TV with new LCD technology
Service innovations	**Architectural innovation**
No frills airlines	Sony Walkman (reconfiguration of
Process innovations	existing components in a new way)
Transacting business online	**Incremental innovation**
Business model innovation	iPod Mini/Nano
Digital banking	

principles of the business thinking of Mr Jobs, who was the co-founder and CEO of Apple, and what others can learn from this great innovator. One (common-sense) principle put forward by Mr Gallo is "Create Insanely Great Experiences".

Apple managed to do that in different ways, including the "cool" design of its stores where customers are served by product experts rather than insufficiently trained service staff with poor attitudes. Comparing the Apple way with service standards in Asia, one may argue that we still have a long way to go before we can claim to be experts in enriching the lives of customers innovatively.

Much has been written about the enablers of innovation which refers to the implementation of a new or significantly improved service, product or business processes that exceed customers' needs at an affordable price. Two key enablers include the ability to mitigate pain points of customers and to ensure that they experience pleasure.

Everyday pain points such as having to deal with cramped space situations at home when trying to dry a load of washed clothing or long queues in banks or at taxi stands indicate that Mr Jobs' common-sense principle of "creating insanely great experiences" is not commonly practised here despite the fact that Singapore is among the most innovative countries on planet Earth according to the Global Innovation Index, co-published by Cornell University, INSEAD and the World Intellectual Property Organization (WIPO).

One possible reason for this shortcoming is the lack of conceptual understanding of both the principles and action steps of effective innovation management in business, entrepreneurship, creative arts, construction or social enterprises.

While innovation processes are seldom linear, four inter-related phases or main activities of the innovation value chain can be differentiated (Table 2).

Strategic Idea and Concept Development is characterised by searching for the strategic intent and value-added innovation needs triggered by the constantly changing ecosystem in which the organisation is embedded.

Once there is clarity about the overall strategic direction of the innovation efforts, the stage of idea generation or ideation management kicks in to systematically gather, share, analyse and execute on innovative ideas generated within the organisation and its collaborative networks.

After ideas have been ranked, conceptualised and their feasibility assessed, they need to be turned into viable business models and aligned

Table 2:   Phases of the Innovation Value Chain

Strategic Idea & Concept Development	Development of Innovative Products, Services, Processes & Business Cases	Market Launch & Successful Commercialisation	Managing Risk, Sustainable Growth & Value Extraction
Opportunity recognition & Ideation management	Organizational aspects of making innovation work	Managing service innovations	Business acceleration & Growth strategy (scaling)
Turning concepts into business cases (Innovation Development)	Managing technology innovation	Value selling as driver of business growth	Intellectual property management and value extraction

with the business models of partners. We refer to this second idea conversion phase as *Development of Innovative Products, Services, Processes & Business Cases.*

The main objective of the third phase is the successful implementation of the innovation. This includes prototype production, testing and validation, production, finance, market launch, roll-out management, Sales management etc. This stage is categorised as *Market Launch and Successful Commercialisation.*

The "final" phase *Managing Risk, Sustainable Growth and Value Extraction* puts emphasis on the business acceleration aspect of innovation management, sustainable growth and continuous value extraction.

Across all stages of the innovation value chain, innovation managers play a crucial role in making innovation work. Table 3 features some of the key managerial tasks during the innovation management process, ranging from idea generation and idea evaluation to the intricacies of innovation project management.

While these tasks may not look very daunting, many organisations find it difficult to make innovation work. Reasons include lack of high quality ideas, insufficient screening of relevant ideas or budgetary constraints. Management gurus Morten T. Hansen and Julian Birkinshaw (2007) have systematised these challenges with regard to *idea-poor, conversion-poor* and *diffusion-poor* organisations as summarized in Table 4.

Hansen and Birkinshaw (2007) distinguish between three types of organisational innovation management challenges: (i) "idea-poor organisations" fail to create a climate where internal or externally-sourced, "sound ideas" can be nurtured; (ii) "conversion-poor organisations" lack

Table 3: The Innovation Management Process

Idea Generation		Idea Evaluation	Innovation Project Management	
Strategic Innovation Areas	Championing Ideas	Ideation (Cont'd)/ Design Thinking	Concepts	Innovation Project Management
Identify key innovation needs of the organization.	Ensure that the ideas generated are aligned with sponsor-led opportunities and problems.	Generate ideas, insights and potential solutions to "pain points".	Turn top ideas (and challenges) into concepts.	Develop a "phase/stage gate" process with steps to monitor the transformation of concepts into concrete innovation project activities with milestones, metrics (e.g. financials), risk matrix etc.
Agree on the most important strategic targets (growth, quality, efficiency, customer satisfaction).	Connect sponsors with the "right" (wise) crowd and vice versa.	Capture problems, (bad) customer experiences etc.	Develop deeper business cases to ascertain the feasibility of turning selected (top) concepts into viable business outcomes.	
Discuss: Where can we make the most difference/create the most value?		Prioritise ideas that are aligned with sponsor's requirements.		
		Vote and select top ideas for further advancement.		

Table 4:   Issues and Remedies of Idea-Poor, Conversion-Poor and Diffusion-Poor Organisations

Type of Organisation	Issue(s) and Remedies
Idea-poor organisations do not promote internal or externally-sourced, sound ideas.	• Building external networks and improve internal cross-unit networks • Creating portfolios with "high quality" ideas
Conversion-poor organisations do not screen or develop ideas properly.	• Implementing proper screening processes (stage-gate approach) • Knowing how to get buy-in for funding radical ideas
Diffusion-poor organisations find it difficult to monetise good ideas.	• Promoting idea evangelists to increase awareness internally and promote ideas to customers • Creating "safe havens" to shield good ideas from budget constraints and short-term thinking

Source: Morten T. Hansen and Julian Birkinshaw (2007). The Innovation Value Chain, Harvard Business Review (June Issue).

a screening system that would allow ideas to be converted into prototypes; while (iii) "diffusion-poor organisations" find it difficult to scale (see Table 4).

In many organisations, tight budgets, risk-averse thinking, and formal bureaucratic procedures grind execution to a halt. Attempts to build a culture of innovation often amount to little more than innovation theatre, despite top management's best intentions.

While there are numerous innovative organisations here which have mastered the management of the innovation value chain such as Singapore Airlines, Qian Hu or DBS, there is no doubt that Singapore's potential for innovation can be further harnessed if one considers the hundreds of small and medium-sized enterprises (SMEs) which do not make use of official enterprise development schemes.

One reason is arguably the difficulty in practising what is common sense elsewhere, namely the systematic integration of stakeholders into innovation planning activities. The *open-innovation approach* does not only characterise the innovation frameworks of big multinational companies such as the US giant, IBM or Germany's skin-care leader, Beiersdorf; it can also be a key competitive differentiator for SMEs operating in volatile business environments whether in manufacturing or services.

An interesting example from the world of finance is Fidor Bank[4], an innovative German social banking enterprise which leverages Web 2.0. Customers sign on to the platform through Facebook Connect, can see all of their accounts on one page and are able to influence the bank's interest rate on savings by the number of likes on their Facebook page. Crowdsourcing is also integrated into the bank's business model.

It proactively leverages its user community to enable peer-to-peer support, sharing of experiences and cooperation in order to tackle all sorts of financial issues. Innovators such as Fidor's Co-Founder Matthias Kroener do challenge the status quo through their queries, constantly observe the ecosystem in which they operate (customers, services, products, technologies, firms) to generate ideas for new ways of doing things (and easing pain!), network with a very diverse group of people to get feedback for ideas, constantly pilot new ideas and frequently visit new places to get inspired.

While it takes time to master transformational business model innovation processes, rapid change "out there" suggests that a change in mindset is imperative. A "wait and see" attitude will do more harm than good as the failures of Rollei Singapore, Kodak, Sony, Borders etc., have shown.

While denial and ignorance will persist, the good news is that more and more enterprise development agencies and tertiary education institutions are rolling out support schemes and competency development programmes in order to enhance innovation management capabilities in business and society. Such programmes provide a great launch platform for innovators eager to "create insanely great experiences" for customers and to avoid disruption by competitors. One example is the Business Excellence initiative of Enterprise Singapore.

Making Innovation Work

Enterprise Singapore is a government agency championing enterprise development[5] under the Ministry of Trade and Industry. Its *Business Excellence (BE) Framework* helps companies build their business

---

[4]https://www.fidor.de/.
[5]https://www.enterprisesg.gov.sg.

capabilities, improve their organisational strengths and identify areas for improvement. The BE initiative was launched in Singapore in 1994 to help organisations assess which stage they are at on the excellence journey and what they need to do to achieve a higher level of performance. This is done by an assessment of organisational performance against the requirements of the BE framework which provides a holistic standard that covers all critical drivers and results for business excellence. It illustrates the cause and effect relationships between the drivers of performance, what the organisation does, and the results it achieves. It covers the following areas as indicated in Figure 1.

The organisational profile sets the context for the way the organisation operates and serves as an overarching guide for how the framework is applied. So-called "attributes of excellence" describe key characteristics of high performing organisations and are embedded throughout all critical drivers of the framework. These are: 1. Leading with Vision and Integrity, 2. Creating Value for Customers, 3. Driving Innovation and Productivity, 4. Developing Organisational Capability, 5. Valuing People and Partners, 6. Managing with Agility, 7. Sustaining Outstanding Results, 8. Adopting an Integrated Perspective, and 9. Anticipating the Future.

Together, the organisational profile and the attributes of excellence form the context and foundation that encapsulate the entire framework as shown in Figure 1. To achieve excellence, an organisation needs strong

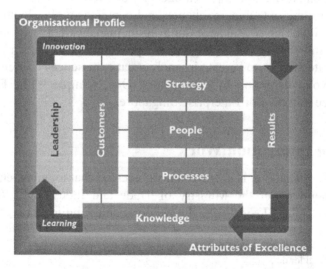

Figure 1:   Areas Covered by the Business Excellence Framework

"leadership" to drive the mind-set of excellence and to set a clear strategic direction. "Customer-centricity" is positioned after leadership to demonstrate the focus on anticipating customer needs and creating value for them. "Strategy" is developed based on understanding internal and external stakeholder requirements to guide "people" and "process capabilities" required to drive desired "results". To sustain excellent performance, organisations need to continually learn, improve and innovate. Continuous learning and innovation is demonstrated through acquiring "knowledge" from the lessons learned and the measurement of results, and using them in a closed feedback loop to support decision-making and drive improvements.

The *Singapore Innovation Class* is one of four standards and certification programmes based on the BE framework interested companies can choose from (based on the same seven dimensions of excellence, namely, Leadership, Planning, Information, People, Processes, Customers, and Results). Singapore Innovation Class (I-Class) offers certification for business excellence in innovation aimed at helping organisations to develop their innovation management capabilities.

Launched in 2001, the Innovation Excellence Award (I-Award) recognises organisations for outstanding innovation management capabilities resulting in breakthrough or impactful innovations observed in areas such as business models, processes, and products and services. More details about the Business Excellence Niche Standard (InnoVation), which features an "Innovation Scorecard for Business Excellence (I-Score)", can be found on the website of Enterprise Singapore.[6]

Catalyzing Innovations for a Sustainable Future: Bite-Sized Commentaries and Revelations

This reader contains several "op-eds" (op-ed = short for "opposite the editorial page") on innovation and urban sustainability matters written between 2012 and 2021[7] aimed at providing interested readers with

---

[6]https://www.enterprisesg.gov.sg.
[7]The author is grateful to Singapore Press Holdings (SPH) for allowing him to reproduce these articles (previously published in The Straits Times, The Business Times, Lianhe Zaobao and Tabla) in his book.

deeper insights into some of the enablers of effective innovation management and selected dimensions of "smart" cities.

The bite-sized commentaries on innovation presented in the following are loosely structured with regards to the business excellence (BE) initiative of Enterprise Singapore — which we regard as a useful tool to develop a governance system for innovation. Key BE categories include Leadership, Strategy, People, Processes, Knowledge, and Governance.

We added some **case materials** on selected aspects of innovation management and sustainable smart cities such as the remarkable innovation stories of Singapore Airlines (SIA) and the National Library Board (NLB).

We also shed light on the poorly understood uniqueness of innovation governance in local family-based businesses, the role of entrepreneurial leadership for achieving innovation outcomes and the educational benefits of UAV technology (small drones) for future-proofing university students with reference to digital sustainability management and urban heritage preservation.

The case study *Innovation Governance in Chinese Family Business: A Case Study* (with Ong Geok Chwee) provides insights into the innovation management capabilities of Qian Hu, an integrated ornamental fish service provider incorporated in Singapore in 1998. Based on half-structured interviews with its Executive Chairman Mr Kenny Yap, we exemplify the key components of Singapore's Innovation Excellence Award (I-Award) and how Qian Hu made them work. Corporate innovation governance can be defined as a systematic approach to align goals, allocate resources and assign decision-making authority for innovation, across the company and with external parties. While the dos and don'ts of innovation governance approaches in non-Asian firms are fairly well researched, little is known about the Chinese way of governing innovation in Asian family firms. The paper attempts to shed light on some of the unique innovation management approaches in Chinese family-owned enterprises, e.g. with regard to family involvement in boards which divert to some extent from formal business excellence standards. The paper is part of an on-going research project aimed at examining the specifics of innovation governance in Asian enterprises.

In *The Impact of Entrepreneurial Leadership on Innovation Outcomes* (with Neo Kin Kah and Chay Yue Wah), we discuss experiences at the Singapore Management University (SMU) with a Master of Science in Innovation programme (MI) aimed at creating novel and viable business ventures as part of so-called Capstone Projects. Given concerns about the somewhat mediocre nature of ideation and business model creation outcomes of some of the students' capstone projects vis-à-vis a couple of very successful, award-winning innovation projects, emphasis is put on understanding a key antecedent of *high-quality* new ventures, namely *entrepreneurial leadership* and its role in creating innovative new business ventures as outcome of students' capstone projects. In addition, we examine two other critical factors which have often been highlighted as reasons for start-up success: (i) the strength of the innovation team in terms of *diversity* and (ii) the overall *team climate*. Based on semi-structured interviews with MI graduates, we develop three key hypotheses about the impact of entrepreneurial leadership and team matters on innovation outcomes in preparation for a major survey to empirically test these assumptions.

Due to rapid technological developments in the area of unmanned aerial vehicles (UAVs), the application of UAVs is becoming increasingly popular in heritage preservation and urban management projects. Examples include the visual documentation and inspection of standing monuments such as lighthouses or the detection of subsurface archaeological remains. Asian countries arguably lack behind the UK or the USA in leveraging UAVs for such purposes despite the increase in drone-related recreation activities on open fields and in parks. Against this background, the article *Drones over Singaporean Heritage Sites: Exploring the Potential of Small UAVs (Drones) for Educational Smart City Projects and Heritage Preservation* makes a case for utilising small drones for educational "smart city" projects in institutions of higher learning aimed at enabling students to appreciate not only the importance of a nation's urban heritage in general but also how "good" urban planning has contributed to urban development.

Recent experiments with low altitude drones in two courses (IDIS103 Understanding Drone & Robotics Technology — History, Usage, Ethics & Legal Issues, and MGMT320 Innovations for Asia's Smart Cities) on UAVs and smart city management at the Singapore Management University suggest that the integration of UAV images captured through the drone's camera into pedagogical projects can be highly instrumental and motivating in ensuring that students do indeed appreciate past physical planning effects on our dynamic urban environment. A related proposition is that UAV activities help students to acknowledge the role of active heritage preservation with regard to area conservation or revitalisation of "old" places aimed at enriching "the character of places where we live, work and play". Based on several potential pilot project sites such as Tanjung Rhu, SMU, and the Lorong Halus Wetland, we are currently examining the pedagogical usefulness of small UAVs/drone photography and visualization projects with regard to enhancing students' appreciation of Singapore's heritage and its preservation with reference to Singapore's on-going smart nation development efforts in general and "historical place evolution" in particular. We argue that students' active involvement in a technology-rich learning environment with a historical place-making component qua "map-knitting" software and other tools such as Adobe Movie Maker is instrumental in acknowledging how important heritage is in building a sense of belonging in a "smart" city.

To sum up, making innovation work in order to enhance a firm's competitiveness by creating and capturing value requires "total innova-tion", i.e. innovation leadership and a *winning* innovation strategy aligned with corporate strategy. An innovation strategy is a sort of roadmap of efforts to support overall strategy. An organization without a holistic inno-vation framework is like "a tanker without a propulsion engine". Pulling the right levers and enablers of both business model and technology inno-vation is critical for strategizing innovation efforts. An innovation frame-work must stand on strong pillars such as a robust innovation culture (with the "right" people), meaningful incentives and trusted collaboration processes (internally and externally).

As the ongoing global student strikes remind us, greater action on climate change is no longer an option. It is an absolute necessity because the time to halve our global greenhouse gas emissions is running out. Catalyzing innovations for a sustainable future is therefore one of our greatest challenges.

Chapter 2

Smart Singapore

From Smart Cities to Start-up Hubs

Singapore is on track towards being a successful start-up nation, but there are some hurdles to clear.

An interesting element of the Singapore story is the city-state's transformation into a "smart" city. A city can be defined as smart when urbanites enjoy a high quality of life, good education, jobs, health, connectivity, security, mobility and so on, enabled by good governance and relevant technologies (for example, sensors) aimed at enhancing urban sustainable development. One milestone in Singapore's journey towards a smart city is Gardens by the Bay with its stunning Supertrees (tree-like structures stretching up to 50 metres into the sky). Looking from one of the sky bridges within the Cloud Forest (one of two cooled conservatories) in the Bay South Garden at Singapore's skyline, the Marina Barrage built across the Marina Channel or the city's new cruise terminal, one can only marvel at the determination of the Republic's planners to turn it into "a great place to live, work and play".

Unlike other small countries whose economies are heavily dependent on just one or two sectors, Singapore started its diversification programmes early on the basis of a cluster-based development approach. A new cluster is currently in the making. Policymakers are determined to turn Singapore into a successful start-up nation as evidenced by the planned expansion of an existing start-up cluster (located in a 200-hectare science-cum-business park developed by JTC Corporation to attract R&D

and high-tech firms in the biomedical, ICT and media industries) to be known as LaunchPad @one-north, and an increasing number of venture capitalists.

Three new Web businesses which have attracted investors include: (i) restaurant reservation site Chope led by CEO Arrif Ziaudeen, who raised S$1.1 million in 2011 from Innosight Ventures, a venture-capital firm, and angel investor Hian Goh, co-founder of Asia Food Channel (in 2013 it managed to raise another S$3.2 million from a subsidiary of Singapore Press Holdings and some individual investors); (ii) online motoring portal sgCarMart (founded by Vincent Tan and Tan Jinglun), which was acquired by Singapore Press Holdings for up to S$60 million in April 2013 and (iii) online video website Japanese e-commerce giant Rakuten for an undisclosed sum that insiders believe is close to S$300 million).

A big hurdle in sustaining Singapore's ambition to become one of the world's most innovative, smart cities is arguably its hierarchical culture. In The New York Times bestseller Start-Up Nation-The Story of Israel's Economic Miracle, authors Dan Senor and Saul Singer pointed out that (its growth story notwithstanding) "Singapore's leaders have failed to keep up in a world that puts a high premium on a trio of attributes historically alien to Singapore's culture: initiative, risk-taking, and agility". They believe that Israel, on the contrary, is full of vivid entrepreneurial success stories because of its adversity driven culture which has created a fertile ground for innovation and entrepreneurial mindsets.

While Singapore is shifting gears towards a less hierarchical societal system, the fear of failure is still a barrier deterring many young Singaporeans from starting a company despite new policy measures introduced recently (for instance, in higher education) to nurture creativity, entrepreneurship and new ventures (Germany is facing similar issues). A related challenge faced by every new entrepreneur is to develop an innovative business model. Both geeks and founders need to be well versed in monetising skills. A popular approach is Internet advertising, which delivers ads to Internet users via Websites, e-mail, ad-supported software, text messaging or Smartphones, Website owners, for example, receive payouts based on the number of times a link on a Web page is clicked compared with the number of times it is displayed (note: this can be risky, especially if it is the only source of income generation). Even giants such as Google whose money-making foundation is advertising via AdWords and Adsense or Twitter, and whose main revenue source is also advertising are not 100% future-proof. Weak revenue models caused many new tech firms to fold during the dot.com bust. Making innovation work by successfully innovating the customer value proposition can be learnt as indicated by the entrepreneurial journeys of Asian and Western innovators such as Anthony Tan, CEO of Grab Holdings Inc., a Singaporean multinational ride-hailing company, or Germany's start-up star Lars Hinrichs, the founder of Xing, a platform for business networking.

Proven revenue-generating business approaches include: (1) *freemium* (Amazon Web Services, for example, introduced a free usage tier for customers of its cloud services; if they exceed the free usage amount as stipulated under the offer, standard charges apply); (2) *subscription* (as practiced by Netflix, a subscription-based movie and television show rental service that offers media to subscribers via Internet streaming and via US mail); (3) *affiliate marketing* (payouts depend on whether customers click ads as well as the respective marketing formula which could be based on pay-per-click, pay-per-sale, or pay-per-lead; note: if the majority of customers do not make a purchase or use affiliate links, the business may go bust); or (4) *sense and respond strategies* as pursued by many integrated resorts who track and follow up on customers' online purchasing patterns via special rewards cards and game applications. Leveraging on new innovation frameworks such as collaborative innovation, new social models or smart city technologies can help to create new successful business ventures. Wash & Coffee, a new laundromat and social gathering place with an integrated café in Munich[1] and Facebook presence,[2] provides a great new experience for customers with dirty clothes. The new service features clean designs, energy efficient programmable Bosch washers and dryers, sustainably produced detergent products from Henkel (Persil brand) and entertainment. It's a successful example of the power of collaborative innovation between two big firms who combined their expertise for the benefits of specific customer segments such as singles, students and commuters. Online charity DonorsChoose.org (US) enables contributors to select and financially support a particular school project (initiated by educators) listed on its website.

---

[1] http://wash-coffee.com/.
[2] facebook.com/washcoffee.

According to FastCompany, DonorsChoose.org has raised US$225 million from more than one million citizen philanthropists since it was established by Charles Best in 2000 for the benefit of more than 175,000 teachers, some 400,000 class projects and about 10 million students.

(The Business Times, 19–20 April 2014)

Paying the Singapore Path to Innovating Professionally

This will make organisations more profitable and the Republic a truly smart city.

As part of Singapore's national efforts to prepare its citizens for the demands of the knowledge-based society and to nurture the city-state's economic clusters, educational institutions continue to roll out new master degree programmes ranging from business analytics to clinical investigation. An interesting case in point is the management of innovation.

The term innovation refers to the implementation of a new or significantly improved product, service or process that meets/exceeds customers' needs at an affordable price. Examples include mobile phones with GIS map capabilities, digital marketing methods (social media), new organisational methods in business practices such as open innovation and so forth. The word itself is derived from the Latin words novus ("new") and innovatio ("something newly created"). Innovations can range from small incremental improvements, such as Nabisco's extension of the Oreo product line, to radical breakthroughs, such as Toyota's battery-fuelled Prius. While invention forms part of the innovation process, the latter goes far beyond invention because it embraces the critical process of commercialisation so that new products, services or processes can be successfully introduced into the market. As in the case of a root-canal treatment or when it comes to stitching up a wound, making innovation work is best left to the professionals.

While this may sound like common sense, it is arguably not common practice. Although empirical studies about the number of professionally educated "chief innovation officers", "innovation development managers" or "organisational excellence specialists" in Singapore-based organisations are hard to come by, anecdotal evidence suggests that concerns about their organisations' ability to innovate effectively do keep many chief executives awake at night as real innovation talent is still rare.

Can corporate Singapore afford not to innovate professionally? The answer is obvious. Whether smart(er) business models, smart(er) traffic, smart(er) health, smart(er) banking or smart(er) ageing, innovation opportunities exist across all sectors of the economy but are not always seized due to the lack of awareness or strategic innovation know-how. There is also reluctance at times to utilise available support schemes provided by government agencies such as Enterprise Singapore which supports a wide range of capability upgrading initiatives for SMEs as part of its Capability Development Grant (CDG) scheme, and the Workforce Skills Qualifications (WSQ) training programmes funded by the Singapore Workforce Development Agency (WDA) which are customised to develop deep, vertical and horizontal skills across various industry disciplines and job functional areas.

Three well known, award-winning firms which practise good synergistic innovation management are *Biosensors Interventional Technologies*, *Qian Hu* and *Singapore Airlines* with their differentiation through service excellence, innovation and superior levels of operational efficiency. What does it take so that more organisations implement management systems that deliver the desired innovation results consistently with similar levels of cutting-edge professionalism?

One strategy to trigger improvements in innovation work is to attract, retain, develop and reward professionally trained innovation specialists who are able to think beyond current paradigms and to turn strategically sound innovation ideas and concepts into tangible new products, services, processes, and business cases.

Provided they have received proper competency-enhancing innovation management education, they will be instrumental in managing commercialisation challenges and market launch with confidence, whether they work for MNCs, financial services firms, statutory boards, hospitals, government agencies, or small and medium-size enterprises. And once the market has accepted the innovation, these specialists will know how to accelerate further growth and create sustainable value through appropriate business development, risk management, financing and value extraction strategies. To support the innovation culture and, in particular, innovation for service excellence, the Singapore WDA has offered several scholarship places for innovation programmes at tertiary levels under its Service Excellence-Step (Skills Training for Excellence Programme) funding initiative. One key goal of this initiative by the Ministry of Manpower and WDA was to help professionals, managers and executives (PMEs) update their skills, knowledge and expertise to remain competitive in today's global business climate.

Service innovation is just one of several areas where strategic innovation learning needs exist. Other innovation forms include product innovation (e.g. Dyson's bagless vacuum cleaner), process innovation (e.g. Walmart's product distribution system) and business model innovation (e.g. Amazon's online platform). And then, there are the various types of innovation such as radical innovation (e.g. Samsung's flat-screen TVs with new LCD technology), architectural innovation (e.g. Sony's Walkman, which was based on reconfiguring existing components in a new way) and incremental innovation (e.g. Apple's iPod Mini/Nano). Properly trained innovation professionals will be able to drive managed innovation on the basis of winning innovation strategies and a balanced innovation portfolio comprising both incremental and breakthrough innovations in order to extract good value out of innovation-related investments.

Innovation experts know how to create real value for customers and to capitalise on that, ensuring that the organisation retains some percentage of the customer value it creates in every transaction of the revenue stream. A good example is LinkedIn whose revenues are based on the premium subscriptions it sells to users. Its talent and marketing solutions are attractive to recruiters as well. As the war for talent continues, it is likely that demand for its services will further increase.

Besides the need to support business managers in driving their innovation teams to greater success by effectively organising internal (or open) innovation management systems, there are other target groups that would benefit from systematic innovation management programmes such as engineers, scientists and designers (by equipping them with commercialisation skills), entrepreneurs to enable them to apply design thinking principles), fresh graduates (who can reap benefits if they are paired with experienced business mentors), health professionals (to leverage new developments in connectivity and monitoring and social entrepreneurs who wish to dive deeper into the world of sustainable innovation on the basis of new social models. Seizing available opportunities for innovation management education here will not only be instrumental in making organisations more profitable but also help to further improve Singapore's status as a truly innovative, liveable smart city.

(The Business Times, 5 June 2014)

"Senseable S'pore" — Driving Air-Con-Less in a "Smart City"

Driving is a bit of luxury in Singapore, and it can be a real challenge at times. It's not only expensive but also stressful due to congestion during peak hours, the sporadic aggressive motorist, (some) drivers not indicating, unbuckled kids, etc. When my vehicle's air-con broke down recently, I seriously considered selling my continental car and using (cheaper) public transport modes (however, old habits die hard; after the air-con was fixed, I changed my mind and kept the car). Driving around in tropical Singapore without the air-con for a couple of days (in a convertible) inspired me to reflect on the meaning of "sheer driving pleasure" (BMW's tagline) in a "smart, senseable city" which Singapore aspires to be in order to enhance competitiveness, innovation, liveability and sustainable development.

The malfunctioning of my air-con came as a real surprise given the fact that the car was relatively new with a proper service record. Nobody alerted me, unlike the other day when two of my car's sensors came on almost simultaneously, signalling an almost empty fuel tank and a worn-out rear brake pad (which was threatening my safety and potentially that of others) that had to be replaced. "Such an air-con issue would have been preempted from happening during Singapore's F1 night race on the Marina Bay Street Circuit" — I told myself while driving to the workshop (after several aircon-less, hot and sweaty driving days) due to its superior electronic control unit (ECU). The ECU manages all the data transmitted live via telemetry from a smart F1 car with its more than 120 sensors, enabling engineers to predict the right time for pit stops, changing tyres etc. Can't cities be like F1 cars? Yes, they can.

Like other urban centres around the globe, Singapore is leveraging technology and innovation to turn Smart city visions aimed at enhancing liveability into reality. A key driver is the iN2015 masterplan developed in 2005 under the guidance of Singapore's Infocomm Development Authority with its new Smart City Programme Office. The plan represents the blueprint for turning Singapore into an intelligent nation and a global city with a well-connected society powered by Infocomm.

Smart mobility is one of several dimensions of Smart city concepts implemented here and elsewhere. It envisions that a city is always on the move without major hiccups. Emission of air pollutants, traffic jams, poorly-planned public transport systems and even potholes can lead to frustration and urban chaos which can be prevented by integrated mobility solutions, including controlling (and limiting as in the case of Singapore) the number of cars on the roads through electronic road pricing alternative transport modes, sound infrastructure investments (or snapping a picture of that pothole and patching it up as practised by a group of city dwellers in Boston called the New Urban Mechanics). The *Land Transport Authority* works hard to ensure that Singapore's infrastructure meets the needs of a growing population so that people can make hassle-free multi-modal journeys (potholes do not pose a problem here due to effective monitoring and continuous 24/7 efforts of road surfacing teams who keep Singapore's roads in good shape).

Like modern racing cars in F1, cities can benefit from the use of wireless sensors installed at static points such as roads or buildings or in taxis and buses to anticipate (and prevent) traffic jams or to save electricity and energy costs. *MIT's SENSEable City Lab*[3] is piloting several smart and innovative infrastructure solutions such as the visual exploration of urban mobility patterns. Via the LIVE Singapore project (a collaborative effort of SENSEable City Lab, the Alliance for Research and Technology/ SMART and the National Research Foundation of Singapore), it aspires to empower people by giving them visual and tangible access to real-time information about their own city so that they can make better decisions about healthier routes to work, convenient (empty) parking lots, attractive dining options or the nearest bicycle for rent.

(Tabla, 6 December 2013)

---

[3] http://senseable.mit.edu/.

Chapter 3

Leadership & Strategy

What Makes Leaders of Innovation?

Research on innovation leadership competencies suggests that there are about 100 different skill requirements.

Strong leadership from senior management is crucial to make innovation work. Competent innovation leaders have the knowledge, skills and abilities to influence employees to develop and implement new or significantly improved products, services or processes that meet or exceed the needs of customers.

Their key tasks include defining and aligning innovation and business strategy, selecting the right innovation portfolios, and to determine the targets for innovation-driven value creation. Despite the large number of books on innovation matters, there is still widespread confusion when it comes to the identification of key innovation leadership competencies.

Innovators such as Reed Hastings who started Netflix, an innovative provider of on-demand Internet streaming media or Tim Berners-Lee, the inventor of the World Wide Web (which turned 25 this year) are characterised by distinct attributes such as a high achievement drive, empathy, courage, determination and hard work. These are just a few of the critical attributes innovation novices must acquire in order to effectively manage innovation efforts.

Associational Thinking

In their 2011 book *The Innovator's DNA*, university dons J.H. Dyer, H.B. Gregersen and C.M. Christensen have proposed a couple of other behavioural skills innovation leaders must possess in order to come up with new ideas (propelled by the willingness to take smart risks). They include questioning (defined as passion for inquiry and challenging the status quo); observing the external business environment, including customers, technologies, products and services; relentless networking with diverse individuals; and experimenting, e.g. by initiating pilot projects to test new ideas.

An important enabler to synthesise and to make sense of novel inputs generated with the help of these skills is associational thinking by making connections across seemingly unrelated issues or knowledge assets. Innovative building designers such as the Spanish Dante of architecture, Antoni Gaudi (1852–1926), have a sharp eye for details and the habit of observing the everyday World around them. Nature often provides inspiration for creative minds. Gaudi found many of his models by studying the branches, twigs and leaves of trees as can be seen in the central part of the impressive Sagrada Familia in Barcelona designed as a forest of pillars which branch out and upward in several directions. Companies can benefit from associational approaches to innovation by using nature as a model for inventions or cross-pollination. One of the most commercially successful examples of biomimicry — i.e. the imitation of models, systems, and elements of nature aimed at solving human problems — is the Velcro hook and loop fastener, This innovative product was invented by Swiss engineer George de Mestra who "discovered" it during a hunting trip in the Alps in 1941 after his dog was covered in burdock burrs.

Corporate cross-pollinators do connect the dots between seemingly unrelated ideas to create something new. As idea champions, they are curious and highly motivated to share external lessons learnt inside the organisation. They know how to build support so that new ideas are implemented. They inspire and energise others with their innovation vision and personal conviction. Most importantly, they have decision-making discretion and good power skills to get things done.

Can such traits and competencies be taught and learnt? Absolutely! Associating skills, for example, can be acquired by looking at things differently via role-playing in combination with creativity training (e.g. by the formation of associative elements into new combinations). Reconstructing the evolution of existing product innovations such as biochips for cancer detection via blood samples (which were developed by combining biomedical and electronics knowledge) serves similar purposes.

A key challenge is to focus learning efforts on the most important innovation competencies given the complex nature of the job of an innovation leader.

Research on innovation leadership competencies suggests that there are about 100 different skill requirements, ranging from the ability to learn and identify innovations, effective team leading by example in conjunction with high energy levels and perseverance, to expertise in planning and project management, emotional intelligence and commitment, and the need to establish a robust trust culture.

Which leadership approach works best? Studies have shown that "transformational leaders" who practise a "collaborative leadership style" are particularly effective at fostering innovations. Such leaders are skillful in changing peoples' frames of reference so that they recognise new opportunities, hold teams accountable to the organisation's vision and mission, and thereby create new organisational capabilities.

Leadership behaviours such as the provision of individual support or intellectual stimulation of associates increase employee trust which results in greater commitment to diffuse innovations within the organisation.

Culture of Innovation

The latter is particularly important in knowledge-intensive contexts such as neurodegenerative research (e.g. Alzheimer's) where a leader's personality, traits, charisma, out-of-the-box thinking, international reputation, organising skills, and decisive leadership style are crucial to obtain buy-in from diverse groups of scientists to join forces in new types of collaborative research aimed at making therapeutic advances that could help tackle these diseases.

Does transformational leadership automatically lead to greater innovativeness? Absolutely not! One important precondition is the existence of a robust culture of innovation. Leaders who are unwilling to frankly evaluate the effectiveness of their own innovation management behaviour and negate the importance of reflecting how their personality traits might facilitate or complicate sustainable innovativeness, will not succeed. Innovators such as Richard Branson stand out because of their openness to experience — they have a particular cognitive style that distinguishes imaginative, creative people from down-to-earth, conventional people.

Open-minded people are intellectually curious, appreciate art, and tend to act in non-conforming ways. The more closed-minded people an organisation has hired, the more difficult it might be to make innovation part of the corporate DNA. Given the need to exert strong leadership on innovation strategy, a robust selection tool for innovation leaders is indispensable in order to create and sustain successful innovations.

(The Business Times, 6 December 2014)

Developing Global Leaders with an Asian Focus

Mastering mindfulness will ensure that more Asians successfully claim leadership roles.

Given the volatility in current global markets, highly capable leadership in both public and private sectors is a key requirement to steer emerging Asia to greater heights.

While there is still a large number of multinational corporations whose chief executive officers are reluctant to empower local Asian managers as bosses, an increasing number of firms located in Asia are keen to implement strategic leadership development (LD) programmes to ensure a sustainable talent pipeline.

This is easier said than done. While substantial research has been conducted to identify the required attributes of effective leaders such as visionary thinking, courage or resilience, there is still widespread confusion when it comes to defining what is "Asian" in "Asian" leadership. When asked about this, executives sometimes construct a simple dichotomy between the "assertive Western" and the "risk-averse Asian" corporate leader. "Asian" leadership traits arguably include humility and collectivism. Humility refers to the quality of being modest, reverential and politely submissive which is in stark contrast to being arrogant and rude.

Collectivism implies that group goals have priority over individual goals. In everyday corporate life which is increasingly complex, such traits can sometimes be in conflict with competing value systems imported through foreign talents.

What are the challenges when it comes to developing global leaders with an Asian focus? A key challenge is to figure out what is meant by Asian leadership and to incorporate that into needs-based leadership development programmes to ensure leadership effectiveness across cultures.

One study which has helped to shed light on this is the Global Leadership and Organisational Behaviour Effectiveness Study (in short GLOBE) conceived by Robert House from the Wharton School of Business. The GLOBE team surveyed over 17,000 middle managers from 951 organisations in the food processing, financial services and telecommunications services industries in 62 societies across the globe to establish the essence of Asian leadership.

Building on Geert Hofstede's classic studies of how values in the workplace are influenced by culture, GLOBE analysed the responses of thousands of middle managers around the globe to 112 leader characteristics, such as modest", "decisive", "autonomous", and trustworthy", based on the following definition of leadership: *An outstanding leader is a person in an organisation or industry who is exceptionally skilled at motivating, influencing or enabling you, others or groups to contribute to the success of the organisation or task.*

The research helped to identify universally desirable key leadership competencies and attributes such as integrity, inspiration, vision, performance-orientation, team integration, decisiveness, administrative competence, diplomacy, collaborative team orientation, self-sacrifice, and modesty. Among six empirically established typical leader styles ranging from participative (with regard to decision-making, delegation, and equality) to autonomous independent implying an individualistic, self centered approach to leadership, the team-oriented style with its emphasis on pride, loyalty, collaboration, and team cohesiveness turned out to be the most preferred leader style in the so-called "Confucian cluster", comprising Singapore, Hong Kong, Taiwan, China, South Korea, and Japan. Another challenge is to accept the limits of both communitarian and individualistic variants of leadership. The still nascent Asian leadership research suggests that there is an urgent need for aspiring corporate leaders in East and West who want to succeed in Asia to develop a broader range of skills in line with the increasingly diverse and globalising business environment. This may include the need to be more collaborative, assertive or focused depending upon the particular leadership moment and situational demands.

One source of inspiration for discussions about effective leadership development with an Asian focus is mindfulness, which can be defined as a sort of enlightened state of being in which greed, hatred and delusion are absent from the mind. Coupled with clear comprehension of what is taking place now and here, i.e. present moment-awareness, mindfulness can help leaders to transform other people's fears and anxieties into hope which some consider as the hallmark of good leadership. Research conducted by Professor Jochen Reb at the Singapore Management University (SMU) has shown that a leader's mindfulness is associated with higher well-being and performance of subordinates. Full awareness of current activities (i.e. not running on autopilot" etc.) or paying full attention to a follower's problem brought up during an unplanned conversation without being preoccupied with thoughts about the next appointment represent strengths of mindful leaders.

The acquisition of mindfulness is challenging. It requires the willingness for personal stocktaking in terms of self-awareness and openness towards frank feedback. Another necessity is to regularly pause and to make time available for in-depth reflections. For example, if a leader regularly puts off others by appearing to be in attentive or cold, a self-evaluation of one's psychological strengths might help him or her become a better, more mindful leader.

Meditation, yoga, in-depth introspective discussions, reflective techniques, or exercises such as journaling or interdisciplinary group reflections about difficult leadership events where each member identifies and evaluates personal challenges and coping strategies in the context of others and then jointly reflects about outcomes achieved represent useful tools. The mastery of mindful leadership will not only enhance effectiveness at individual, team and organisational levels. It will also enrich the development of global leaders with an Asian focus and ensure that more Asians successfully claim leadership roles in East and West.

(The Business Times, 25 April 2012)

The Impact of Entrepreneurial Leadership on Innovation Outcomes

With Neo Kin Kah and Chay Yue Wah

Introduction

Singapore, a 50-year-old island state country, has been able to survive and prosper due to its strategic location in the heart of South East Asia and because it is a major maritime port connecting Asia to Europe trade. Singapore's success has been largely credited to a stable political environment and a business-friendly government. Singapore has attracted an enormous number of FDIs and foreign companies to set up regional headquarters and manufacturing facilities. As of 2017, the Singapore Stock Exchange (SGX) had a total of 754 firms with 40% overseas listing value at US$700 billion.

Despite the economic success of Singapore, home grown successful entrepreneurs have been rare in Singapore. Many Singaporeans prefer to work for multinational companies, then start their own businesses. Singapore's GDP growth has slowed down to 2–4% during the past 10 years after growing at double digits from the 1960s to 2000. As the economy matures, Singapore's government is looking at ways to grow the economy. Over reliance on foreign companies for growth can potentially cause issues, as neighbouring countries develop and improve their infrastructure. There is also the danger that foreign companies may be moving out of Singapore as the cost of doing business is so much higher here as compared to neighbouring countries (Webb, 2017).

Since 2000, Singapore's government (realising the importance of entrepreneurship in creating jobs and growing the economy) has invested heavily in creating a strong start-up environment, with heavy investment into R&D, tax exemption credits for start-ups, a strong patent law, and the provision of government-led funding ("Funding & Grants", 2015). This has resulted in an increase in entrepreneurial activities, and in 2015 more companies were created annually as compared to 2005 (Narasimhalu, 2015). Universities in Singapore have started to establish innovation centres as incubators, and collectively this has helped to incubate hundreds of companies since 2001.

Local Universities have also created several novel innovation and entrepreneurship-related degree programs.

What does it take to create successful entrepreneurship? Scholars have been debating the question whether entrepreneurs are born or whether they can be taught (Colette *et al.*, 2005) for a long time. There is evidence that entrepreneurship education does in fact stimulate participants to create new ventures, but it can also be argued that participants who signed up for such programs already had the intention of starting their own business (Matlay, 2008). In entrepreneurial education contexts, students are usually put into a group project environment to ideate business ideas and to create a successful venture. Successful start-ups are often created in a team environment with strong leadership. Successful firms in the technology sectors are known for their innovation leaders. Examples include Bill Gates, Steve Jobs and Mark Zuckerberg. They all have something in common: they dropped out of college. While one could argue that they were not in the correct degree program that trains entrepreneurs, we cannot deny the importance of entrepreneurial leadership as enabler of successful entrepreneurship as outcome (Beh and Shafique, 2016).

In this research study, we intend to shed light on some of the antecedents of successful and innovative capstone project outcomes based on the case of the Masters of Science in Innovation programme at a Singapore University that trains students to become "entrepreneurial leaders" capable of creating new businesses. The programme has been running since 2012 with about 180 graduates. This master course is a 12-month weekend-based course attended mostly by working adults. The broad objective of the course is to enable the students to appreciate what it takes to make innovation work within an organization and to come up with a viable start-up business (plan). The capstone innovation project cycle mimics a start-up process. The students must pitch their project ideas to both professors and potential investors several times after they have gathered external advice from mentors and resident entrepreneurs — similar to what start-up founders do when they pitch for funding. Project groups can submit their capstone project ideas at international entrepreneurial competitions. Over the years, a few groups enrolled in the programme have won awards in such international start-up competitions. Others have not been so successful. What makes success and failure tick?

Research Questions

Does "Good" Entrepreneurial Leadership Matter in Creating Innovative New Business Ventures as Outcome of Students' Capstone Projects?

Start-up success is rare. Nearly 50% of start-ups do not survive after one year, and less than 80% survive more than 4 years. Those who survive and become successful are known for their innovation and entrepreneurial leadership quality. Non-home grown successful entrepreneurs in Singapore such as Forrest Li of Garena or Anthony Tan of Grab both helped to lead the successful tech start-up Unicorn. Other successful home-grown tech entrepreneurs include Tan Min-Liang of Razer and Quek Siu Rui of Carousell. These companies are all known for innovation and their entrepreneurial leaders.

For a start-up to survive and be successful, it must be innovative broadly speaking, and that arguably requires a unique type of leadership as motor: *entrepreneurial leadership* (see Table 1 below). That this type of leadership is not always present in young start-up teams was confirmed during several half-structured interviews conducted during the pre-survey stage of this study by several graduates of the MI programme. As the team leader of a particularly successful MI group emphasized, good entrepreneurial leaders need to focus in order to lead their members to create innovative outcomes and win awards in competitions:

I tell you why we have won so many competitions. I am very focussed on what I am doing. The young people in the class are not focused on what they are supposed to do. The way I look at it is that students need to be realistic, think whether it is workable in the real world. Some of my classmates' projects are not workable and practical at all. When you talk to investors you will have a problem.

The significance of entrepreneurial leadership as a key variable in the area of entrepreneurship is well established in the literature as indicated in Table 1 (Leitch and Volery, 2017) below.

Recent developments in entrepreneurial leadership research suggest that it can be considered as a new paradigm that cuts across leadership and entrepreneurship (Leitch and Volery, 2017). What makes it so

Table 1:   Entrepreneurial Leadership Research

Cunningham and Lischeron (1991)	Entrepreneurial leadership involves setting clear goals, creating opportunities, empowering people, preserving organisational intimacy, and developing a human resource system.
Nicholson (1998)	Entrepreneurial leaders can differ from other leaders and non-leaders in specific respects including traits such as high risk-taking behaviour, openness, need for achievement and low deliberation. Entrepreneurial leadership is also about being resistant to the socialisation that shapes managerial personality and the willingness to escape management into leadership.
Ireland *et al.* (2003)	Entrepreneurial leadership entails the ability to influence others to manage resources strategically in order to emphasize both opportunity-seeking and advantage-seeking behaviors.
Cogliser and Brigham (2004)	Entrepreneurial leadership should involve idea generation, idea structuring and idea promotion, where idea generation is critical in the early stages of a venture and idea structuring and promotion in the latter stages. Therefore, an entrepreneurial leader does not only need to recognise opportunities, but he or she must also be able to marshal the resources necessary to reach the potential of that opportunity.
Gupta *et al.* (2004)	Leadership that creates visionary scenarios that are used to assemble and mobilize a supporting cast of participants who become committed by the vision to the discovery and exploitation of strategic value creation.
Kuratko (2007)	Entrepreneurial leadership is a unique concept combining the identification of opportunities, risk taking beyond security and being resolute enough to follow through.
Surie and Ashley (2008)	Leadership capable of sustaining innovation and adaptation in high-velocity and uncertain environments.
Leitch *et al.* (2013)	Entrepreneurial leadership is the leadership role performed in entrepreneurial ventures, rather than in the more general sense of an entrepreneurial style of leadership.
Renko *et al.* (2015)	Entrepreneurial leadership entails influencing and directing the performance of group members towards the achievement of organisational goals that involve recognising and exploiting entrepreneurial opportunities.

powerful? As Renko *et al.* (2015) have convincingly argued, entrepreneurial leadership entails influencing and directing the performance of group members towards the achievement of organisational goals that involve recognising and exploiting entrepreneurial opportunities.

Renko's ENTRELEAD Scale

In the following set of questions, think of your immediate manager (or team leader). How well do the following statements describe him/her? (If you have many immediate managers, please pick one):

1. Often comes up with radical improvement ideas for the products/services we are selling
2. Often comes up with ideas of completely new products/services that we could sell
3. Takes risks
4. Has creative solutions to problems
5. Demonstrates passion for his/her work
6. Has a vision of the future of our business
7. Challenges and pushes me to act in a more innovative way
8. Wants me to challenge the current ways we do business.

If leaders fail to lead a team towards the successful commercialization of innovative business ideas qua attractive business products or services, a start-up will not be successful (Renko *et al.*, 2015). Besides the need for effective ideation and opportunity recognition, execution is important, too, as stressed by the leader of an innovation team that discontinued after graduation:

> *I think the successful part is that as a team we came together and created a business idea that has an impact on the society ... We saw a need and tried to come up with a business idea to solve it. The conceptualisation was good but what I felt was not good or unsuccessful was the execution part. How do you take an idea and make it into reality? That was the part where we stumbled, so it didn't end so well.*

Asked how well some of the ENTRELEAD scale items describe her such as "coming up with radical ideas for new products/services" or the need to "challenge and push team members to act in a more innovative way", she replied ("No — team") that this was a collective effort rather than based on a singular competency. However, with regard to other scale items such as "risk-taking" or "demonstrating passion for the work", she answered in the affirmative. Eventually, her capstone group project came to an end after graduation because they "didn't find it feasible". Team members moved on to other challenges.

In view of the importance of entrepreneurial leadership for capstone project success, we hypothesize the following:

Hypothesis 1: Entrepreneurial leadership has a positive impact upon the success of innovation projects.

To What Extent Do Team Attributes Such as Diversity Support the Creation of Innovative New Business Ventures as Outcomes of Students' Capstone Projects?

Most successful start-ups are created by a group of individuals rather than one person alone. In our research, we were baffled by the varied experiences of capstone project teams ranging from those who received external funding or won competitions to those who failed to create sustainable new venture success. We have categorised the MI teams into (i) average (mediocre), (ii) award-winning teams, and (iii) drop-outs.

Average teams

Average teams are teams that passed the general requirements of the capstone course but did not win any awards. These teams arguably had somewhat mediocre (incremental) business ideas and were not always able to demonstrate how they would commercialize the outcome of their projects in a sustainable manner. Often these teams had a common profile in terms of age and educational background, i.e. they were less diverse than others. As one of these team leaders stressed, a key challenge for such groups lies in the area of commercialization. Students were guided to master the commercialization process during the course through lectures, case discussions and guest presentations. They also had to repeatedly pitch their proposals to professors and outside consultants during the capstone project phase. While entrepreneurial training was provided, something was arguably lacking amongst these teams, namely strong entrepreneurial (team) leadership. When asked about the importance of leadership for innovation success in general, one interviewee reflected about her shortcomings and associated struggles:

> *Was I radical in my thinking and did I challenge my team member as their leader? I think that is where as an entrepreneur I have weaknesses. I don't challenge or push enough. Whereas if I look at my current boss, he always thinks about more radical stuff and always challenging and*

pushing us on how things can be done. I think that is very critical for any leader in business.

Diversity often came up during the interviews. As one respondent argued, more homogenous groups (in terms of age) seemingly spent more time during the ideation process creating new ideas but lacked focus when it came to creating an innovative outcome that could be commercialized. More diverse groups appeared to be less creative but more effective in terms of execution:

In the all senior and diverse group, the idea seems to be more rigid or less creative, but their execution is very good. I look at the younger group, perhaps there is more creativity but the execution doesn't seem to be so good.

Award winning teams

Award winning teams refer to MI teams that stood out in terms of their competitive entrepreneurial orientation. These teams were diverse in terms of age, education and work experience. Reflecting on their success, one team member talked about the diversity of the group in terms of disciplines represented and the importance of leading groups in creating an innovative outcome:

We have a team of diversity experts. We have a medical engineer; we have a strategic planner, an IP consultant and me as a design consultant. We have a hardware and software engineer. Diverse in skillsets and diverse in age ranging from 24 to 42. It is really rewarding as we get to be exposed to different trains of thoughts, different perspectives and also different kinds of expertise — that is why it was rewarding to me.

It was emphasized that there was a positive team climate in the team and that members appreciated other younger and older group members as well as their different educational backgrounds.

We do have a high appreciation for people from different age groups. From an entrepreneurial journey perspective, not everyone from different age groups has the same drive. First thing, when some of the older ones get tired, the younger ones can take on the load. To the young it's something new they want to try. Second thing, it is about experience, the older people in the group have gone through a lot of mistakes. We can actually advise the younger guys in the team so that they will not take the long road to discovery and they really appreciate that.

Drop outs

Very few team members had dropped out from the course in order to start their own company but then joined an established firm as employees. One of them reflected about his struggle working with younger teammates, stressing that he preferred a less diverse group to reduce infighting:

Senior people are able to handle diverse ideas better than young ones. I see people in their 30s who are more mature and more open to accept different ideas. Even if there are debates, we always come to an agreement but for large age diverse teams I see a lot of debates and people get into fights. The results were not so satisfying in those groups.

Diversity in groups can be helpful in terms of ideation and problem solving as such groups are able to create solutions from diverse ideas and backgrounds. But diverse voices can also cause conflict and in-fighting. As a result, the overall team climate may suffer and a negative tone may appear in team discussions. Another respondent pointed out that leadership is important to ensure that diverse groups perform well but in reality he often observed the opposite happening:

The thing is different people have different ideas. How can you maintain democracy? Allow different people with different ideas but centralize the idea and consolidate it to move forward. I saw many cases where discussions are going on forever. The team couldn't align, and I agree it is very important to have a leader.

Without an entrepreneurial leader able to push the innovation idea forward and to nurture a positive team climate, groups may never become "real" teams and as a result may suffer from lack of focus and execution. This concern was apparent in our conversations with MI graduates. In view of the importance of a good team climate for team success, we argue that teams with weak entrepreneurial leaders and a poor team climate will not succeed in creating successful new ventures and innovation outcomes:

Hypothesis 2: Entrepreneurial leadership has a positive effect on a positive team climate and the appreciation of a team's age diversity.

Does Age Diversity Matter in Creating Innovative New Business Ventures as Outcomes of Students' Capstone Projects?

An interesting observation which emerged in the cause of the MI programme is the notion that particularly successful student teams (e.g. as evidenced by cash awards they received) often comprised very diverse team members in terms of age, education and working experiences. The overall importance of team diversity was highlighted by several graduates of the MI programme (insert more quotes here).

As a member of an age diverse, award winning team pointed out:

I must say diversity does help because of our different ages and experiences. It provides some dynamics. You can see that Jay is very energetic. He will do things after midnight. Ron is in his mid-30s and still very energetic. Ken is a bit more laidback. He has his ideas but let us take the lead on different things. We will throw a lot of ideas at him, and he will say "yes workable" — then we will proceed. Me and Ben are in our late 40s. We are more stable. We try to balance enthusiasm and creative ideas versus the practical aspect.

While diversity is generally seen as an asset when it comes to ideating diverse and innovative ideas, it can also make innovation harder to work or cause conflicts with negative effects on team climate unless a "strong" entrepreneurial leader steps in who is able to achieve a high degree of team identification qua a positive team climate which in turn is beneficial for a high degree of group/team effectivity and high quality innovation outcomes.

Our interviews suggest that a key factor is how motivated and satisfied team members are, both individually as well as collectively. As another graduate pointed out:

The satisfaction level in itself tells you how much efforts are put in to churn out the solution. It also tells you how strong the dynamics of the team are when members are dealing with issues. Sometimes, success is dependent on sheer luck of having "like-minded" personalities that can work with one another. Sometimes, it is due to the charm of the overall leader in the group or sub-group, and at times it is also due to the fact that the process of getting the job done was developed and approved collaboratively.

Making innovation work effectively across various generations requires the willingness to understand what everyone's expectations and points of view are right at the start of the journey which could be a job interview to recruit a team member or an initial brain-storming session. A good job fit, positive team dynamics and a sound balance of multi-generations in a team are all essential to achieve innovation goals in age-diverse innovation teams:

> *Identify the end state objectives clearly before you start. Ensure over-arching leadership or supervisory expertise which understands the higher intent and priorities, e.g. greater emphasis of building culture vis-à-vis a fast and effective solution. Be aware of the nuances of different generations in terms of their approaches to tackle problems, their attitudes towards authority, their means and preferences of communications, what makes each generation ticks and so forth.*

Encouraging team members to reach-out to the other generation and reverse mentoring can be instrumental in building A-teams. Therefore, we centre hypothesis 3 on the interplay between entrepreneurial leadership, team identification and performance-related team effectivity:

Hypothesis 3: Entrepreneurial leadership has a positive effect on team identification and performance-related team effectivity.

Towards a Model

A framework model is proposed for creating/predicting a successful inno-vative outcome by a team that undertakes a start-up activity as shown in Figure 1. In a successful innovation team, members should ideally experi-ence and benefit from strong entrepreneurial leadership while in reality members' capability to do so may vary due to differences with regard to age, educational and/or work experiences. We posit that entrepreneurial leaders will be able to nurture a positive team climate with a high appreciation of the team's age diversity. This in turn will have a positive impact on team iden-tification, group/team effectiveness and high quality innovation outcomes. The dependent variable centres around the innovation outcome level. We intend to assess group/team effectivity in achieving teams' (high quality) innova-tion outcomes with the help of objective goal attainment scores such as capstone project-related assessment scores provided by external judges.

These scores were obtained during the final project presentations (10 min presentation plus 10 min Q&A) scheduled at the end of each

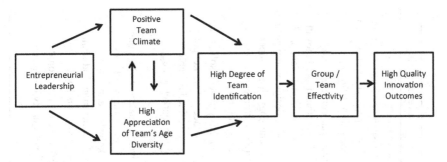

Figure 1: Conceptual Model of Entrepreneurial Leadership in Age-Diverse Innovation Teams as Driver of Effective Innovation Outcomes

programme cycle. Judges, Faculty, and other experts acted as judges and provided feedback. Project outcomes were graded on a pass-fail basis. A poor grade required rework and could lead to graduation delays. Table 2 contains the Feedback Sheet (rubrics) which has been used in the programme for assessing the final capstone project presentations based on altogether five evaluation criteria.

Methods

The foundation of this research paper is provided by several in-depth exploratory interviews with MI graduates representing different capstone project teams, i.e. those who won awards, those who passed the programme, and those who dropped out of the course to pursue other ventures. Exploratory in-depth interviews were conducted with five ex-students. Leadership and commercialization challenges were topics that came up repeatedly. Students from the award-winning team were selected to understand how they perceived their own success in creating innovative outcomes. Students from average teams and drop out students were selected to understand their limitations and challenges of creating an innovative outcome. Team leaders and members were selected for the interviews from the same group to obtain information about their leader and member perspectives. Interviews were conducted separately. Each interview took about 45 to 60 minutes. The interview findings provide us with a better understanding of critical factors that dictate new venture success with special emphasis on entrepreneurial leadership and team matters in the innovation process. With our interim findings, we will proceed to design a quantitative research study to examine the various variables by using

Table 2:   Rubric for Assessment of MI Capstone Project

Evaluation Criteria	Level 1 (Poor)	Level 2 (Average)	Level 3 (Good)
Definition & Under-standing of Business Opportunity (incl. Business Case and Customer Value Proposition)	Not able to define the business opportunity, incl. business case and customer value proposition	Business opportunity (incl. business case and customer value proposition) has been satisfactorily defined	Business opportunity (incl. business case and customer value proposition) has been very well defined
Differentiation with regard to innovative Business Model/ Plan, Product/Service Design (clarity of prototype) and Technology (e.g. vis-à-vis leading competitors)	Unable to come up with a differentiated, innovative and competitive business model/ plan, product/service design prototype and technology (vis-à-vis leading competitors)	Team has come up with a (mediocre) business model/ plan, product/service design prototype and technology	Team has come up with a differentiated and innovative business model/plan, product/ service design prototype and technology that is superior (e.g. with regard to leading competitors)
Market Potential & Viability of Go-to-Market Strategy, incl. anticipated Market Acceptance	Fails to provide any data/evidence for market potential and a viable go-to-market strategy	Some attempts have been made to provide data/evidence for market potential and a viable go-to-market strategy but gaps remain	Team has provided solid data/ evidence for market potential and outlined a viable go-to-market strategy
Overall Quality of Capstone Project Team in terms of Knowledge, Passion, Determination and Team Dynamics	Overall poor quality of Capstone Project Team in terms of knowledge, passion, determination, and team dynamics	Overall quality of Capstone Project Team in terms of knowledge, passion, determination, and team dynamics is satisfactory	Overall quality of Capstone Project Team in terms of knowledge, passion, determination, and team dynamics is good
Clarity and Effectiveness of Presentation Delivery, incl. Quality of Q&A	Presentation delivery, incl. quality of Q&A is substandard	Presentation delivery, incl. quality of Q&A is adequate but can be further improved	Effective presentation delivery, incl. quality of Q&A

established scales on entrepreneurial leadership (Renko *et al.*, 2015), age diversity (Hentschel *et al.*, 2013) and team climate (Anderson and West, 1998). Whether the examination of group affective tone via the use of job-related affective well-being scales (Van Katwyk *et al.*, 2000) makes sense needs to be ascertained. An online survey will be sent to all graduates of MI in addition to 30 already existing survey forms collected earlier.

Conclusion

This article is part of an ongoing research project on age-diverse innovation teams aimed at establishing what it takes to harness the innovation potential of age-diverse work teams comprising members of different generations. Based on half-structured interviews with graduates of a Master of Innovation programme at an Asian university, several hypotheses about team innovation and age diversity were generated to guide a future quantitative survey on the topic. Based on our interim findings, we derived the following recommendations for harnessing the innovation potential of age-diverse teams as well as for more effective (innovative) capstone projects in higher education (master programme level):

- Ensure that age-diverse innovation teams are led by effective innovation team leaders (with entrepreneurial leadership skills) capable of nurturing a positive team climate where age diversity is appreciated.
- Acknowledge that entrepreneurial leadership of age-diverse innovation teams requires special competencies in order to leverage the multi-generational strengths of teams which need to be acquired and honed.
- Ensure that team members have a high appreciation of age diversity in their team and that they know what that entails in practical terms in order to generate positive effects with regard to team identification and overall innovation outcomes.

Other studies suggest that team success correlates with the degree of age-diversity salience, i.e. the degree (high/low) to which diversity is indeed observed by group members and ensure that associated conflicts are nipped into the bud so as to avoid negative consequences for team success. Whether this matters in the context of our study needs to be examined.

Both our on-going capstone project evaluations and team diversity research suggest that it is important to tackle potential inter-generational issues within an organization context through effective inter-generational communication strategies. One practical approach could be to conduct special workshops so that employees understand the basic values binding each generation and to promote a culture of (reverse) mentoring and knowledge sharing comprising different generations. Setting-up age-diverse project teams as communities of practice (Wenger and Snyder, 2000) can help to enable the division of responsibilities between generations, leveraging their capabilities to ensure innovation success. A key challenge is to convince top decision-makers that age diversity management frameworks actually make a difference.

With regard to the achievement of robust innovation outcomes on the basis of special (innovative) capstone projects as part of (post) graduate level courses on innovation, we argue that it is essential to shed more light on the ideal composition of the executive team and the ability of the team leader to inspire age-diverse team members. They also need to understand the intricacies of a particular market, including effective staffing of indispensable roles (e.g. sales and marketing) with "the right people". Strong teams can easily engage in group thinking and fall in love with mediocre ideas. Brutally honest feedback by experienced mentors and the use of a minimum viable product (MVP) to validate the business model can help to avoid prolonged failure. As an angel investor remarked during one of the MI course sessions, "80% of the innovation opportunities we reject do not fail because they do not deliver unique value. They fail because they are not solving a large enough problem that people have. I am sure they deliver some value but how much will people pay for it? They likely would need to monetize via advertising. But you can only do that if you have millions of users …". Building a strong (age-diverse) team and pushing team members in a more innovative way are just two of several ingredients for business scalability. While that may sound like common sense, it's not always commonly practiced by innovation team leaders.

References

Anderson, N.R. & West, M.A. (1998). Measuring climate for work group innovation: Development and validation of the team climate inventory. *Journal of Organizational Behavior*, *19*, 235–258.

Beh, L.-S. & Shafique, I. (2016). Does leadership matter in innovation and new business venturing? Testing the mediating effect of absorptive capacity. *International Journal of Innovation, Management and Technology*, *7*(5), 206–212. doi: http://dx.doi.org/10.18178/ijimt.2016.7.5.674.

Cogliser, C. C. & Brigham, K. H. (2004). The intersection of leadership and entrepreneurship: Mutual lessons to be learned. *The Leadership Quarterly, 15*(6), 771–799. doi: https://doi.org/10.1016/j.leaqua.2004.09.004.

Colette, H., Frances, H. & Claire, L. (2005). Entrepreneurship education and training: Can entrepreneurship be taught? Part II. *Education + Training, 47*(3), 158–169. doi: doi:10.1108/00400910510592211.

Cunningham, J. B. & Lischeron, J. (1991). Defining entrepreneurship. *Journal of Small Business Management, 29*(1), 45.

Funding & Grants. (2015). Retrieved November 25, 2015, from http://www.nrf. gov.sg/funding-grants.

Gupta, V., MacMillan, I. C. & Surie, G. (2004). Entrepreneurial leadership: Developing and measuring a cross-cultural construct. *Journal of Business Venturing, 19*(2), 241–260. doi: https://doi.org/10.1016/S0883-9026(03)00040-5.

Hentschel, T., Shemla, M., Wegge, J. & Kearney, E. (2013). Perceived diversity and team functioning: The role of diversity beliefs and affect. *Small Group Research, 44*(1), 33–61.

Ireland, R. D., Hitt, M. A. & Sirmon, D. G. (2003). A model of strategic entrepreneurship: The construct and its dimensions. *Journal of Management, 29*(6), 963–989. doi: 10.1016/S0149-2063_03_00086-2.

Kuratko, D. F. (2007). Entrepreneurial leadership in the 21st century. *Journal of Leadership & Organizational Studies, 13*(4), 1–11.

Leitch, C. M., McMullan, C. & Harrison, R. T. (2013). The development of entrepreneurial leadership: The role of human, social and institutional capital. *British Journal of Management, 24*(3), 347–366. doi: 10.1111/j.1467-8551.2011.00808.x.

Leitch, C. M. & Volery, T. (2017). Entrepreneurial leadership: Insights and directions. *International Small Business Journal, 35*(2), 147–156. doi: doi:10.1177/0266242616681397.

Matlay, H. (2008). The impact of entrepreneurship education on entrepreneurial outcomes. *Journal of Small Business and Enterprise Development, 15*(2), 382–396.

Narasimhalu, A. (2015). Singaporean entrepreneurship — Thinking bigger. *Asian Management Insights, 2*(1), 36–44.

Nicholson, N. (1998). Personality and entrepreneurial leadership: A study of the heads of the UK's most successful independent companies. *European Management Journal, 16*(5), 529–539. doi: https://doi.org/10.1016/S0263-2373(98)00030-9.

Renko, M., El Tarabishy, A., Carsrud, A. L. & Brännback, M. (2015). Understanding and measuring entrepreneurial leadership style. *Journal of Small Business Management, 53*(1), 54–74.

Surie, G. & Ashley, A. (2008). Integrating pragmatism and ethics in entrepreneurial leadership for sustainable value creation. *Journal of Business Ethics, 81*(1), 235–246. doi: http://dx.doi.org/10.1007/s10551-007-9491-4.

Van Katwyk, P. T., Fox, S., Spector, P. E. & Kelloway, E. K. (2000). Using the job-related affective well-being scale (JAWS) to investigate affective responses to work stressors. *Journal of Occupational Health Psychology,* 5(2), 219.

Webb, J. (2017). Singapore is Still the Most Expensive City in The World.

Wenger, E.C. & Snyder (2000). Communities of Practice: The Organizational Frontier. *Harvard Business Review, 78,* 139–145.

Case Study

SIA — How Do Innovators Stay Innovative? A Longitudinal Case Analysis*

Sven Tuzovic

School of Advertising, Marketing and Public Relations, Queensland University of Technology, Brisbane, Australia

Jochen Wirtz

Department of Marketing, National University of Singapore, Singapore, and

Loizos Heracleous

Warwick Business School, Coventry, UK

Abstract

Purpose — How can some companies be the innovation leader in their industry over prolonged periods of time, while others cannot? The purpose of this study is to understand a firm's capability to be a successful serial innovator and to generate a constant stream of industry-leading innovations.

Design/Methodology/Approach — The paper uses a longitudinal case study approach to gain an understanding of what and how Singapore Airlines (SIA) sustained service innovation for over 30 years. The study uses triangulation, whereby the core data from in-depth interviews with senior and middle management, and frontline employees were

*Note: This is a reprint of an article originally published in the *Journal of Services Marketing*, Vol. 32, No. 1, pp. 34–45 (https://doi.org/10.1108/JSM-02-2017-0052). The permission of the publisher (Emerald Publishing Limited) and the authors to reprint the article in this edition is gratefully acknowledged.

45

complemented with academic research, case studies, annual reports, observations, and archival documents. 240 single-spaced pages of interview transcripts with over 130,000 words were analyzed and coded using MAXQDA for identifying repeated patterns of meaning.

Findings — We identified three key institutional foundations for service innovation: (1) innovation climate (i.e., leadership and service culture), (2) human capital (i.e., recruitment, training and development, and engagement and incentives), and (3) resource configurations (i.e., systems, structure, and processes). These foundations enabled the organization to build the following four service innovation-related dynamic capabilities: (1) embrace ambidexterity, (2) institutionalize learning and knowledge integration, (3) orchestrate collaboration, and (4) reinvent customer value. Interestingly, these institutional foundations and capabilities remained largely stable across 30 years; what changed were the contexts and specifics, not the foundations and capabilities.

Research Limitations and Implications — Data were collected only from one company. Due to the method of thematic analysis the generalizability of our findings needs further investigation.

Originality/Value — This study is the first to investigate the drivers of industry-leading sustained service innovation over a prolonged period of time. The proposed framework provides a fuller and more integrated picture of sustained service innovation than past cross-sectional studies.

Keywords: service innovation; serial innovation; dynamic capabilities; longitudinal case study; Singapore Airlines

Introduction

"And that every time we reach a goal, we always say that we got to find a new mountain or hill to climb". (Senior Vice President Product & Service, 2001)

How can some companies be the innovation leader in their industry over prolonged periods of time (i.e., are serial innovators; Hamel 2006), while many cannot? Consider the case of *Singapore Airlines* (SIA). Founded in 1972, the airline has over decades routinely been voted the "best airline", "best business class", "best cabin crew service", "best in-flight food", "best for punctuality and safety", "best for business travelers", "best air cargo carrier", even "Asia's most admired company" (Wirtz *et al.* 2001;

Wirtz and Zeithaml 2017), and continues to be one of the most successful and consistently profitable airlines in the world (Deshpande and Hogan 2003; Wirtz and Zeithaml 2017). Evidence of the firm's sustained innovation performance includes the following:

1. In 1979, only six years after being formed, SIA was ranked first among 40 airlines in the Service Index Ratings prepared by International Research Associates (INRA) with a rating of 78 for esteem and performance, compared to an industry average of 62.9 (Wyckoff *et al.* 1989);
2. In 2016, SIA was ranked number 1 for 29 of the past 30 years in the Condé Nast Traveler's World's Best Airline Award (Singapore Airlines 2017);
3. SIA was the top-rated airline in the Customer Satisfaction Index of Singapore (CSISG) since its inception in 2008 (CSISG 2016).

SIA's success was built on its ability to be a serial innovator. *Serial innovation* occurs when an organization is repeatedly successful in adopting change over time (Hamel 2006). The airline pioneered a series of strategic innovations, introducing many firsts in the airline industry that sustained its competitive edge over decades in the face of intense cost pressure, industry crises, and trends towards commoditization (Heracleous and Wirtz 2010; Wirtz and Zeithaml 2017). Yet, even though SIA was well known for its service excellence, it was also one of the industry's most cost-effective operators (Wirtz and Zeithaml 2017).

The crucial question is: What enabled SIA to not only achieve but also sustain service innovation over very long periods of time? We define *sustained service innovation* as a firm's capacity to generate a stream of industry-leading innovations (i.e., multiple new products and services, encompassing both incremental and radical innovations) with a reasonable rate of commercial success (Dougherty and Hardy 1996). Understanding the determinants that allow an organization to be innovative over time has proved to be particularly complex (Corradini 2013).

While the academic literature has studied extensively *dynamic innovation capabilities*, almost all research has been cross-sectional with the notable exception of Damanpour *et al.* (2009) who studied a 4-year period (see Figure 1). Thus, these studies do not provide insights on how an organization can be a serial innovator over long periods of time. Here, our study makes an important contribution by exploring the long-term

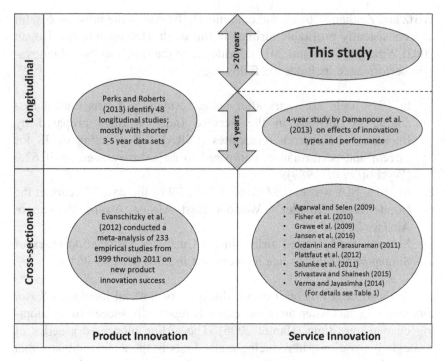

Figure 1:   Overview of the Literature and Positioning of this Study

institutional foundations and service innovation-related capabilities that enabled a firm to persistently innovate and prevail in a hyper-competitive business environment.

Literature Review and Background

Service innovation has been widely recognized as a primary source of competitive advantage (Snyder *et al.* 2016) and as a research priority (Ostrom *et al.* 2010). Historically, the innovation literature has primarily focused on products and technical innovations as opposed to services (Weerawardena and Mavondo 2011). Over the last decade, the body of scholarly research on service innovation has grown considerably (Carlborg *et al.* 2014; Lusch and Nambisan 2015). The research momentum underscores the significance given to service innovation in different fields, including marketing (Nijssen *et al.* 2006), strategy (Verma and Jayasimha 2014), economics (Djellal *et al.* 2013), and information systems (Kim *et al.* 2015).

Service innovation is a broad and loosely-defined concept (Witell *et al.* 2016). Salunke *et al.* (2011, p. 1253) conceptualize service innovation as "the extent to which new knowledge is integrated by the firm into service offerings, which directly or indirectly results in value for the firm and its customers". This view captures both continuous and discontinuous innovation and the improvement of existing services and the creation of radical new services.

In recent years, the topic of innovation persistence has attracted a growing interest by scholars in manufacturing and product contexts adopting a wide range of econometric approaches (see a review of 30 empirical studies by Le Bas and Scellato 2014) but with inconsistent results (Haned *et al.* 2014). Analyses of case studies suggest that "many elements, other than continuous R&D or continuous innovation output, influence the ability of firms to be persistent, successful innovators" (Lhuillery 2014, p. 518). For example, persistent innovators may use the market for technology more efficiently. The available literature on innovation success does not investigate the mechanisms which enable firms to replicate innovation success over time (Lhuillery 2014).

In the strategic management and marketing-related innovation literature, the discussion of *dynamic capabilities* (also referred to as innovation capability or innovative capability, c.f. Hogan *et al.* 2011) has gained prominence in understanding service innovation-based competitive advantage. A number of researchers have proffered different definitions and conceptualizations (e.g., Den Hertog *et al.* 2010; Eisenhardt and Martin 2000; Teece *et al.* 1997; Teece 2007). Teece *et al.* (1997) define dynamic capabilities as the firm's ability to integrate, build, and reconfigure internal and external competences to address rapidly changing environments. Eisenhardt and Martin (2000, p. 1107) provide an alternate view and argue that "dynamic capabilities are the organizational and strategic routines by which firms achieve new resource configurations as markets emerge, collide, split, evolve, and die". Salunke *et al.* (2011, p. 1252) define dynamic capabilities as the "capacity of an organization to purposefully create, extend or modify its knowledge-related resources, capabilities or routines to pursue improved effectiveness". Furthermore, some scholars distinguish between lower- and higher-order capabilities (Winter 2003), while others call those higher-order capabilities also meta capabilities (Collis 1994) or regenerative capabilities (Ambrosini *et al.* 2009). Despite the different definitions and conceptualizations, the dynamic capabilities perspective has become a prominent theoretical lens to study service innovation-based competitive advantage.

Empirical work has identified a number of dynamic capabilities, including strategic orientation, organizational learning, knowledge integration, and collaborative competencies. For an overview see Table 1. Note that these studies are predominantly cross-sectional. However, Le Bas and Scellato (2014) argue that dynamic capabilities co-evolve over time in step with a firm's innovation persistence and conclude that the institutional foundations for dynamic capabilities and firm innovation over time requires further study. We describe next the method we use to address this gap and examined the long-term innovation capability of a leading service organization.

Method

Research Approach

We adopted a longitudinal case study approach for three main reasons. First, case studies are deemed a suitable method when the proposed research is largely exploratory addressing "how" and "why" questions (Gummesson 2017; Yin 2014) and when the research question requires a need for richness of data (Stavros and Westberg 2009). Since dynamic capabilities are difficult to imitate their complex nature makes it also harder to identify them for research purposes (Fischer *et al.* 2010). Matvejeva *et al.* (2014, p. 550) argue that focusing "the analysis on one economic entity (a firm) allows going deeper into the details of internal processes and makes a valuable contribution to the understanding of the emerging relationships based on the qualitative richness of the discovered evidence".

Second, single case research is known for its descriptive power and attention to context, and recommended to study organizations that represent outstanding successes or notable failures (Ghauri 2004). As established in the introduction, SIA was recognized as an innovation and service leader for over 30 years.

Third, scholars have emphasized the importance of longitudinal studies in understanding the management of innovation in organizations (Damanpour *et al.* 2009; Van de Ven and Huber 1990). This view is particularly applicable to this study because the service innovation–performance relationship is path dependent and takes place over time

Table 1:   Empirical Studies of Dynamic Service Innovation Capabilities (DCs)

Authors	Sector/Country	Conceptualization of DCs	Key findings
Birkinshaw *et al.* (2016)	Pharmaceutical, (GSK), automotive (BMW), food (Nestle)	Lower-order (sensing and seizing) and higher-order (transforming/ reconfiguring) capabilities	1. Sensing, seizing and reconfiguring capabilities depend on three modes of adaptation (structural separation, e.g., Nestle, behavioral integration, e.g., GSK, and sequential alternation, e.g., BMW).
Fischer *et al.* (2010)	Capital goods industries; Germany and Switzerland	Sensing, seizing, reconfiguring	2. Companies either exploit or explore opportunities when it comes to service business development. 3. DCs differ between the two approaches and predict which way a company chooses.
Grawe *et al.* (2009)	Electronics industry; China	Customer orientation, cost orientation, competitor orientation	4. Both customer- and competitor-orientation are positively related to service innovation capability. 5. Relationship between cost-orientation and service innovation was not significant.
Janssen *et al.* (2016)	Multi-industry (76% services); Netherlands	Sensing (user needs and technological options), conceptualizing, coproducing/ orchestrating, scaling/stretching	6. Authors develop and validate a new scale of five DCs: (1) sensing user needs, (2) sensing technological options, (3) conceptualizing, (4) coproducing and orchestrating, and (5) scaling and stretching. 7. Sensing user needs and sensing (technological) options are linked to conceptualizing, which in turn is related to coproducing and orchestrating, and scaling and stretching. 8. Capabilities correlate to different extents with firm performance.
Ordanini and Parasuraman (2011)	Hotel industry; Italy	Collaborative competences, dynamic capability of customer orientation, knowledge interfaces	9. Customer collaboration contributes to innovation volume but not radicalness (and vice versa for collaborating with business partners).

(Continued)

Table 1: *(Continued)*

Authors	Sector/Country	Conceptualization of DCs	Key findings
Parida *et al.* (2015)	Manufacturing; global	Developing customer insights, integrating global knowledge, creating global service offerings, building digitalization capability	10. Path towards global service innovation is a gradual, three-step process which requires a distinct focus — (1) collaboration, (2) integration, and finally (3) orchestration.
Plattfaut *et al.* (2012)	IT consulting; Germany	Sensing, seizing and transformation	11. Capabilities of sensing, seizing and transforming vary for "event-dependent" (i.e., consulting projects for clients) and "event-independent" situations.
			12. Current understanding of dynamic capabilities was only partially useful for explaining service innovation at the client organization
Salunke *et al.* (2011)	Project-oriented service firms; Australia	Episodic learning, relational learning, client-focused learning, combinative capability	13. Innovation is an integral component of competitive strategy in project-oriented service firms.
			14. Episodic learning, relational learning, and client-focused learning are key drivers of service innovation.
			15. Building and nurturing these DCs involves three inter-related processes or routines: (1) create, (2) extend, and (3) modify.
Srivastava and Shainesh (2015)	Healthcare; India	Knowledge, technology, institutions	16. Identified four enablers of ICT-based service innovations: (1) obsessive customer empathy, (2) belief in transformational power of ICT, (3) continuous recursive learning, and (4) efficient network orchestration.
Verma and Jayasimha (2014)	Finance and IT consulting; Mexico	Collaborative efforts (customer & business partners), technology (IT infrastructure and knowledge integration mechanisms), organizational resources (market and innovation orientation)	17. DCs have a positive and significant relationship with service innovation success.
			18. Customer orientation strengthens the service delivery–performance relationship.

(Damanpour *et al.* 2009). Thus, the adoption of an innovation at a point in time will not sufficiently explain innovation success over time (Damanpour *et al.* 2009).

Given the widespread recognition of SIA as an innovation leader over the last 30 years, we consider this in-depth study of SIA to be both a unique and revelatory case (c.f., Yin 2014). Aligned with our research question, SIA allowed us to explore patterns of persistent innovation capabilities that are instrumental to achieving sustained industry-leading service innovation.

Data Collection

We analyzed data from a number of sources, both primary research and secondary data. Our primary research consisted of in-depth interviews with SIA's management and staff, and was conducted in four phases (see Figure 2). The interviews were exhaustive, ranging from approximately 45 to 75 minutes, and were conducted by two interviewers simultaneously which facilitated in-depth coverage of issues (c.f., Salunke *et al.* 2011). During the interviews, probing questions were used to clarify and explore participants' responses and to elicit further insights (Creswell 2009). The interviewers followed an emergent design method with the purpose to

Overview of SIA's break-through service innovations:

1) 1970s: SIA was first to offer free drinks, free headsets and choice of meals
2) 1991: First to launch phone and fax services on board
3) 1998: One of first airlines to set up a website
4) 2001: SIA the first airline to provide audio- and video-on-demand to all passengers in all classes
5) 2004: World's longest non-stop flight from Singapore to New York City (SQ-21)
6) 2006: Introduced world's widest First and Business Class seats, which transformed into fully-flat beds
7) 2007: First airline to fly the Airbus A380
8) 2009: First to offer iPod and iPhone connectivity in Economy Class
9) 2013: First airline to introduce 3D games on board
10) 2013: Launched next generation of cabin products, set to be the new industry benchmark for premium air travel
11) 2017: New "Skyroom" Suites on the A380

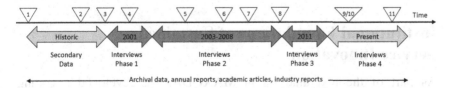

Figure 2:   Timeline of Data Collection and Selected SIA's Innovations

add, delete, and modify questions throughout the research process (Taylor and Bogdan 1984).

Note that the interviews for phases 1 to 3 were conducted for previously published research by Heracleous, Wirtz and colleagues to explore SIA's strategy and competitiveness. Their publications were based on subsets of the interviews using traditional analysis. For this study, we reanalyzed the complete set of interviews with a focus on service innovation using a computer-assisted tool. Table 2 summarizes the sample characteristics.

All interviews were recorded and transcribed resulting in 240 single-spaced pages of transcripts comprising a total of 130,297 words. Transcripts were read for accuracy and then imported into MAXQDA12 (www.maxqda.com), a computer-assisted qualitative data analysis tool (Silver and Lewins 2014). The transcribed interviews were subjected to thematic analysis (Boyatzis 1998), an analytic technique suitable for identifying "repeated patterns of meaning" (Braun and Clarke 2006, p. 86). We followed a systematic step-wise recursive process in the thematic analysis of the data as suggested by Braun and Clarke (2006).

Multiple sources in case research help to validate and triangulate emerging ideas and interpretations (Golden 1992). Therefore, we complemented our primary data with our field notes from observations within SIA, SIA's annual reports, archival records, industry reports, academic publications (e.g., Heracleous and Wirtz 2010; Heracleous, Wirtz and Pangarkar 2009; Wirtz and Zeithaml 2017; Wirtz *et al.* 2003, 2007, 2008) and case studies on SIA (Deshpande and Hogan 2003; Deshpande and Lau 2016; Goh 2005; Wyckoff *et al.* 1989).

We then returned to literature to compare the emergent themes with existing frameworks (Salunke *et al.* 2011). This approach is consistent with Eisenhardt's (1989) observation that tying emergent theory to extant literature enhances the internal validity, generalizability, and theoretical level. Figure 2 illustrates the timeline of data collection and selected SIA innovations.

Institutional Foundations of Sustained Service Innovation

As part of the text analysis in MAXQDA, we developed a coding theme based on the literature (e.g., code: collaboration; keywords:

Table 2: In-depth Interviews Analyzed

Phase	Year	No.	Gender	Position
1	2001		Female	Senior Manager HRD
	2001		Male	Senior Vice President Cabin Crew
	2001		Male	Senior Manager Cabin Crew Performance
	2001		Female	Senior Manager Cabin Crew Training
	2001		Female	Senior Manager Cabin Crew Service Development
	2001		Male	Senior Vice President Product & Service
	2001		Female	Commercial Training Manager
2	2003		Male	Senior Vice President Product & Service
	2004		Male	Senior Manager, Product Innovation
	2004		Male	New Service Development
	2005		Male	Senior Manager, Product Innovation
	2005		Male	Senior Manger cabin crew performance
	2005		Male	Senior Manager, Crew Performance
	2006		Male	Cabin Crew
	2006		Female	Cabin Crew
	2008		Male	VP Company Planning & Fuel
	2008		Male	VP Contracts (former VP Product Development)
3	2011		Male	Acting Senior Vice President Cabin Crew
	2011		Female	Vice President Customer Affairs
	2011		Male	Vice President Product Innovation
	2011		Male	Senior Vice President Human Resources
	2011		Female	Inflight Supervisor
	2011		Male	Inflight Supervisor
	2011		Female	Senior Manager Inflight Services
	2011		Male	Vice President Public Affairs
	2011		Male	Manager Performance Management and Development
	2011		Male	Senior Vice President Product & Services
4	2016		Male	Senior Vice President Customer Affairs
	2017		Male	Senior Vice President Customer Affairs

cross-functional collaboration, collaborating with [business partners/ customers], to engage customers, customer engagement, customer participation, to talk with customers). Our initial themes were guided by dynamic capability theory. We then searched for similarities and differences between the codes to start grouping them into a hierarchical tree structure. New codes were created in an iterative fashion to capture the meaning of groups of initial codes (Thomas and Harden 2007). Next, the interview findings were triangulated with our secondary data.

This analysis suggests that different determinants were responsible for SIA's sustained service innovation success which can be grouped into two broad categories. We labeled the first category *institutional foundations* (also referred to as organizational assets, c.f. Galbreath 2005) consisting of innovation climate, human capital, and resource configurations. The second category was labeled *innovation-related dynamic capabilities* (c.f. Ngo and O'Cass 2009; also referred to as innovative capabilities, Chen 2009). One surprising finding is that these foundations and capabilities seem to be stable over time. While terminology, technology, and contexts changed, the basic underlying foundations and capabilities did not. See Figure 3 for an overview of our findings. We discuss the findings related to institutional foundations in this section.

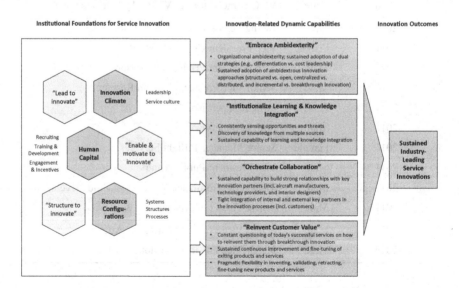

Figure 3:   **Proposed Framework of Sustained Industry-leading Service Innovation**

Innovation Climate ("lead to innovate")

Our case data suggest that SIA built and nurtured a strong *innovation climate*, driven by leadership that consistently over decades emphasized the importance of innovation to retain SIA's industry-leading position. This forceful emphasis on innovation by SIA's leadership resulted in a strong innovation culture that transcended the entire organization. The result was that SIA was involved in "constant innovation" to improve existing products and services as it internalized forward-thinking to push for regular "quantum leap innovations", largely driven by customer needs, technology and the conviction of having to stay ahead of competitors. This focus on innovation was prominent over all decades studied as shown by the quotes below:

> *Because we are SIA we have a brand to support, a brand that says that we have to be a premium carrier, and that we always do better than our competitors. That's why our customers want to fly with us.* (Senior Vice President Product & Service, 2003)

> *[Innovation] is to a large extent governed by ... the need to differentiate, in other words staying ahead as we are a premium carrier.* (Senior Vice President Product & Service, 2003)

> *The culture of innovation is so pervasive in the company that most functional departments have the innovation objective as part of their mission.* (Senior Manager, Product Innovation, 2005)

> *A flight has many, many sub-components. By being better at every one of these sub-components we give our competitors a hard time. By the time they copy, we would already have moved ahead. This means constant innovation, and constant development in all the things we do.* (Senior Vice President of Product and Service Department, 2009)

> *Everyone in this company really understands the value of innovation. ... You always have to stay a step ahead.* (Vice President of Public Affairs, 2011)

Human Capital ("enable & motivate to innovate")

SIA's innovation success was enabled by highly capable human resources. Specifically, SIA consistently invested heavily in human capital over the

30-year period studied, including having a rigorous and well-developed processes relating to recruitment, training and development, and employee engagement and incentives. One interviewee referred to training at SIA as "almost next to godliness". One of the important outcomes of having top quality human capital was its systematic and company-wide innovation capability driven by SIA employees' future and innovation orientation, and their pro-activeness, creativity, and readiness to innovate. These capabilities were supported through a clear innovation component in all human capital-related policies (e.g., constant job rotation to drive improvements and innovation), activities (e.g., training), and targets and incentives (e.g., performance evaluations contain innovation-related KPIs) as is shown in the quotes below:

> *Within the Product Innovation Department there is what we call the innovation lab, where resources are on a one-year basis. This person who comes in can be from anywhere in the company, be it the cabin crew or the engineering division or elsewhere. They would be asked to come into this idea lab, where they will spend one year coming up with ideas.* (VP Contracts, former VP Product Development, 2008)

> *So [there are] a lot of areas for improvement because this is a huge organization. ... So it's ... about process improvement, training, to drive up productivity and quality of the people.* (Senior Vice President Product & Services, 2011)

> *There's a group of them [cabin crew], and we're asking them to brainstorm. We have certain objectives, so ... we do this kind of thing quite regularly.* (Inflight Supervisor, 2011)

> *[The] innovation process can be a bit chaotic. ... We need to be able to think out of the box. And sometimes pressures come in and people are creative when they're under some pressure.* (Senior Manager Inflight Services, 2011)

> *Their KPI is how many good ideas they can come up with. It's not easy, it's very challenging actually* (VP Contracts, 2008)

Resource Configurations ("structure to innovate")

The interviews show that SIA supported its innovation capability through adapting and reconfiguring its structures, systems, and processes. Change in these was a constant to adapt to changing customer requirements, competitor activity and technology. However, throughout the 30-year period, structures, systems and processes were in place to drive innovation as is shown in the quotes below. For example, SIA established the program "Future Works" which was an annual mini boot camp that consisted of some 50 executives from various departments to work on SIA's next breakthrough innovations:

> *The concept is to bring together a group of people from different departments and backgrounds, lock them up for a few days ... and do brainstorming. Participants will have a chance to let their imagination run wild. At the end of the workshop, they will be given a chance to present their ideas to the Venture Board, a selected group of SIA's senior vice presidents. Funds will be provided to develop ideas if the board endorses them.* (Senior Manager, Product Innovation, 2004)

More recently, Future Works was superseded by a different program which places staff from various departments of the company into the innovation lab for a year to come up with new ideas and to involve others in developing and testing them.

Furthermore, SIA internalized the concept of "distributed innovation" (Lakhani and Panetta 2007; von Hippel 2005), also referred to as open innovation, which is decentralized and unstructured in nature. This fluid and flexible approach to distributed innovation enabled and encouraged departments and individuals to take ownership of their innovations. Thus, employees felt more motivated that their ideas contributed to SIA's performance. For example, one initiative that ran for over 10 years globally across all stations and units was Transforming Customer Service (TCS):

> *TCS is a pretty integrated system where you look at not only the processes, but you [also] look at the people. And the customer is the underlying reason why you do those things. Because, basically, what you want is to anticipate the customer's needs, to exceed the customer's wants. And you want to empower your people to be able to do that. And to put into place processes that enable the employees to do that. So it is interrelated. It is seen as one. You cut it down and dissect it. When you do service process reengineering, you actually dissect it into bits where you just examine that. But actually, it's linked together.* (Senior Manager HRD, 2001)

Service Innovation-Related Dynamic Capabilities

The interview analysis suggests four broad clusters of dynamic capabilities that enabled SIA's sustained service innovation (see Figure 3). We describe these capabilities and feature sample quotes below.

Embracing Ambidexterity

The case data suggest that SIA managed to embrace ambidexterity and pursue paradoxical positions. First, its dual focus on differentiation and cost leadership was an important driver and consideration in almost all innovations. For example, SIA's innovation department did not only focus on service innovations but also rigorously emphasized costs. When SIA launched the then-widest business class seat in the industry, it designed it to "wow" travelers. The seat could be flipped over and turned into a flat bed with a duvet and a bigger pillow. As the flipping was done manually, the number of heavy motors in a seat could be reduced which resulted in significant savings in manufacturing, fuel, and repair and maintenance.

Second, SIA sustained innovation by having adopted a seamless combination of centralized (i.e., structured and rigorous) and distributed (i.e., open and emergent), and break-through and incremental innovations. For example, the Product Innovation Department followed a well-defined innovation framework that guided processes, including opportunity identification and selection, concept evaluation, design and development, and new service launches. This central unit focused on ground-breaking, dramatic innovations such as the cabin design of the newly launched A380 in 2007 and its new "Skyroom" Suites in 2017, but also developed more incremental improvements:

> *We launched our new Japanese meal. It has been around with us for many years, but after 10 years or so, we enhance it and give it new look.* (Senior Manager Inflight Services, 2011)

> *We continue to enhance [the] business class seat ... as part of this refresh programme.* (Manager New Service Development, 2011)

While the large, centralized innovation department was key in driving significant and incremental innovations, SIA also showed a strong distributed innovation capability:

The idea is that innovation is not the sole monopoly of one small group of people here. I have only 18 people, how much can we do? Future Works want to tap the resources of the whole company. (Senior Manager, Product Innovation, 2004)

Whether you are in Product Innovation or whether you are in Inflight Services, Ground Services and so on ... they are all very innovation-oriented, so in that sense, it is decentralized to all these departments. (Senior Manager, Product Innovation, 2005)

Institutionalizing Learning and Knowledge Integration

The interviews show that SIA used intensive sensing, discovering and accumulating of knowledge from a wide range of sources, and managed to integrate and synthesize all this information. SIA embedded employees, customers, suppliers, contractors, and design firms in the knowledge accumulation process. SIA constantly monitored customer feedback on current service offerings, tracked competitors' products and service, and used extensively surveys and benchmarking tools. The case data show that SIA managed to implement learning routines and processes (e.g., feedback loops between cabin crew and the service department), and establish knowledge interfaces across the organization, share knowledge across units, and integrate the knowledge to sense opportunities and problems to develop solutions. This capability was visible across the entire 30-year period of observation. The following quotes illustrate this capability:

I am [in] product innovation. So what we have to do is bring in in-flight entertainment people and engineers and cabin crew and so on. Then we will explain what the concepts are [and ask] are you all interested, do you think that for your product this is going to add value? If they say yes, that will be one more endorsement from the users. Then we will sit together and do a business case. (Senior Manager, Product Innovation, 2004)

How we explore that? It's a lot of interactive processes. (Senior Manager Inflight Services, 2011)

One of the things we can do in terms of innovation is not necessarily always coming up with new ideas. If somebody can do [something] very well, we can emulate them and do better. (Senior Manager, Product Innovation, 2004)

Orchestrating Collaboration

Innovation at SIA was generally conducted jointly with key internal stakeholders and a network of external innovation partners, including technology suppliers, aircraft manufacturers, airports, and of course, customers. The case evidence suggests that SIA had recognized the strategic importance of collaborative relationships for a long time and therefore had orchestrated their participation in the innovation process and developed close relationships with these partners. For example, SIA engaged in a strategic partnership with Panasonic for redesigning its inflight entertainment system. They worked closely with external vendors where they sometimes even provided ideas for new products their vendors would develop. The following quotes illustrate how SIA orchestrated internal and external collaboration:

> *In SIA, we used a lot of task forces. We are only the product people, so we work with the engineering department ... there would also representatives from cabin crew and inflight services.* (VP Contracts, former VP Product Development, 2008)

> *Cabin crew can tell us, they feel that this product may not work ... they're [an] important integral of this process, because if they can't deliver, no matter how good the product is, it is useless.* (Senior Manager Inflight Services, 2011)

> *We engage [customers throughout] the stages of the development cycle, we actually call back some of these customers ... I don't think it's done anywhere else in the world.* (VP Contracts, former VP Product Development, 2008)

> *I view the [airport] lounge for us as a place to engage our customers... one of the key concepts is to allow passengers to test and give feedback, and to get them involved in the development process.* (Senior Vice President Product & Services, 2011)

> *[This] collaborative approach, with aircraft manufacturer, Boeing, Airbus, with the design firms, with the seat manufacturers, stakeholders within and cross-division colleagues [is] even more prevalent.* (Vice President Product Innovation, 2011)

> *We have to plant the ideas into the software developers [SIA's vendor] to enable this idea at the end of the day.* (Senior Vice President Product & Services, 2011)

Reinventing Customer Value

SIA was able to constantly transform and reconfigure existing value constellations that oftentimes did not just lead to innovative products and services, but that redefined industry standards. When SIA introduced its first suite in 2007, coinciding with the inaugural Airbus A380 passenger flight, it was a "big deal" as no other airline had ever put a double bed on an airplane. SIA's 2007 annual report described the new Suite Class as "truly a class that goes beyond first". A decade later, SIA was still able to "wow" customers. SIA recently introduced a "massive new suite" for the Airbus A380. This constant questioning and reinventing of its value propositions is shown in the quotes below.

It's very easy to love what we do, and that's the danger. It's easy to say that the customers will surely want what we do. To be a winner, we have to continually strive to provide the very best service when compared with any industry. That's why it's so challenging. Whatever we do, we are in search of excellence and are never willing to settle for what we have already achieved. It's good to be passionate, but I think you must be able to say "I'm willing to kill it with a better program". And that is a huge challenge internally. We have to be able to tell ourselves that, "I love this new thing that I've developed and we'll make sure that it's well implemented". However, we also have to kill it with a better product in X number of months. It could be six months, it could be 12 months, it could be 20 months. But you have got to kill it because the lifestyles of our customers are continuously evolving ... This means constant innovation and constant development in all the things that we do. (Senior Vice President Product & Service, 2003)

When we introduced our new business class called Space Bed on board, it has always been our tradition, every time we do anything we do it in a package. It is a stronger proposition to our customer than to say that I have a better cup. We say that the cup comes with better coffee, better delivery, better design and better software. It is not just talking about the cup. Same thing when we introduced the seat. We talk about our service, our food, our thing. (Senior Vice President Product & Service, 2003)

Everyone can have similar aircraft as long as you have the capital. But for SIA, what makes us different is in our configuration in the aircraft (Senior Manager Inflight Services, 2011)

All our departmental heads, including myself, try to encourage our man-agers to be centres of discontentment! They have to be continuously unhappy with some things. I mean that you just have to have the sense to continually assess everything, and preferably before your boss asks you. As a result of the constant injection of new blood into the company, there is a breath of fresh air. Just asking questions, "why can't I have it, why does it have to be this way". The only problem I see in SIA is that if we stop people from asking those questions. Then we would be in big trouble. (Senior Vice President Product & Service, 2003)

Discussion, Implications and Further Research

Our initial question was "Why are some companies able to innovate time and again, while others cannot?" We selected SIA as a *unique* and *revelatory* case (Yin 2014) and conducted a 30-year longitudinal study to investigate the firm's capability to be a successful serial innovator and to generate a constant stream of industry-leading innovations.

We identified three key institutional foundations for service innovation: (1) innovation climate (i.e., leadership and innovative culture), (2) human capital (i.e., recruitment, training and development, and engagement and incentives), and (3) resource configurations (i.e., structures, systems, and processes). These building blocks were the foundation for four service innovation-related dynamic capabilities of (1) embracing ambidexterity, (2) institutionalizing learning and knowledge integration, (3) orchestrating collaboration, and (4) reinventing customer value.

Theoretical Implications

Despite the growing body of knowledge, the concept of service innovation remains relatively unexplored (Carlborg *et al.* 2014; Salunke *et al.* 2011). Scholars have argued that uncovering the organizational antecedents of service innovation is still one of the main challenges in the literature (Janssen *et al.* 2014; Ostrom *et al.* 2010). We expand the current service innovation literature in several ways.

First, we identified the significance of innovation climate, investments in human capital and resource configurations as key institutional foundational drivers of sustained service innovation in a hyper-competitive and commoditized industry (c.f., Rothkopf and Wald 2011; Wirtz and

Jerger 2017). Our results are consistent with dynamic capability theory which "assigns a prominent role to the firm's strategic leadership in nurturing and building of dynamic capabilities critical to the value generation process" (Salunke *et al.* 2011, p. 1252). While we have not seen an integrated examination and discussion of these three foundational elements in the service innovation literature, these topics have been addressed separately in other areas of the literature. For instance, the critical connection between leadership and resource utilization may not surprise resource-based view theorists in the strategic human resource management literature. They emphasized the critical role of human capital and the "centrality of HR issues to the understanding and development of dynamic capabilities" (Wright *et al.* 2001, p. 713). Our research thus extends the view within the service innovation literature to institutional foundations as drivers of the dynamic capability building process (e.g., Salunke *et al.* 2011) and provides a fuller and more integrated view on the institutional foundations required to deliver sustained service innovation.

Second, our findings related to institutional learning and knowledge integration and on orchestrating collaboration are consistent with prior cross-sectional dynamic capabilities research and confirm their relevance for long-term innovation success. In particular, we see consistent arguments for the importance of the following dynamic capabilities: sensing opportunities (Janssen *et al.* 2016; Plattfaut *et al.* 2012), "technology sensing" (Kindström *et al.* 2013), organizational learning (Salunke *et al.* 2011), knowledge sharing/integration (Srivastava and Shainesh 2015), the importance of continuous recursive learning in improving service delivery and effectiveness (Srivastava and Shainesh 2015), and collaboration (Agarwal and Selen 2009; Ordanini and Parasuraman 2011; Verma and Jayasimha 2014).

Our findings that SIA innovations evolve from joined actions of a network of actors in a service ecosystem is also consistent with extant research (e.g., Lusch and Nambisan 2015; Zhang *et al.* 2015) and confirms its importance for sustained innovation. Customer engagement in particular has gained considerable attention among practitioners and in the academic community (Brodie *et al.* 2011, 2016; Hollebeek *et al.* 2014, 2016) and has been emphasized many times as a success driver of service innovation (e.g., Chen *et al.* 2016). Interestingly, we noted that SIA had a long history of involving customers (e.g., their frequent fliers) in innovation processes. While SIA did not use the term "customer engagement" until more recently, we see clear evidence that SIA had a customer centric culture and was following customer needs and wants, and was closely engaged with its various key customer segments.

Third, our findings suggest that ambidexterity is an important capability related to service innovation which can lead to sustained service innovation performance (c.f., Gibson and Birkinshaw 2004; O'Reilly III and Tushman 2013). A paradox involves "contradictory yet interrelated elements that exist simultaneously and persist over time" (Smith and Lewis 2011, p. 382). Specifically, we found that SIA managed consistently to follow "dual strategies" (c.f., Wirtz and Zeithaml 2017) and challenged paradoxical extremes in its approach to innovation. For example, SIA simultaneously pursued differentiation through service excellence and cost orientation, adopted a seamless combination of centralized (i.e., structured and rigorous) with distributed (i.e., open and emergent) innovation, and pursued ground-breaking, dramatic innovations and incremental improvements at the same time. Our findings confirm past research that demonstrated a positive relationship between ambidexterity and innovation (c.f., O'Reilly III and Tushman 2013). However, it appears that the discussion has mainly focused on the comparison between exploration versus exploitation and less on differentiation (e.g., SIA's premium positioning) versus cost leadership. Furthermore, our findings emphasize the importance of ambidexterity, which has hitherto not received much attention in the service innovation literature.

Finally, an important and to us somewhat surprising finding is that the three identified institutional foundations and four dynamic capabilities seem to be stable over time. While terminology, technology, and contexts changed, the basic underlying foundations and capabilities remained largely constant. SIA consistently adapted to changing conditions in the service ecosystem. For example, SIA embraced new technologies (e.g., Internet, CRM systems, biometrics, mobile and RFID technology) to improve existing service processes and to engage customers more actively in the ideation and testing of new services. However, the basic blocks such as SIA's focus on building an innovation climate, human capital and supportive structures, systems and processes remained firmly in place, and the four dynamic capabilities where clearly present throughout the 30-year period studied. These findings align to the views of institutional theorists who contend that "because institutional elements (structures, actions, roles) are authorized to legitimate other elements, institutionalized aspects are simultaneously highly stable and responsible for creating new institutional elements" (Zucker 1987, p. 446).

Managerial Implications

The literature suggests that managers in high-velocity markets face not only external pressure of competition, but also the internal challenge of collapsing dynamic capabilities (Eisenhardt and Martin 2000). Our study offers managers a roadmap to examine a pathway to sustained service innovation performance which consists of two blocks. First, managers need to focus on institutional foundations, beginning with leadership to build an innovation climate. This goes in hand with "aligning skills, motives, and so forth with organizational systems, structures, and processes" (Wright *et al.* 2001, p. 710) in order to achieve organizational capabilities (c.f. Hamel and Prahalad 1994; Wright *et al.* 2001). Oftentimes, organizations tend to focus their innovation efforts on short-term practices and episodic innovations. In order to achieve sustained service innovation performance, firms need to have visionary leaders that inspire employees and cultivate a service-centric culture.

Second, our framework offers managers a fuller and more integrated picture than past cross-sectional studies on the dynamic capabilities required to sustain service innovation. There are four categories of dynamic innovation capabilities managers should examine and build in their own organization. Specifically, managers should (1) evaluate their current strategic orientations and embrace organizational ambidexterity, (2) establish a framework for developing and managing knowledge and enhance the learning processes in the organization; (3) invest in collaborative ideation processes involving all relevant stakeholders internally (especially frontline employees) and externally (including customers and business partners); and (4) foster a culture of discontent with current services and solutions to constantly reinvent the customer value offered in ongoing incremental innovation and periodic break-through new services.

SIA had a long tradition of service excellence and organizational ambidexterity. Thus, managers cannot expect to swiftly change their organizations overnight to become serial innovators. As research shows, "firms are to some degree stuck with what they have and may have to live with what they lack" (Teece *et al.* 1997, p. 514). Nevertheless, we hope that our research helps managers to understand a fuller and more integrated view of how to move their organizations towards becoming sustained innovation leaders in their respective industries.

Limitations and Future Research

This study has several limitations that offer avenues for further research. First, qualitative data were collected from a single organization. To generalize our findings and validate the proposed framework, a necessary next step is to conduct in-depth case analyses of other leading serial innovators, followed by a quantitative study. Second, our results highlighted that SIA is an ambidextrous organization. More research is needed to investigate how different types of organizational ambidexterity (i.e., temporal, structural, and contextual) at the different organizational levels (i.e., organization, group, and individual) influence sustained service innovation. Third, we developed a framework that integrates institutional foundations and dynamic capabilities as drivers of sustained service innovation. Further research is needed to study the interrelationships between innovation climate, human capital, and resource configurations on the development of innovation-related dynamic capabilities.

In conclusion, this study offers a broadened view of sustained service innovation and identified three institutional foundations and four dynamic capabilities that allowed SIA to be the innovation leader in its industry over a prolonged period of time. The proposed framework provides a fuller and more integrated view than what is available in the extant literature on what it takes to for an organization to deliver sustained service innovation. We hope that the emergent framework will encourage future research on this important topic.

References

Agarwal, R. and Selen, W. (2009), "Dynamic Capability Building in Service Value Networks for Achieving Service Innovation," *Decision Sciences*, 40(3), 431–475.

Ambrosini, V., Bowman, C. and Collier, N. (2009), "Dynamic capabilities: an exploration of how firms renew their resource," *British Journal of Management*, 20(S1), S9–S24.

Birkinshaw, J., Zimmermann, A., and Raisch, S. (2016), "How Do Firms Adapt to Discontinuous Change?" *California Management Review*, 58(4), 36–58.

Boyatzis, R.E. (1998), *Transforming Qualitative Information*, Sage: Cleveland.

Braun, V. and Clarke, V. (2006), "Using thematic analysis in psychology," *Qualitative Research in Psychology*, 3(2), 77–101.

Brodie, R.J., Hollebeck, L.D., and Conduit, J. (2016), *Customer Engagement: Contemporary Issues and Challenges*, Routledge: London.

Brodie, R. J., Hollebeek, L. D., Jurić, B., and Ilić, A. (2011), "Customer Engagement: Conceptual Domain, Fundamental Propositions, and Implications for Research," *Journal of Service Research*, 14(3), 252–271.

Carlborg, P., Kindström, D., and Kowalkowski, C. (2014). "The evolution of service innovation research: a critical review and synthesis," *The Service Industries Journal*, 34(5), 373–398.

Chen, J.S., Weng, H.H. and Huang, C.L. (2016): "A multilevel analysis of customer engagement, its antecedents, and the effects on service innovation," *Total Quality Management & Business Excellence*, 1–19.

Chen, C. -J. (2009), "Technology commercialization, incubator and venture capital, and new venture performance," *Journal of Business Research*, 62(1), 93–103.

Collis, D.J. (1994), "Research note: how valuable are organizational capabilities," *Strategic Management Journal*, 15(1), 143–152.

Corradini, C. (2013), *Serial and persistent innovation in UK small companies*, Ph.D. thesis, University of Nottingham.

CSISG (2016), *Customer Satisfaction Index of Singapore: Scores and Ranking*, https://ises.smu.edu.sg/csisg-release-schedule (accessed on March 18, 2017).

Creswell, J.W. (2009), *Research design: qualitative, quantitative, and mixed methods approaches*, 3rd ed., Thousand Oaks: Sage.

Damanpour, F., Walker, R.M., and Avellaneda, C.N. (2009), "Combinative Effects of Innovation Types and Organizational Performance: A Longitudinal Study of Service Organizations," *Journal of Management Studies*, 46(4), 650–675.

Den Hertog, P., van der Aa, W. and de Jong, M.W. (2010), "Capabilities for managing service innovation: towards a conceptual framework," *Journal of Service Management*, 21(4), 490–514.

Deshpande, R. and Hogan, H. (2003), *Singapore Airlines: Customer Service Innovation*, Boston, MA: Harvard Business School Publishing.

Deshpande, R. and Lau, D.H. (2016), *Singapore Airlines: Premium Goes Multi-Brand*, Boston, MA: Harvard Business School Publishing.

Djellal, F., Gallouj, F., and Miles, I. (2013), "Two decades of research on innovation in services: Which place for public services?" *Structural Change & Economic Dynamics*, 27, 98–117.

Eisenhardt, K.M. (1989), "Building Theories from Case Study Research," *Academy of Management Review*, 14(4), 532–550.

Eisenhardt, K.M. and Martin, J.A. (2000), "Dynamic Capabilities: What are they?" *Strategic Management Journal*, 21, 1105–1121.

Evanschitzky, H., Eisend, M., Calantone, R. J., & Jiang, Y. (2012), "Success Factors of Product Innovation: An Updated Meta-Analysis," *Journal of Product Innovation Management*, 29(S1), 21–37.

Fischer, T., Gebauer, H., Gregory, M., Ren, G., and Fleisch, E. (2010), "Exploitation or exploration in service business development: Insights from a dynamic capabilities perspective," *Journal of Service Management*, 21(5), 591–624.

Galbreath, J. (2005), "Which resources matter the most to firm success? An exploratory study of resource-based theory," *Technovation*, 25(9), 979–987.

Ghauri, P. (2004), "Designing and Conducting Case Studies in International Business Research," in *Handbook of Qualitative Research Methods for International Business*, Rebecca Piekkari and Catherine Welch (Eds.), Chapter 5, Edward Elgar Publishing: Northampton.

Gibson, C.B. and Birkinshaw, J. (2004), "The Antecedents, Consequences, and Mediating Role of Organizational Ambidexterity," *Academy of Management Journal*, 47(2), 209–226.

Goh, A.L. (2005), "Fostering Innovation through Knowledge-Centered Principles: A Case Analysis of Singapore Airlines," *International Journal of Knowledge Management* (IJKM), 1(4), 73–90.

Golden, B.R. (1992), "The past is the past — or is it? The use of retrospective accounts as indicators of past strategy," *Academy of Management Journal*, 35(4), 848–860.

Grawe, S. J., Haozhe, C., and Daugherty, P. J. (2009), "The relationship between strategic orientation, service innovation, and performance," *International Journal of Physical Distribution & Logistics Management*, 39(4), 282–300.

Gummesson, E. (2017), *Case Theory in Business and Management. Reinventing Case Study Research*, Thousand Oaks, CA: Sage.

Hamel, G. (2006), "The why, what, and how of management innovation," *Harvard Business Review*, 84(2), 72–84.

Hamel, G. and Prahalad, C.K. (1994), "Competing for the future," *Harvard Business Review*, 72(4), 122–129.

Haned, N., Mothe, C., and Nguyen, U. (2014), "Firm Persistence in Technological Innovation: The Relevance of Organizational Innovation," *Economics of Innovation and New Technology*, 23(5–6), 490–516.

Heracleous, L. and Wirtz, J. (2010), "Singapore Airlines' Balancing Act — Asia's Premier Carrier Successfully Executes a Dual Strategy: It Offers World-Class Service and is a Cost Leader," *Harvard Business Review*, 88 (7/8), 145–149.

Heracleous, L., Wirtz, J. and Pangarkar, N. (2009), *Flying High in a Competitive Industry: Secrets of the World's Leading Airline*, Singapore: McGraw-Hill.

Hogan, S.J., Soutar, G.N., McColl-Kennedy, J.R., and Sweeney, J.C. (2011), "Reconceptualizing professional service firm innovation capability: Scale development," *Industrial Marketing Management*, 40(8), 1264–1273.

Hollebeek, L., Glynn, M.S., and Brodie, R.J. (2014), "Consumer Brand Engagement in Social Media: Conceptualization, Scale Development and Validation," *Journal of Interactive Marketing*, 28, 149–165.

Hollebeek, L., Srivastava, R., and Chen, T. (2016), "S-D logic–informed customer engagement: integrative framework, revised fundamental propositions, and application to CRM," *Journal of the Academy of Marketing Science*, 1–25.

Janssen, M. J., Castaldi, C., and Alexiev, A. (2016), "Dynamic capabilities for service innovation: conceptualization and measurement," *R&D Management*, 46(4), 797–811.

Kim, M., Song, J., and Triche, J. (2015), "Toward an integrated framework for innovation in service: A resource-based view and dynamic capabilities approach," *Information Systems Frontiers*, 17(3), 533–546.

Kindström, D., Kowalkowski, C., and Sandberg, E. (2013). Enabling service innovation: A dynamic capabilities approach. *Journal of Business Research*, 66(8), 1063–1073.

Lakhani, K.R., and Panetta, J.A. (2007), "The Principles of Distributed Innovation," *Innovations*, 2(3), 97–112.

Le Bas, C. and Scellato, G. (2014), "Firm innovation persistence: a fresh look at the frameworks of analysis," *Economics of Innovation and New Technology*, 23(5–6), 423–446.

Lhuillery, S. (2014), "Marketing and Persistent Innovation Success," *Economics of Innovation and New Technology*, 23(5–6), 517–543.

Lusch, R.F. and Nambisan, S. (2015), "Service Innovation: A Service-Dominant Logic Perspective," *MIS Quarterly*, 39(1), 155–176.

Matvejeva, A. (2014), "Determinants of persistence in innovation: evidence from the case study of the 'Eye Microsurgery' Complex," *Economics of Innovation and New Technology*, 23(5–6), 544–562.

Ngo, L.V. and O'Cass, A. (2009), "Creating value offerings via operant resource-based capabilities," *Industrial Marketing Management*, 38, 45–59.

Nijssen, E.J., Hillebrand, B., Vermeulen, P. A., and Kemp, R.G. (2006), "Exploring product and service innovation similarities and differences," *International Journal of Research in Marketing*, 23(3), 241–251.

O'Reilly III, C.A. and Tushman, M.L. (2013), "Organizational Ambidexterity: Past, Present, and Future," *The Academy of Management Perspectives*, 27(4), 324–338.

Ordanini, A. and Parasuraman, A. (2011), "Service Innovation Viewed Through a Service-Dominant Logic Lens: A Conceptual Framework and Empirical Analysis," *Journal of Service Research*, 14(1), 3–23.

Ostrom, A.L., Bitner, M.J., Brown, S.W., Burkhard, K.A., Goul, M., Smith-Daniels, V., Demirkan, H., and Rabinovich, E. (2010), "Moving Forward and Making a Difference: Research Priorities for the Science of Service," *Journal of Service Research*, 13(1), 4–36.

Parida, V., Roenneberg Sjoedin, D., Lenka, S., and Wincent, J. (2015), "Developing Global Service Innovation Capabilities. How Global

Manufacturers Address the Challenges of Market Heterogeneity," *Research-Technology Management*, September/October, 35–44.

Perks, H. and Roberts, D. (2013), A Review of Longitudinal Research in the Product Innovation Field, with Discussion of Utility and Conduct of Sequence Analysis, *Journal of Product Innovation Management*, 30, 1099–1111.

Plattfaut, R., Niehaves, B., and Becker, J. (2012), "Capabilities for Service Innovation: A Qualitative Case Study in the Consulting Industry," *Pacific Asia Conference on Information Systems (PACIS) Proceedings*, Paper 58.

Rothkopf, M. and Wald, A. (2011), "Innovation in Commoditized Services: A Study in the Passenger Airline Industry," *International Journal of Innovation Management*, 15(4), 731–753.

Salunke, S., Weerawardena, J., and McColl-Kennedy, J. R. (2011), "Towards a model of dynamic capabilities in innovation-based competitive strategy: Insights from project-oriented service firms," *Industrial Marketing Management*, 40(8), 1251–1263.

Silver, C. and Lewins, A. (2014), *Using Software in Qualitative Research, A Step-by-Step Guide*, 2nd edition, London: Sage.

Singapore Airlines (2017), Our Awards, https://www.singaporeair.com/en_UK/sg/flying-withus/our-story/awards/(accessed November 20, 2017).

Smith, W. K., & Lewis, M. W. (2011), "Toward a Theory of Paradox: A Dynamic Equilibrium Model of Organizing," *Academy of Management Review*, 36(2), 381–403.

Snyder, H., Witell, L., Gustafsson, A., Fombelle, P., and Kristensson, P. (2016), "Identifying categories of service innovation: A review and synthesis of the literature," *Journal of Business Research*, 69(7), 2401–2408.

Srivastava, S.C. and Shainesh, G. (2015), "Bridging the Service Divide Through Digitally Enabled Service Innovations: Evidence from Indian Healthcare Service Providers," *MIS Quarterly*, 39(1), 245-A19.

Stavros, C. and Westberg, K. (2009), "Using triangulation and multiple case studies to advance relationship marketing theory," *Qualitative Market Research: An International Journal*, 12(3), 307–320

Taylor, S.J. and Bogdan, R. (1984), *Introduction to qualitative research methods: The search for meanings*, 2nd ed., New York: Wiley.

Teece, D., Peteraf, M., and Leih, S. (2016), "Dynamic Capabilities and Organizational Agility: Risk, Uncertainty, and Strategy in the Innovation Economy," *California Management Review*, 58(4), 13–35.

Teece, D.J., Pisano, G., and Shuen, A. (1997), "Dynamic capabilities and strategic management," *Strategic Management Journal*, 18(7), 509–533.

Thomas, J. and Harden, A. (2007), *Methods for the thematic synthesis of qualitative research in systematic reviews*, ESRC National Centre for Research Methods, NCRM Working Paper Series, 10/07, London.

van de Ven, A.H. and Huber, G.P. (1990), "Longitudinal Field Research Methods for Studying Processes of Organizational Change," *Organization Science*, 1(3), 213–219.

Verma, R. and Jayasimha, K. (2014), "Service delivery innovation architecture: An empirical study of antecedents and outcomes," *IIMB Management Review*, 26(2), 105–121.

von Hippel, E. (2005), *Democratizing Innovation*, Cambridge, MA: MIT Press.

Weerawardena, J. and Mavondo, F.T. (2011), "Capabilities, innovation and competitive advantage," *Industrial Marketing Management*, 40(8), 1220–1223.

Winter, S. (2003), "Understanding dynamic capabilities," *Strategic Management Journal*, 24(10), 991–995.

Wirtz, J. and Jerger C. (2017), "Managing service employees: Literature review, expert opinions, and research directions," *Service Industries Journal*, 36(15–16), 757–788.

Wirtz, J. and Johnston, R. (2003), "Singapore Airlines: What it takes to sustain service excellence: A senior management perspective," *Managing Service Quality*, 13(1), 10–19.

Wirtz, J. and Zeithaml, V. (2017), "Cost-effective service excellence", *Journal of the Academy of Marketing Science*. Published Online first. DOI: 10.1007/s11747-017-0560-7

Wirtz, J., Heracleous, L., and Menkhoff, T. (2007), "Value creation through strategic knowledge management: the case of Singapore Airlines," *Journal of Asian Business*, 23(1), 249–264.

Wirtz, J., Heracleous, L., and Pangarkar, N. (2008), "Managing human resources for service excellence and cost effectiveness at Singapore Airlines," *Managing Service Quality*, 18(1), 4–19.

Witell, L., Snyder, H., Gustafsson, A., Fombelle, P., and Kristensson, P. (2016), "Defining service innovation: A review and synthesis," *Journal of Business Research*, 69(8), 2863–2872.

Wright, P.M., Dunford, B.B., and Snell, S.A. (2001), "Human resources and the resource based view of the firm," *Journal of Management*, 27(6), 701–721.

Wyckoff, D.D., Hart, C.W.L., and Lytle, L.N. (1989), *Singapore Airlines*, Boston, MA: Harvard Business School.

Yin, R. (2014), *Case Study Research*, 5th ed., Los Angeles, CA: Sage.

Zhang, T., Kandampully, J., and Bilgihan, A. (2015), "Motivations for customer engagement in online co-innovation communities (OCCs): A conceptual framework," *Journal of Hospitality and Tourism Technology*, 6(3), 311–328.

Zucker, L.G. (1987), "Institutional Theories of Organization," *Annual Review of Sociology*, 13(1), 443–464.

Letting Younger Employees Take The Lead

Reverse mentoring harnesses the innovation potential of a multi-generational workforce.

Be honest. If you were in charge of governing innovation in a bank, who would you entrust the leadership of innovation to: "the old guard" who seek and strive for stability, security and predictability or the younger "fintech trailblazers" who can help to combat the big bang disruptors that enjoy a huge advantage over corporations that have yet to install customer-centric, digital service channels? A smart answer may sound like this: "Well, it depends — ideally both groups should work together for the benefit of the organisation". Unfortunately, common sense is not always commonly practised in business despite the trend of a rapidly ageing population with a shrinking workforce. As a result of shifting age demographics, many companies employ members of four to five different "generations". This rather imprecise term refers to groups of people categorised as belonging to a particular age cohort and who have lived during significant socio-historical events. Millennials Generation Y are born roughly between 1981 and 1994, Generation X are generally born between 1965 and 1980; Baby Boomers born from 1946 to 1964. Then we have Traditionalists, born between 1930 and 1945, and the Silent Generation, those born between 1900 and 1929. The last two groups may include those who have been re-employed by their employers. Add the Facebook generation born after 1994 (the so-called Linksters), and the list is complete.

Innovation Potential

How can the innovation potential of a multi-generational workforce be harnessed? One strategy is *reverse mentoring*, i.e. the practice of pairing older executives as the tees with younger employees as their mentors, e.g. in areas such as social media. This has proven to be an effective approach to bring older, experienced employees up to speed for the benefit of the organisation. The word mentoring has been linked to the story of Mentor in the ancient Greek epic poem The Odyssey (attributed to Homer) who took care of Odysseus' son Telemachus while he was in fighting in the Trojan War (1260–110 BC). A mentor, according to the Merriam-Webster dictionary, is someone who teaches or gives help and advice to a less experienced and often younger person". Various examples of mentoring relationships include Socrates and Plato, and former Minister Mentor Lee Kuan Yew and his younger ministers. A reverse mentorship relationship implies that "younger people" can rise to become the trusted mentors of "older people", supporting their growth and capabilities (e.g. helping with their Facebook or Instagram pages) — just like some of my students have done. While I was born in the era of typewriters, most of my students grew up attending technology-savvy schools where they were given a digital learning device so that they could "learn anywhere and anytime". In his 2001 article "Digital Natives, Digital immigrants", education consultant Marc Prensky called these kids "digital natives" (note the terms are not mutually exclusive as one could argue that the real natives are the technology inventors who made the digital revolution possible). In my case, however, I confess that I do sometimes feel like a "digital immigrant" when I compare my social media capabilities with those of my digital technology mentors who are several decades younger than me. Recently, one of them "refreshed" my knowledge about the cloud-based Google Drive (a file storage and synchronisation service) which assists users with file storing and sharing, as well as editing documents, spreadsheets and collaborative presentations. When I remarked that this was indeed a case of reverse mentoring, my younger mentor urged me to stay focused on what he was "teaching" me.

Jack Welch, former CEO of General Electric (GE), has been credited with propagating the practice of reverse mentoring in business. He discovered the concept during a business trip to London in 1999 and subsequently introduced it to the senior management at GE to learn more about the Internet through younger and tech-savvy employees. Mr Welch said that it was "one of the best ideas (he) had heard in years". Reverse mentoring is not always an easy Journey, especially in hierarchical workplace cultures where seniority practices prevail. However, success stories of digital reverse mentoring programmes at Bosch, AXA or Kimberly Clark, Asia-Pacific, show that this type of mentoring has significant benefits such as higher staff engagement, provided the top leadership team understands its value and walks the talk as mentees of younger coaches themselves. One local small and medium-sized enterprise (SME) which has benefited from having a mix of young, old and middle-aged employees (56% of the staff are above the age of 40) in the form of greater staff loyalty and experience sharing is Han's (F&B) Pte Ltd.

For a reverse mentoring relationship to be beneficial for both mentee and mentor, several ingredients are critical. First of all, both parties must be transparent with regard to their fears and concerns. These should be openly discussed prior to the start of the mentoring process so that both mentee and mentor are at ease. Older and younger employees have different values and communication preferences that have to be clarified to avoid miscommunication.

Secondly, mutual trust is key, without which reverse mentoring will not be effective, because the acceptance of "vulnerability" is part and parcel of a reverse mentoring process. Finally, the willingness to learn from each other is crucial, too, because both sides have substantial resources which can benefit the other. Movies such as The Intern have illustrated the benefits of reverse reciprocal mentoring programmes in terms of mutual learning, experience sharing, empowering younger leaders and generational proximity.

No Complex Formal Processes

Reverse or reciprocal mentoring can be implemented within an organisation without complex formal processes. Besides the need to pay close attention to the (needs-based) matching process, it is important to nurture a community of trusted mentors and mentees as a foundation of robust, adaptive and resilient organisation all culture. To build a strong culture, a transformational innovation leadership style is required so that employees of all generations are encouraged and inspired to co-create in order to come up with the next big idea.

(The Business Times, 21 May 2016)

Innovation Coaching Has Become More Popular

Effective coaches are able to create a climate of trust which helps to develop a relationship-based, collaborative, high performance culture.

A recurring challenge in business is to create and implement innovations — usually a new or significantly improved product, service or process -which meet customer needs or exceed expectations, hopefully at an affordable price. Examples include smart banks like the German Web 2.0

bank Fidor, with its focus on social media, e-commerce, games, and mobile internet; Dropbox, which allows users to store files in the cloud; or the latest jetpack — like a motorised backpack — developed by New Zealand-based Martin Aircraft Co.

For many companies, it is essential to overcome barriers to creativity and innovation coaching can be a suitable solution to meet this challenge. Effective coaches can help managers understand the entire innovation value chain from strategic idea to the development and launch of a better product, service, or process which then delivers sustainable value.

Such coaches must possess the right personality traits and attributes such as emotional intelligence, people skills, and the ability to get others thinking, but should also have a track record of guiding real innovations. They need to listen closely, motivate positively, demand the very best, challenge assumptions, and give honest, non-offensive feedback. This approach will benefit the individuals being coached and the organisation as a whole.

Effective coaches are able to create a climate of trust which helps to develop a relationship-based, collaborative, high performance culture. Research suggests that those who have received innovation coaching view it as an effective developmental tool with good payoffs.

If considering good role models in this area, a few immediately come to mind. There is Silicon Valley's Bill Campbell who worked with Steve Jobs for several years. Campbell was Columbia University's head football coach in the 1970s before joining the business world. There is also design thinker David Kelley who founded product development firm IDEO (Palo Alto) which built the first mouse for Apple. Sports and educational coaches can also provide ideas about innovations, notably Bob Bowman who trained Olympic swimmer Michael Phelps to plan goals and visualise success and, thereby, achieve results few thought possible.

Quality innovation coaching can help everyone from start-up entrepreneurs to senior managers in established industries to excel in their jobs. The focus can be the creation of a collaborative culture of creativity or to convince the boss to finance the setting-up of a design thinking lab. With the help of candid conversations about the barriers to innovation, such as defensive reasoning along the lines of "we have never done this before", it becomes possible to generate new ideas and get around all sorts of road-blocks to creativity.

Such coaching, though, requires time, openness and commitment. It also takes a willingness to reflect about insights, lessons learned and execution tactics. However, it is increasingly important for managers and entrepreneurial leaders to have the relevant competencies, and companies which ignore this trend could face serious issues regarding productivity and competitiveness.

Whether in the east or west, innovation coaching is not about analysing past mistakes. It is about creating and nurturing robust cultures of innovation and a better sustainable future.

(Education Post, 29 November 2013)

To Make Innovation Work, You Must Pull The Right Levers

Knowing how to "rewire" the value network by changing the supply chain or the revenue, cost and margin model can be very effective in generating and implementing new profitable solutions.

The task of making innovation work can be overwhelming due to insufficient value creation know-how or confusion about the right innovation levers that need to be pulled in order to come up with new ways of selling and delivering value to customers. While mastering innovation is certainly not rocket science, it does require solid innovation management skills. Competent innovators know how to identify and seize innovation opportunities triggered by changes in industry and market structures such as the rapid growth of the sharing economy — consider Carousell (a Singaporean e-commerce company), Uber, and BMW's car-sharing service, DriveNow. Company leaders who recognise the need to innovate and the danger of "big bang" disruptors "out there" without effectively strategizing and structuring innovation efforts both internally and externally are well advised to re-examine the failure stories of Rollei, Kodak, Borders, or Apple's PDA device, Newton. Often, however, those in charge are unwilling or unable to reflect on the past, to proactively anticipate disruptive challenges ahead, and to further develop innovation capabilities which would allow them to create a powerful portfolio of incremental and radical innovation initiatives with the "right" balance so that the organisation remains on top.

Almost a decade ago, Harvard Professor Rosabeth Moss Kanter systematically analysed some of these innovation management and leadership challenges in her Harvard Business Review article titled Innovation *The Classical Traps*. Looking at the current innovation landscape in Asia, one wonders why so many companies can get away with "strategy mistakes" (unwillingness to risk failures), "process mistakes" (strangling innovation with tight controls and budgeting), "structure mistakes" (maintaining organisational silo cultures), and "skills mistakes" (appointing weak innovation leaders with poor relationship skills).

Critical for commercial success is the capability to pull the right innovation levers in the form of effective technological process capabilities in combination with new product and service offerings on the basis of an innovative business model-for example, based on a networked (digital) platform. Amazon is truly outstanding in that respect. Its cloud computing division, Amazon Web Services, offers third parties various remote computing services, and the company continues to roll out efficiency-improving innovations (which revolutionise the eBook experience) such as its new army of robots, which enables the rapid picking and delivery of products for customers' orders.

One way of achieving "innovation management mastery" is to study and dissect successful network models of other "great" firms in order to understand how they leverage resources — for example, through enabling technologies, alliances, agreements and contracts with third-party organisations. An interesting case is the network innovation approach Apple used when it developed the iPod in collaboration with partners such as Toshiba (1.8-inch hard disk drive), PortalPlayer (CPU), Wolfson (DAC/digital-to-analog converter), Pixo Inc (operating system that runs the user interface of the iPod), and others. As the systems integrator, Apple took care of the entire innovation and cooperative development process.

Convincing Value Proposition

The digital success story of *Airbnb* is also based to a large extent on its innovative platform system, which connects hosts and travellers in novel ways (without it owning any rooms itself) fuelled by effective information technologies. But the key is its convincing value proposition, which explains much of its success: it enables homeowners to earn income from their underutilized property assets and provides price-sensitive travellers more flexibility in deciding where to stay. Knowing how to "rewire" the value network by changing the supply chain or the revenue, cost and margin model can be very effective in generating and implementing new profitable solutions. The value network lever was pulled by *Ryan Air*, whose commercial success rests on its unique business model and pricing strategy, including fare-conscious target customers ("lowest fares), superior value architecture (use of secondary airports with lower charges), bulk acquisition of aircraft, lowest ex-fuel costs, and so forth. Non-customers can also be of value, as illustrated by the development of *Tata Motors'* *Nano car* in India-an outcome of a business model whose conception was fuelled by the desire to meet the needs of the many road users who ride two-wheelers.

Corporate innovation contexts are increasingly characterised by uncertainty (how will customers react?), complexity (how to manage the diversity of participating groups of internal and external experts from different discipline areas and age groups?), and low degree of predictability (who might disrupt our business and how can we cope with such a threat?). Therefore, those in charge of innovation need frameworks and tools to determine the goals of innovation efforts, to structure and organise related working relationships to "get things done", to create a compelling strategic innovation vision, and to build a robust innovation culture so that folks are motivated and willing to drive innovation. One guidance system which can be easily deployed by companies to manage innovation more effectively is the Business Excellence (BE) initiative by Enterprise Singapore. The internationally benchmarked BE framework provides a "roadmap for excellence" and helps managers enhance organisational performance. Of particular interest here is the Singapore innovation Class (l-Class). Niche Standard, which provides managers of private or public sector organisations with a holistic, criteria-based assessment approach to further develop their innovation management capabilities. Winners of the -Class Award — which recognises organisations with outstanding innovation and value-creation capabilities — include the Defence Science and Technology Agency, Agency for Science, Technology and Research (ASTAR); Biosensors interventional Technologies Pte Ltd, Qian Hu Corporation Ltd and Nanyang Polytechnic. Their summary reports (another wonderful resource for managers) are freely available on the website of Enterprise Singapore, and underscore the benefits organisations can obtain when they pull the right innovation levers.

(The Business Times, 19 February 2016)

Take a Leaf out of Library Board's Book

Strategy implementation and execution will not succeed if leaders do not speak with one voice about their vision.

With Jochen Wirtz and Frank Siegfried

According to management textbooks, strategy matters because it helps organizations to be different. While many firms succeed in asking the right questions as part of their strategic management process such as "do we aspire to play to win?", others fail to align value propositions and internal capabilities with new mega trends, future-ready scenarios and the right strategic choices as evidenced by innovation flops such as Apple's Lisa Computer (Lisa was one of the first computers with a graphical user interface — but it turned out to be too costly). Visionary organizations often lack the internal capabilities to support their strategy. Strategy implementation and execution fail if leaders do not speak with one voice about the vision thing; if goal-oriented program objectives are detached from leadership accountabilities and future-oriented metrics; if early warnings such as an idea-unfriendly culture or the denial of major quality problems are not escalated to the top; or when team-related, intra-organisational interdependencies are poorly managed.

Corporate leaders who want to make innovation work need a winning innovation strategy. Innovation strategy is about the big decisions surrounding innovations, e.g. whether, where and when to innovate and enter a (new) market. The failure of Borders and the success of Amazon underline the importance of strategic innovation aligned with corporate strategy in an era of digitization and accelerated innovation. One local organization which has managed to close the strategy-to-execution gap with a robust innovation strategy is the award-winning *National Library Board* (NLB), a statutory board established in 1995 to play a defining role in setting up a world class library system in Singapore. If one looks at the innovation strategy development process as a series of cascading stages where each stage derives from or acts upon the results of the preceding stage, NLB managed to ask the right questions and decisively followed-up step by step.

Seven Critical Aspects of a Strategic Innovation Cascade

1. **What's Our Purpose?**
   Why to innovate on the basis of what kind of objectives?
2. **Where To Play (Where Not To Play)?**
   Where should the innovation focus and scope be?
3. **With What Intensity?**
   How much innovation (e.g. incremental or radical) is wanted?
4. **How to Win?**
   How to pursue corporate innovation goals based on which unique value proposition?
5. **With Whom To innovate?**
   With whom to collaborate (e.g. internal partners and/or external complementors) and where are the innovation boundaries?
6. **With What Capability Assets?**
   How to ensure that people in the organization are capable and motivated to make innovation work?
7. **With What Management Systems?**
   How to structure and organise working relationships to "get things done" innovatively?
   What business processes need to be built in order to create and capture innovation value?
   How to keep tabs on strategic innovation matters and evaluate innovation efforts?

What Is Our Purpose/Where Should We Play? NLB's mission ("We make knowledge come alive, spark imagination and create possibilities") and innovation objectives were indicated in several master plans envisioning the establishment of a world class library system. These plans provided strategic purpose for both NLB's leadership team and staff. National aspirations such as becoming an intelligent nation or the computerisation of the civil service paved the way for NLB to find "the right playing field" in terms of its vision, mission, localities, product and service categories, customer segments, channels etc. Driven by the "Library 2000" vision, which aimed to bring library and information services closer to the citizens and introduce a wide range of services to different communities, NLB underwent a major transformation from the 1990s onwards which redefined the roles of the library and its key stakeholders — staff and library users. The focus of these early transformation efforts was to develop the infrastructure of a world-class public library in Singapore aimed at enhancing the learning capacity of the nation. This gave way to Wave 2 ("Library 2010"), where technology was adapted and mastered to bring libraries to the next level of knowledge services, deepening capacity building to focus on specialised capability-building. 2016 heralded in Wave 3 ("Library 2020") with the vision to create "Readers for Life, Learning Communities, and a Knowledgeable Nation", enabled by a new generation of public and digital libraries, including 24/7 online access to materials from the National Archives of Singapore. The main fundamentals underpinning these visionary changes include(d) effective strategic leadership, an enduring culture of innovation and a strong focus on user-centric service delivery.

Important questions which NLB's management team had to answer concerned the intensity level of innovation efforts (How much incremental or radical innovation do we want?) and the strategic approach towards pursuing innovation goals on the basis of a compelling value proposition (How to Win?). NLB is a pioneer of deploying Radio Frequency Identification (RFID) technology to enable self-service borrowing and returning. It has also developed a new mobile application enabling library members to borrow materials using their mobile devices on-the-go. One of NLB's numerous strategic innovation approaches is service co-creation, an efficient way to meet the needs of stakeholders and to identify internal and external service opportunities.

With Whom To Innovate? An example of NLB's boundary-spanning collaboration approach is the library@chinatown which opened in 2013 (its whole day-to-day operations are fully run by volunteers). Through this novel approach, NLB involved community members and public organisations such as CP1 Pte. Ltd. (the property developer for the Chinatown Point shopping centre) and Kwan Im Thong Hood Cho Temple based on the 3Ps sector motto (3Ps = People, Public and Private). It enabled NLB to tap into the knowledge, inputs and resources of the wider community, contributing to improved public service delivery. Gradually, NLB further strengthened its customer value proposition with a focus on "non-customers" and the ability to create and capture new demand as evidenced by its "Verging All Teens" programme rolled out in the Jurong Regional Library (the first library space created for teens by teens) or "My Tree

House", the world's first green library for children (created in collaboration with City Development Limited) to promote the habit of learning and reading for life in line with the Library 2020 vision.

With What Capability Assets? All this wouldn't have worked if not for a strong foundation comprising a set of reinforcing capabilities and competency-enhancing activities such as the Master of Science in Library Science programme for library staff (developed together with NTU) embedded in a robust culture of learning and innovation.

With What Management Systems? Besides good innovation governance and strategy execution in general, one needs to acknowledge the establishment of various supporting management systems, e.g. for innovative IT deployment such as the OneSearch service which enabled NLB's transformation towards a project-centric organization. Rather than focusing on traditional librarianship duties, staff across all levels can provide ideas for innovation and engage in new initiatives such as crowdsourcing, a core component of NLB's Citizen Archivist Project which enables the public to contribute to the nation's intellectual memory. NLB's innovation success rests upon numerous value-adding business processes such as rapid prototyping or open innovation and an integrative performance measurement approach. A recently deployed novel tool is the use of geo-spatial analytics to understand the borrowing behaviour of library users across the island.

(Business Times, 29 September 2017)

Creating New Value through Smart Innovation Strategies

According to management textbooks, strategy matters because it helps organizations to be different. Strategy is about "choosing what not to do" (Michael Porter) and how to respond to the new era of disruption. While many business leaders succeed in asking the right questions as part of their strategic management process such as "do we aspire to play to win?", others fail to align value propositions and internal capabilities with new mega trends, future-ready scenarios and the "right" strategic choices as evidenced by innovation flops such as Apple's Lisa Computer (Lisa was one of the first computers with a graphical user interface — but it turned out to be too costly), the two-wheeled Segway or Colgate's frozen meals. Research suggests that few (visionary) leaders are good at both creating good strategies and putting them into practice. In their book *Strategy That Works* (Harvard Business Review Book, 2016), Paul Leinwand and Cesare Mainardi have shown that gaps between strategy and execution are often created unintentionally. Strategy implementation and execution fail if leaders do not speak with one voice about the vision thing; if goal-oriented program objectives are detached from leadership accountabilities and future-oriented metrics; if early warnings such as an idea-unfriendly culture or the denial of major quality problems are not escalated to the top; or when team-related, intra-organisational interdependencies are poorly managed. Performance tracking and communication of early wins can help to drive confidence. But once morale has declined, it's an uphill battle to restore staff's confidence into the power of innovation as source of value creation. The authors also shed light on some of the strategy secrets of successful companies such as white goods maker *Haier* or *IKEA* who have managed to skillfully connect strategy and execution based on "strategic focus", "customer-centricity", a "winning innovation culture", and so forth. So, where do we go from here?

Technology and business model innovation are great levers which business leaders can pull in order to be(come more) different and find new revenue sources. *Amazon* is a shining example of impactful strategic innovation leadership. As a new product and service offering, its cloud computing division "Amazon Web Services" offers third parties the highly responsive "on demand" IT infrastructure that had been originally created for amazon.com's own developers. As part of its continuous business model optimisation, it created "Amazon Author Central" which provides independent authors with online exposure and a source of additional sales that can be linked to the writer's Twitter account, blog and other social media. Amazon's founder Jeff Bezos also set up the aerospace manufacturer and spaceflight services company *Blue Origin* for a new type of affluent customer eager to be sent on a brief journey into space at a suborbital altitude. Some regard Blue Origin as the most ambitious "transformational" innovation in Amazon's overall innovation portfolio.

The key to strategic innovation is to have a well-defined business idea which excites (almost) everyone in the organizational network, the iron will to include the inclination to innovate in the business strategy and to utilise information and communication technology (ICT). Business as usual is not sustainable in an era of Big Data, A.I., and big bang disruptions (remember Kodak?). The next step is to translate strategy into concrete innovation processes. This may imply more regular idea meetings with staff, systematic observations of the innovative behavior of competitors and/or stronger collaborations with new partners such as technology specialists or deep smarts in institutions of higher education in the innovation process. Finally, the leadership team needs to come up with clear procedures of how to implement the various process elements such as rapid prototyping and risk assessment while maximizing time and resources.

Rose, a German bicycle retailer, recently opened a new "Bike Town" 300 square metre "concept store" in a Munich mall where customers can use iPads to create their customised dream bikes and virtually experience the final 3D design of their new products via large touch screens and digital displays. The combination of the traditional bricks and mortar retail business with modern ecommerce solutions and (configurated) service offerings is a clever innovation approach that leverages both technology and business model innovation. Another innovative example from Germany is fashion retailer *Solebox* (Berlin) where a robot (stationed in the stock room) picks the right shoes as per the customer's shoe size and delivers them safely to shoppers.

Creating new value through smart innovation strategies is not rocket science. Business leaders who want to make a difference are well advised to (i) challenge the status quo and seek new information, (ii) to systematically observe customers (human centric design can help to gain insights into pain points in order to ideate how things could be done differently), (iii) to network with diverse individuals to get and validate new ideas, and (iv) to cautiously experiment with new concepts and ideas before going "live" with pilot tests. Creating and capturing new value requires a smart innovation strategy propelled by an innovative business model and "smart" technology, well-managed innovation processes, a motivating change culture and effective execution. Enterprise Singapore's innovation award framework can help to come to terms with the complexity of "good" innovation management.

(Translated version published in Lianhe Zaobao,
5 October 2017)

Chapter 4

People & Culture

To Innovate, Hire the "Wrong People"

Business leaders must use diagnostic frameworks to examine the extent to which entrepreneurialism, creativity and continuous learning is promoted within their organisation.

Innovation success is often attributed to individuals with outstanding attributes. Examples of such so-called innovation champions include Rudolf Wanzl Senior who started the corporate success story of the world leader in shopping carts and airport baggage carts (*Wanzl*) as a locksmith in Giebau (Sudetenland) in 1918; Nespresso's former CEO Jean-Paul Gaillard who turned Nespresso into a very profitable luxury brand; and the "Father of the Digital Revolution", Steve Jobs.

The champion concept can be traced back to MIT professor Donald A. Schoen who observed in a 1963 study on radical military-related innovations that they were often driven by extraordinarily engaged persons who played a key role throughout the entire process from ideation to implementation: "The champion must be a man willing to put himself on the line for an idea of doubtful success".

Champions are the individuals who emerge to take creative ideas (which they may or may not have generated) and bring them alive. Their role is critical as innovation implies change (innovations can range from small incremental improvements, such as Nabisco's extension of the Oreo product line, to radical breakthroughs, such as Toyota's battery-fuelled Prius), insecurity, resistance and risks.

Strong Self-belief

A famous risk-taking innovator is German physician Werner Theodor Otto Forssmann (1904–1979) who received the 1956 Nobel Prize in medicine (together with A Court and D. Richards) for performing the first human cardiac catheterisation in 1929. The story goes that he ignored his department head when he passed the catheter into his heart via a vein of his arm, a risky self-attempt which could have cost him his life. A similar narrative surrounds the development of the laser printer by Xerox researcher Gary Starkweather who faced enormous headwinds from colleagues and his own manager who regarded this new laser technology as impractical and too expensive. Research has shown that innovation champions have unique personality traits, such as high self-esteem in combination with extraversion and an unwillingness to adjust their behaviour in line with social norms.

While these so-called low self-monitors with their somewhat uncompromising traits can drive their bosses and colleagues crazy, they add very significant value to a firm's creativity and innovation performance, for example in terms of new product development. The problem is that they are not seldom regarded as difficult employees, as outlined by Stanford Professor Robert Sutton in a 2001 Harvard Business Review article entitled *The Weird Rules of Creativity*. Such perceptions are in stark contrast with their actual behaviour as they seek to foster cross-functional communication and collaboration within the organisation, stimulating discussions and decisions about innovation projects or ensure that scarce resources are distributed correctly in support of strategic development and commercialisation objectives.

Organisational research has shown that innovation champions display very effective transformational leadership behaviour such as knocking down barriers to the innovation, getting problems into the hands of those who can solve them or not giving up when others say that it cannot be done.

This often requires a combination of pursuing new ideas independently and gathering support by colleagues horizontally rather than vertical authorisation through superiors.

Real Champions

Depending on the culture of an organisation, bosses who are being consulted by their employees with regard to new ideas aimed at authorising then may consider such employees as uncreative and unimaginative.

"Real" champions take charge and challenge complacency. If they are in senior management positions, they provide a compelling innovation vision, including the necessary resources to get things done. They walk the "innovation strategy talk" with a clear sense of purpose, command and conviction. They are enthusiastic and confident about the success of the innovation and persist under adversity (e.g. in cases where they decide to disobey their "ignorant" superiors and get the right people involved in the organisation).

Unfortunately, corporate reality often differs from such a scenario. Often, insufficient attention is given to the people-oriented determinants of innovative culture, i.e. values, behaviours and organisational climate. Business leaders who wish to check the innovative health of their own corporate culture are well-advised to utilise diagnostic frameworks to examine the extent to which entrepreneurialism, creativity and continuous learning is promoted within the organisational culture or to shed light on the ability to effectively ideate, seeing the gaps, prototyping going to market and making deals.

The success or failure of any innovation initiative, whether accidental or intentional, is contingent upon the respective organisational (business) model. Organisational culture, communications, power distribution, human resource engagement, etc., has an impact upon what works and what doesn't.

Focus and Diversity

In their book *Making Innovation Work*, Tony Davila *et al.* listed nine levers of culture that affect innovation. One of these levers is what the authors call focus and diversity. Innovative organisations must master these conflicting goals of focus and diversity if they want to create and extract sustainable value from innovations while being focused adds value in a stable business environment, extreme focus can lead to inflexibility and slow responsiveness in times of rapid change as illustrated by the corporate decline of German camera maker *Rollei*. Embracing diversity in talent, ideas, and methods can ensure that the organisation excels in periods of change as evidenced by the success of Google. Attracting and retaining the "wrong" (diverse) people such as enthusiastic and "bull-headed" innovation champs can be a wise approach to combat groupthink in favour of greater innovativeness — provided trust, collaboration and cultural diversity are managed optimally.

(The Business Times, 14 March 2015)

Make Innovation Work by Overcoming the Ingroup-Outgroup Bias

Imagine this: you have a great idea to make innovation work in your organisation, but nobody listens. While there could be many reasons why this is the case — such as the lack of a formal ideation management framework or your personal inability to get the attention of key decision-makers — let us look at this challenge from the perspective of a particular leadership concept, the so-called Leader-Member Exchange (LMX) theory.

LMX puts emphasis on the interaction process and dyadic relationship between leaders and followers. First conceived by US academics Fred Dansereau, George Bear Graen and William J. Haga, it draws attention on the existence of in-groups and out-groups within organisations and how that may affect organisational outcomes related to performance, job climate, organisational citizenship behaviour, or innovation.

While members of in-groups are often regarded as "good" organisational citizens who are doing more than their job specs require, out-group members engage in business as usual as stipulated by their job contracts. They get less attention from their leaders and, over time, often turn out to be less engaged.

Becoming part of the in-group is based to some extent on the quality of the relationship between boss and subordinate. Supporting a leader through mission-critical project works, for example, can be instrumental in becoming part of the leader's "inner circle". If the quality is high, in-group members may benefit in terms of favourable performance evaluations or faster career progress, which in turn might lead to greater organisational commitment.

LMX research posits that in-group members receive more information and concern from their leaders, which correlates with greater involvement and extra-role taking. As time progresses and roles become more formalised, a supportive staff member may advance into a powerful position. The flipside is that subordinates in the out-group may feel less recognised. They receive less attention from the boss due to the comparatively low quality of their relationship.

While "negotiating" with the leader may help to make an individual part of the (seemingly more privileged) in-group, in reality, the pathway towards a high-quality leader-member exchange might be blocked for those categorised as out-group members due to insufficient opportunities to interact with the boss, or simply because the leader does not know how to manage the "leadership making process". The number of bosses who really make time to get to know employees and to create a deeper relationship beyond town hall events or routine staff meetings is still rather small, despite decades of leadership development research and training. The peak of the leadership making process is a "mature" partnership phase characterised by a high degree of mutual trust and respect, and responsibility that transcends traditional hierarchy.

While LMX is a rather "old" theory with some inconsistencies (such as its measurement validity), the core concept does provide valuable insights into "good" leadership principles, such as the need to be more responsive to followers' requests for participation or the importance of being mindful in allocating newly created, interesting job opportunities to the "right" candidate(s), regardless of any potential ingroup-outgroup bias.

Six Building Blocks

The conceptual heritage of LMX is visible in more recent, both prescriptive and diagnostic innovation management frameworks such as the innovation assessment tool "How Innovative Is Your Company's Culture?" by Jay Rao and Joseph Weintraub.

Relevant items of the building block "Leadership Behaviour" (one of six building blocks of a robust innovation culture) include "Our leaders inspire us with a vision for the future and articulation of opportunities for the organisation", "Our leaders model the right innovation behaviours for others to follow" or "Our leaders provide support to project team members during both successes and failures".

Innovation leaders are well advised to "energise", "engage" and "enable" followers in order to make the organisation more innovative and to avoid what innovation expert Scott Anthony has termed "innovation inbreeding". This can happen when innovation efforts are consistently led by the same group of people.

Research has shown that major inventions often occur in the "wrong place", for example, by people in out-groups. To avoid innovation inbreeding, leaders can bring in external ideas in order to innovate the firm's business model, initiate co-creation of new products and services together with customers or establish internal innovation jams to leverage on diverse talent pools. Related management instruments are so-called skunkworks project teams led independently of normal research and development operations.

So what could you do if you belong to an out-group in your organisation with little or no influence on innovation matters? Don't accept the ingroup-outgroup dichotomy as a given. Attempt to change it.

Arrange for your own personal "meet-the-boss session" and voice your concerns and innovative ideas. Take the initiative and open up so that the boss can learn more about you (personality compatibilities have been identified as potential drivers of a hi-quality dyad relationship between a leader and follower) and vice-versa.

Just like subordinates, bosses also need cooperation, reliability and honesty. Try to figure out what may impede or facilitate effective communication, and act on that insight. By taking responsibility for improving the relationship between leader and follower, problems can be removed so that both parties can play a more constructive role in making innovation work.

(Business Times, 7 December 2017)

Why Are Kopitiam Tables Round?

Coffee shop — or cafe — culture can promote interaction and learning, boosting innovation.

"A coffee dessert, yes, you know it's good news", so proclaimed The Beatles in their song *Savoy Truffle* released in 1968 as part of their famous White Album. One of the hallmarks of good musicians is improvisational jamming (the art of playing without meticulous preparation or predetermined agendas) which helps band members to create new songs, come up with novel arrangements, or simply to bond and feel good. A closer look at Singapore's kopitiams (coffee shops), both old and new, reveals that these social institutions can and do perform similar functions. The Singapore kopitiam can be found across the island both in the heartland as well as in the city's dynamic business hubs. The Malay word *kopi* means coffee and *tiam* (a Hokkien word) refers to shop. Kopitiam customers can enjoy various types of coffee, tea and other drinks as well as kaya toast, soft-boiled eggs, etc. Singapore's kopitiams are great localities for inter-ethnic communication and social gatherings. They offer traditional drinks and dishes from different ethnicities and dietary habits which allow members of different social groups to eat and socialise in a common place (and often at a common table, despite the infamous tissue paper reservation system prevalent in some local food courts).

The majority of tables in traditional kopitiams are round. Why? In Asian society, eating and drinking coffee is usually done in social groups. A round eating table can accommodate many people, friends and/ or relatives, and enables the host to effectively manage social occasions if situational demands warrant it. Another reason is that it facilitates the sharing of food and the process of eating it. If there are many diners, a round table enables each person to easily pick up the food regardless of their seating position. Roundedness has deep cultural meanings in Asian society. The respective Chinese characters symbolise "reunion" and "success" (in the sense of being "united", "rounded", and "complete") whose significance can be observed during cultural festivities such as the annual reunion dinners during Chinese New Year. With regard to interaction, brainstorming and new knowledge creation, coffee shops are ideal places for the exchange of the latest gossip, problem solving and idea production.

Sitting cross-legged (if one's fitness allows it), sipping coffee and leaning forward in order to hear the others better (or to whisper something patrons at other tables should not hear) are all familiar activities performed by Asian coffee shop patrons. The fertile mix of caffeine, the joy of being in good company as well as mental stimuli created by the proximity of fellow coffee shop patrons during a lively coffee shop discussion (in short: coffee shop talk) can give rise to a conducive, organic culture of knowledge sharing and innovation which cannot be easily dictated qua sheer managerial authority, as respective "buzz-creating initiatives" in new knowledge-intensive agglomerations have shown, such as science parks (with their healthy juice bars). It's all about connection, authenticity (and roundness).

One popular knowledge sharing and creation tool which is based on this insight is the knowledge cafe method pioneered by collaborative learning specialist Elizabeth Lank, from Britain, in the 1990s. It was popularised by British knowledge management expert David Gurteen who convincingly argues that the best way to share knowledge has always been by conversations.

A recent, local example of effectively utilising the informal atmosphere of coffee chats is Member of Parliament Grace Fu's "eavesdrop" (ST, Oct 3, 2012), as part of her Jurong East dialogue (linked to the

Singapore Conversation) during which she met up with some 150 elderly "aunties" and "uncles" who shared their worries and concerns, such as health-care costs and the cost of living, with her. When discussing coffee shops or cafe culture, one may ask if there is a difference between "Asian" kopitiams with their round tables and "non-Asian" coffee houses with their predominant rectangular tables. Do people behave differently in these different settings? One might argue that the degree of new knowledge creation qua sharing is lower when patrons are seated at rectangular tables.

One may also wonder whether Singapore's Gen Y appreciates their own cultural coffee shop heritage. Anecdotal evidence suggests that non-Singaporeans are more willing than Singaporeans to spend big bucks for a "grande mild with room" (that is, a large, hyper-caffeinated coffee with cream and sugar) while older kopitiam patrons enjoy their *kopi si siew dai* (coffee with evaporated milk, less sugar) at a much lower price. Gen Y on the other hand seems to prefer an air-conditioned environment, a cosy sofa to lounge around and convenient plug-ins for their laptops, something most kopitiams do not provide. If these different social groups do not meet in "local" coffee places, the lack of social contact (and thereby foregone communication and innovation potential) could lead to socio-economic dysfunctions in the long run, for example, by perpetuating both mental and physical boundaries between "us" and "them".

Against such a rather gloomy scenario, I would argue based on observations in coffee shop hot spots (and dessert bars) in Holland Village or Bras Basah that Singapore's increasingly diverse coffee shop scene is alive and kicking. Collectively, the city-state's coffee shops represent a powerful social institution whose integration, knowledge creation and innovation potential is enormous.

(The Straits Times, 9 October 2012)

Mastering Effective Collaboration

It underpins the entire innovation process from ideation to the successful commercialisation of a novel product or service.

Collaboration is an important asset that differentiates highly innovative organisations from laggards. Essential are collaborative teams, i.e. units of two or more people with complementary skills, committed to a common purpose and performance goals. A classical case is Walt Disney's team of cartoon animators who created not only a new art form but also a lucrative business innovation. Collaborative innovation feeds on unifying goals, complementary capabilities, respectful communication, trust and diversity. "A-ha" moments are more likely to happen if team members are markedly different from one another and when potentially inevitable destructive conflicts are nipped in the bud.

A structured innovation environment is the hallmark of most Hidden Champions, i.e. those (mostly family-run) private companies with up to 500 employees and US$5 billion in revenues who are among the top three in the global market. An example is *DELO*, a world-leading manufacturer of industrial high-performance adhesives. A core element of its award-winning innovation system is the project information team — comprising members from top management, research & development, engineering product management, marketing and distribution. This diverse group of specialists is involved throughout the innovation process from idea generation to market launch and decides every step during the various project phases. Customer wishes, collected globally, serve as impulses for innovations. Reputable pilot customers are invited to test new products very early during the development phase which in turn facilitates the go-to-market process. The use of collaboration tools is critical throughout the innovation process. Right at the start of the ideation phase aimed at defining the innovation content, collective gap analyses can be conducted to discover new insights and to determine how to win. Ideas for innovation can be generated with the help of associational thinking practices, insights from science & technology or lab work. Related tools include structured idea management or communities of practice to connect teams of scientists, researchers and for consumers. To source for the best strategic innovation ideas, sufficient time must be devoted for diverging i.e. moving or extending in different directions from a commonly perceived market gap. Strategic management tools can help to spot new trends, anticipate hidden organisational inflexibilities or create blue oceans of uncontested market space. Collaborative workshops such as the visualisation of cultural archetypes (extracted from stories collected through anecdote circles) are useful to identify and combat barriers towards change. Jointly drawing characters who typify one's organisational culture (e.g. the overly cautious "lurker" who is careful of what he or she says) can be effective to unfreeze an organisation towards a more collaborative innovation culture.

Models and Prototypes

The goal of the development stage is to construct models and prototypes of the innovation. Functional prototypes allow for experimentation and testing to find out whether the new product works well in line with consumers' expectations. Computer-generated 3D models illustrate how the final outcome of the innovation effort might look like. If a "rapid prototype" is poorly constructed, chances are that its creators did not perform well as a collaborative team. The power of multidisciplinary teamwork in creating innovative prototypes based on systematic research and user feedback has been documented in a video, featuring the efforts of *IDE0* (a design and consulting firm from Palo Alto, California) to develop a new, cost-effective shopping cart concept and creating better manoeuvrability, more enjoyable shopping behaviour, and enhanced child safety. The recording[1] provides insights into IDEO's design approach and key ingredients of collaborative innovation, such as trusting relationship or openness towards internal colleagues and external stakeholders. Team members trained in ethnography and solution-focused design thinking are critical to translate unmet needs into innovation opportunities. Figuring out how to make money from an innovation is a key concern from the design phase onwards. Prototypes and models without a viable business model are doomed to fail. The business model canvas by A.Osterwalder *et al.* is a great visualisation tool to chart the value proposition of a new product or service and to align business activities around during the market evaluation stage. Any sustainable revenue generating mechanism requires some form of collaboration management — be it to identify suitable hosts as in the case of Airbnb a website for people to rent out lodging or when entering into a licensing agreement with licensees.

Network Innovation

Once the business model is established, the innovator has to figure out how to manufacture the innovation. The production engineering stage requires specific capabilities such as good contracting and platform development know-how as exemplified by Apple's network innovation approach when it developed the iPod together with external partners such

---

[1]Available at: https://www.youtube.com/watch>v=taJOV-YCiel.

as Sony, Toshiba, Telas Instruments, etc. During the final market testing, full-scale manufacturing and market launch stages of the innovation process, close collaboration with customers and other stakeholders are just as important as during the initial steps. Sometimes people in organisations experience collaboration overload as a result of unclear priorities or the absence of well-documented business procedures which require informal workarounds in order to get things done. Team members may find themselves overwhelmed with requests to "work together" and to innovate, a difficult challenge even with tech tools designed to enhance intra-organisational connectivity, such as social networking sites, due to the reactive nature of this type of remedial collaboration. Progressive collaboration, in contrast is more value-added and durable as collaborators are committed and know what to shoot for. They are passionate about sharing and expanding their knowledge driven by visionary shared innovation goals as well as the desire to learn from one another. In case innovation managers are clueless about internal collaboration patterns and the whereabouts of subject matter experts capable of innovatively addressing pain points of customers and their diversities, a social network analysis can help to map them in support of strategic innovation.

To sum up, the entire innovation process from ideation to the successful commercialisation of a novel product or service depends crucially on working well with others and the mastery of collaboration tools.

(The Business Times, 12 September 2015)

Innovation Through Organisational Climate Change

An innovative climate challenges people to take risks within a safe environment.

Organisational climate change is often seen as a key driver of a more successful and sustainable organisation. The term itself is vague and arguably hard-to-measure which is why managers do not always give it the necessary attention. Organisational climate refers to the recurring behavioural patterns, attitudes and feelings that characterise the workplace life. Communication patterns (open communication versus allowing rumours), leadership behaviour (participatory-visionary versus practicing favouritism) or organisational structure (hierarchical versus entrepreneurial) determine the "climate" of an organisation and with it whether employees are engaged or have low morale.

According to Jay Rao, a professor of technology and innovation at Babson College in the US, an innovative climate "cultivates engagement and enthusiasm, challenges people to take risks within a safe environment, fosters learning and encourages independent thinking".

To appreciate an innovation culture, let us first deal with corporate culture — which has been defined as shared assumptions, values and beliefs considered to be the correct way of thinking about and acting on problems and opportunities facing the organisation.

As a source of organisational identity, it provides employees with a sense of who or what the organisation stands for. One of the eight core values of renowned US Mayo Clinic, for example, is "healing". The respective value statement reads as follows: "Inspire hope and nurture the wellbeing of the whole person, respecting physical, emotional and spiritual needs".

Google's use of retention algorithms to manage attrition rates is part of its data-oriented corporate culture. It helps employees to understand why the organisation does what it does and how it intends to accomplish its goals. A motivating value which is instilled in employees at Southwest Airlines is "a fun-luving attitude". Job applicants who do not reflect such a value do not get hired. For innovation to flourish, a cultural environment is required that supports imaginative thinking with visible efforts to create and extract value from knowledge. A strong culture of innovation entails a shared set of values and mutually reinforcing beliefs about the strategic importance of innovation. However, a strong organisational culture is no guarantee for success. In fact, success is often the best threat to innovation as successful companies may become complacent and conservative in order to preserve core competences as illustrated by Kodak, Borders, and more recently Yahoo! So what needs to be done in order to make innovation work through organisational climate change?

In one of their studies entitled *How Innovative Is Your Company's Culture?* (MIT Sloan Management Review, 2013), Jay Rao and his co-author Joseph Weintraub present a useful assessment tool featuring "6 Building Blocks of an innovative Culture" which managers can easily use to measure, assess and monitor the strengths and weaknesses of corporate innovation cultures.

Climate is just one of three so-called "people-oriented" determinants of innovative culture besides *values* and *behaviours*. The other (more tangible) three building blocks of an innovative culture include *resources*, *processes*, and the *measurement of success*. The tool helps to lay out a pathway towards greater innovation and the way forward in terms of climate change.

(Tabla, 12 August 2016)

Incentives for Motivating Radical Innovation — How to Make It Work?

While rewards and recognition are critical in encouraging a robust innovation culture, they can also backfire. Designing an optimal and strategic incentives system is key.

An important question for academics and business leaders is how best to motivate innovative behaviour in organisations. In one of my research studies on knowledge sharing behaviour in knowledge-intensive contexts, rewards and recognition turned out to be critical management tools to encourage employees to innovate. But top management does not always see the need to incentivise to introduce actionable new ideas for many reasons, such as the belief that too many positive, tangible incentives might backfire. And then there are corporates who go all out: tech firms empower their employees to award peer cash bonuses to innovative colleagues without approval (one's own team members excluded); banks motivate staff with special bonuses and long-term incentive awards, such as profit-sharing plans which sometimes outweigh their fixed remuneration components. To avoid frustration among those who got too little or nothing, it is important to check whether the chosen approach leads to a robust innovation culture or the opposite: envy and disengagement. Even the best intended practices can provide disincentives for the right (innovative) behaviour. The promise of tangible monetary rewards can erode one's intrinsic motivation which is critical for breakthrough innovations. The rise and fall of the dotcom bubble has been partly attributed to too much focus on downstream financial rewards. Limiting the risks of failure inherent in innovation efforts requires specific skills to enable "those who did not deliver" to quickly bounce back without career setbacks. Competitive innovation tournaments are no panacea for greater innovativeness if risk-averse leaders fail to implement newly proposed ideas. Firms may forgo the chance to achieve greater performance outcomes unless people relentlessly innovate, driven by passion alone. Psychologists describe this as a strong inclination towards a self-defining activity that one likes or loves, and in which one invests time and energy. The story of Steve Jobs suggests that such behaviour can be so self-defining that it represents a central feature of one's identity. Most of us are not extremely self-motivated co-founders of multinational tech firms. Despite being dutiful and conscientious, we do need some carrots. If there is no outlet for our passion, or worse, if compensation is below market price, and driving new ideas is not recognised in one way or another, some people might look for better prospects elsewhere. What does it take to create an organisational incentive framework that supports radical innovative behaviour?

When designing an incentive framework to support innovativeness, managers need to appreciate the temporal distinction between two motivational tools: incentives, such as funding or financial compensation, which kick in before an innovation project starts; and rewards, such as recognition in the form of publicly showcasing innovative employees, which are doled out after the interim results of the innovation effort have been achieved. This might then encourage people to continue to innovate, provided the right carrots are in place.

Incentive systems must specify and reinforce strategic and long-term innovation goals in order to achieve the desired corporate results. For instance, in contrast to incremental innovation, the goal posts of radical innovation projects such as SpaceX (founded in 2002 with the ultimate goal of enabling humans to live on Mars) are distinct but much less specific. This requires a unique reward management approach based on subjective metrics, such as attaining intermediate roadmap targets, rather than objective measures, such as speed to market or percentage of sales derived from "new products".

Initially, radical innovation projects have a very high level of uncertainty associated with high costs. CEOs keen to achieve greater product innovation are advised not to stifle risky new development initiatives and flexibility by prescribing narrow, specific business goals. The development of Logitech's IO Digital Pen, for example, has been attributed to broad goals set by former CEO Guerrino de Luca aimed at creating new last-inch products at the interface between human and technology.

Once formulated, innovation goals and exploration activities need to be integrated into the corporate performance measurement system. Innovation experts suggest coming up with stretch goals which inspire employees beyond a narrow project mentality in contrast to (potentially demotivating) measurable goals. "Bill Gates a PC in every home" and Netflix CEO Reed Hastings' vision to reach out to the five billion people on mobile fall into this category. Innovation KPIs incorporated into a balanced innovation scorecard must leave enough room for trial and error, experimentation, exchange of ideas and learning. If individual innovation efforts can be pinpointed and measured but remain unrecognised, personal effort will decrease. Likewise, it is essential to reward collaborative value creation because the success of breakthrough products of services newly developed by one team often depends on other units. To ensure equity and to prevent social loafing, team-based performance measures, such as on time project completion, can be combined with individual performance evaluations, such as 360-degree feedback based on a holistic portfolio approach across several innovation projects, to measure efforts and outcomes over time. According to Kenny Yap, executive chairman of Qian Hu Corporation Ltd, it is of utmost importance to prevent office politics in order to maintain a work environment conducive for innovative behaviour. Team efforts can be rewarded through gain-sharing which links actual team-based rewards with the long-term value of innovation outcomes throughout a particular gain-sharing period. Sharing monetary savings (gains) from improved performance with employees, for example in the form of deferred bonuses, can potentially increase a sense of ownership.

Finally, the determinants of innovation measures and rewards are all contingent upon business model, profitability, and organisational culture. For CEOs and corporates, the challenge is to measure what is important for their businesses. Rewards can take the form of "failure rewards" (for teams whose failures taught valuable lessons), "gamification-linked point systems" (aimed at incentivising great new ideas) or "long-term stock-based incentive systems" (deemed suitable by experts to drive radical innovation). One interesting takeaway of recent strategic management research on rewarding innovation is this: rather than providing highly incentive-intensive rewards, such as financial compensation which is tied closely to the value that very few outstanding people have created (which leads to rivalry and potentially corrodes innovative behaviour), a better option might be to stimulate the process of value-creating ideation through a robust culture of innovative intrapreneurship, in conjunction with a weaker incentive intensity. This might then lead to many incremental innovations — and a few (albeit very valuable) radical ones as fresh drivers of more innovation breakthroughs.

(The Business Times, 20 May 2015)

Solving Asia's "Creativity Problem"

Educators need to stimulate and reward curiosity, encourage risk taking or providing opportunities for discovery.

Some Asian Countries arguably have creativity and innovation-averse cultures which makes it difficult to break out to higher income-country status. What is the "real" challenge and what can be done to further nurture imaginative speculation and the capability to bring ideas to life?

In 2003, US linguist William Hannas blamed (in a somewhat stereotypical book titled "The Writing on the Wall: How Asian Orthography Curbs Creativity") the character-based writing systems of China, Japan, and Korea for East Asia's "creativity problem", that is its difficulty to achieve significant scientific and technological innovations compared to the West. One puzzling argument put forward was that unlike the more abstract, alphabet-based languages such as English, the use and rote memorisation of graphic symbols implies a lesser degree of abstract thinking and ultimately creativity.

While Mr Hannas' propositions remain highly contentious (one might argue that it is the combination of knowledge and great minds that produces creativity, not the orthography) and out of tune with reality in view of ancient Chinese innovations such as the sternpost rudder or contemporary ones such as Creative's sound blaster sound card, the book points to the wider question how Asia's creativity and innovation potential can be further harnessed. This is not only a challenge for high-income countries such as Singapore but also for countries such as Brazil, China or Malaysia which have yet to master the transition from resource-driven growth towards a higher value-added, knowledge-intensive type of economic system.

Studies by the World Bank underline the importance of STEM (science, technology, engineering, and mathematics) education in achieving economic growth. STEM occupations are among the best-paying and fastest growing jobs. Problems include lack of rigorous K-12 mathematics and science standards, shortage of qualified teaching staff, inability to motivate students' interest in mathematics and science or the misalignment between STEM job demands and the structure of the post-secondary STEM system.

Data on the quality of STEM education can help countries stuck in the middle to identify potential disconnects between supply and demand parameters. Information on trends in international mathematics and science (TIMSS) is provided by the International Association for the Evaluation of Educational Achievement.

The TIMSS 2007 International Mathematics Report, for example, summarised fourth and eighth-grade students' mathematics achievement in over 50 participating countries and several benchmarking participants. The TIMSS trends in mathematics achievement data showed great differences between countries such as Malaysia, Indonesia or the Philippines in terms of mathematics and reading. Collectively, these nations continue to lag behind students in more developed economies such as Hong Kong, Japan, South Korea, Macau, or Singapore. STEM data suggests that strong mathematical competencies can be instrumental in escaping the middle-income trap.

Research on education and economic growth shows a correlation between both cognitive and non-cognitive competencies for individual earnings and careers. Important cognitive skills include attention skills, the ability to store and recall information (memory), logic and reasoning, the ability to analyse, blend and segment sounds, visual processing and the competency to perform simple or complex cognitive tasks quickly. Relevant non-cognitive skills include motivation, effort, engagement, persistence, or self-esteem. Without an inquisitive mind and focused attention, creativity (and thereby the courage to effect change) will be restricted. Curricula reviews can help to identify related gaps and mis-matches.

Creative skills are in high demand by employers who wish to hire employees "who can think outside the box". While I am convinced that everybody can be creative through individual nurturing, my experiences of confronting business students in the region with problems that do not have well-defined answers (which is one way of enhancing creativity in the classroom) suggest that more can be done to impart creativity skills into young learners.

Lack of intrinsic motivation, the pressure to conform and the fear to fail sometimes act as deterrents to greater use of one's imaginative speculation and originality.

Learning by Mistakes

Those who "win" are often those who excel in exams, and these students are unlikely to work in the creative industries which represents a key future growth driver according to US urban studies theorist, Richard Florida. Educators can work against such trends by stimulating and rewarding curiosity, encouraging risk taking or providing opportunities for discovery. Mistakes are great learning opportunities!

For Asia's future creative class to rise, a new leadership paradigm is required, too, one which puts a premium on providing talent with meaningful challenges, sufficient autonomy, suitable resources (for example, attractive collaboration space to think outside one's cubicle), effective teamwork and plenty of encouragement.

Our studies at SMU indicate that a lot of creativity is lost in Asian business because it remains hidden in people's brains as tacit knowledge resource. While more and more organisations embrace the need to proactively manage creativity and innovation as exemplified by the recent "Neighbourhood Police Post for the Future" design competition (where tertiary students came up with new ideas about aesthetic NPPs) organised by the Singapore Police Force, the search is still on for (more) Asian equivalents of Google or Facebook, including their creative and innovative founders.

At the same time, we have to be mindful of not becoming addicted to all these new and convenient technological tools such as smart maps which might seduce us to rely on other people's brains rather than our own as this could really stifle creativity in both Asia and the West.

(The Business Times, 16 August 2012)

Bike-Sharing Chaos and Out-of-the-Box Thinking

"I want to ride my bicycle … I want to ride my bike … I want to ride my bicycle… I want to ride it where I like". Although a bit dated, these lyrics (which originate from the song *Bicycle Race* released by British rock band,

Queen in 1978) came to my mind recently when I observed the clumsy attempts by a fellow baby boomer to master one of these new bikes-for-share which have popped up all over the island — almost overnight.

Many of us have seen them "standing around", and there is intense coffee-shop talk about the need for proper bike rental etiquette. "How could he abandon the bike here? So inconsiderate!" a commuter might think if a bicycle is left behind near a bus stop (or worse, if it is spotted next to someone's home — chained).

Rather than analysing now why people throw bicycles from HDB blocks (as happened recently), let us take a step back and analyse the new bike-sharing phenomenon positively from the perspective of innovation and creativity.

Just like Uber, Nespresso, and Airbnb, the business models of bicycle-sharing companies oBike, ofo, and Mobike feature a unique customer value proposition which continues to propel these new bike-share services forward. (one day they might help to achieve the dream of a "car-lite" Singapore.)

The bicycles can be "parked" almost anywhere, and it is very convenient for another person to pick one up — provided it is functioning and safe to ride.

As a service innovation, bicycle-sharing systems help to solve the so-called "last-mile problem" in cities by enabling (some) people to move from a transportation hub to their final destination.

From an innovation point of view, the new bike-sharing phenomenon arguably provides an opportunity to appreciate the power of divergent thinking and doing, which can be a catalyst for creative value creation.

While I have yet to use this mode of transportation, having cycled regularly when I was younger, I am always pleased to see these colourful bikes "standing around" — often at places where we would least expect them. I have even made mental plans to use one of them to explore various interesting places near my office which depict Singapore's rich heritage. I do like them because they spice up our urban landscape a little. They symbolise a little messiness and creative chaos which, according to creativity experts, urban innovation hubs require in order to function well.

From an innovation point of view, this new bike-sharing phenomenon arguably provides an opportunity to appreciate the power of divergent thinking and doing, which can be a catalyst for creative value creation in an environment geared towards greater entrepreneurial risk-taking.

In contrast to convergent thinking which is about finding the "correct" solution to a problem (for example, highlighting the moral obligation to "dock" such bikes at a docking station) or answering standard questions that do not require much creativity, divergent thinking and doing is a method which helps to generate creative ideas by exploring many possible solutions.

The distinction between convergent and divergent thinking can be traced back to the research works conducted by American psychologist J.P. Guilford (1897–1987). It is about spontaneity, out-of-the-box thinking and non-linearity — that is, an environment where "blue sky ideas" can emerge. Isn't that what the joy of cycling is about, at least if it is not too hot? Isn't that what our Singapore society, which is so well organised, needs in order to remain relevant in an era of VUCA (volatility, uncertainty, complexity and ambiguity)?

Divergent thinking is often found among people with personality traits such as non-conformity, curiosity, and the willingness to take risks. So, could those "errant cyclists", who seemingly do not care about returning their bikes in a "proper manner" (for example, at a docking station) and leave them wherever they wish, be labelled as "divergent users"?

While our common analytical (convergent) sense would tell us that these non-conformists must be disciplined, perhaps we can stop for a moment and conduct a little thought experiment so as to try and acknowledge the creativity potential of such "socially disruptive" behaviour.

One could put oneself in the shoes of a cyclist who might have found unexpected serendipity (that is, a fortunate discovery by accident) during cycling while looking at a particularly beautiful cloud formation. Spotting several "abandoned" bikes in a park might imply that this particular spot may have served as an urgently needed resting place for exhausted, sweaty and dehydrated bikers — and perhaps indicating the potential demand for a pop-up drink stall and/or a pop-up shower facility in this particular space or community.

While these scenarios may sound unrealistic, "thinking divergently about cycling" may help to drive home the point that we should, from time to time, question our routinised, convergent ways of thinking in order to appreciate the power of transformational, out-of-the-box thinking which is critical to make innovation work. In that sense, one may also applaud the creative business behaviour of bike-share companies which are strategically placing their bikes at the least expected of locations, to encourage the public to use them.

While getting out of the box may be risky because "the boss might not be pleased!", remaining inside the box all the time is hardly an option in an era of big bang disruptions. Coming up with new actionable ideas is paramount to kick-start innovation.

Coming back to the theme of "improper" bike rental etiquette (within the confines of the law), one may go a step further and argue that such perceptions are outcomes of our own tight mental boundaries. Out-of-the-box, divergent thinking can open up new ways of perceiving reality and help to develop more creative ideas, which in turn can give us a competitive edge in differentiating ourselves and the organisation we work for. Going against some of the accepted ways of doing things, as perhaps subtly suggested by Queen's Freddy Mercury in his Bicycle Race song, might be one way of doing so.

Safety, of course, cannot be compromised. Leaving a bike on a footpath and blocking a wheelchair user who is unable to push it away is unacceptable. So, one's "divergent behaviour" should not be at the expense of another person's safety. Also, abandoning a malfunctioning bike "divergently" on a grass patch (and thereby passing on the problem to someone else) would indeed be very inconsiderate.

(The Straits Times, 22 July 2017)

Bright Future for Solar Power Entrepreneurs

With the need to save power and disruption in the energy sector, there are plenty of opportunities for the Smart-er players.

In an era of climate change and scarce fossil fuels, there is an urgency to make people more aware of the need to save energy and to think about the wiser use of power — whether from traditional sources (95% of Singapore's electricity comes from gas) or alternative power, such as solar, wind, or thermal.

Singapore's Smart Nation vision represents a great lever to make the most of newly arising business opportunities in the field of green energy and to change consumer behaviour. There can be no "smart city" without smart(er) energy, a more sensible use of clean renewable energy sources and "good" energy-saving habits.

Indeed, energy-saving tips can be found on the website of Singapore Power (SP): Clean your air-con filters regularly; use more LED bulbs;

use a fan instead of air-con; audit your daily electricity usage; set the temperature at 25°C (rather than 23°C or lower); switch off the water heater immediately after showering and so forth.

In addition, though, wouldn't it be nice to harness the power of the sun by putting a small mobile solar energy storage facility in our homes (it usually takes a couple of hours to dry my laundry outside when the sun is shining)?

In search of an answer, I checked out the websites of Singapore Power (which oversees solar development in Singapore) and Singapore's Energy Market Authority (EMA).

According to the EMA, the number of "Solar Photovoltaic (PV) Installations and Grid Connected Solar Photovoltaic Installations by Residents" in Singapore is still quite small. It grew from just 13 in 2009 to 500 last year; the non-residential take-up rate increased from 46 in 2009 to 1,280 last year.

Unfortunately, I failed to get the information I wished for when I activated the "how to install a solar PV system for your business or home" link on the EMA website. Instead, I was directed back to the website of SP (Singapore Power) group.

As a consumer, I would like to establish quickly if (and if yes, where and how) I can buy my own "solar energy supply system" here and what it takes to link it to the national grid.

Reading the *Handbook of Solar PV Systems* put together by the Building and Construction Authority and EMA is worthwhile as it contains important technical details, but in the end we wish to know which system is available on the market, is it endorsed by the regulator, is it reliable, how much does it cost, and who can safely install it.

Singapore Catching-up

One pioneer in providing grid-connected PV systems here is Sunseap, Singapore's biggest renewable energy provider, which was started by Mr Frank Phuan and Mr Lawrence Wuin.

Singapore is catching up with renewable energy leaders such as Germany, and with the vision of energy disruptors such as Mr Elon Musk with his idea of "integrated solar roof tiles" or Google's futuristic Titan-Solara 50 drone.

The goal is to have solar power contributing 350 megawatt peak to Singapore's system by 2020, making up 5% of the projected electricity demand. The Government's tender for PV (photovoltaic) panels, the Housing Board's efforts to equip more HDB blocks with solar panels, Nanyang Technological University's evolving Cleantech hub, and the large floating solar photovoltaic cell test bed at Tengeh Reservoir are recent manifestations of an envisaged greener future. However, more can be done.

The corporate story of Germany's giant electric utility E.ON (once a monopoly), which has seen its share price fall by more than 50% in eight years, is perhaps indicative of the risks in delaying to innovate in the area of renewables (which are getting cheaper and cheaper, in line with changing customer preferences). This is especially important in an era of climate change and at a time when there is potential to have a more open, innovative business model which leverages renewable forms of energy such as wind and solar instead of fossil fuels.

However, E.ON has recently started its own energy acceleration programme by supporting several energy start-ups such as digimondo ("a cloud for every information"), Radbonus (a reward scheme for cycling) and pixolus (meter reading via smartphone camera).

E.ON's stakeholders can easily get information on its user-friendly website — for example, there are tips on how to install a solar system in one's home, and there is also a tap to calculate the cost of doing so.

Trends Provide Opportunities

Several trends are disrupting the traditional structure of the energy sector, such as grid parity of solar-distributed generation. This refers to the time when an emerging technology such as solar power will produce electricity at the same cost to consumers as traditional approaches.

These trends represent promising new business opportunities. Questions which energy entrepreneurs need to ask themselves include: How could established utilities monetise green energy trends (and avoid becoming extinct like Kodak, Borders and many others before)?

Other questions: How could a new energy-related start-up team leverage energy-related technological advancements, such as in areas like micro grids, lithium batteries, storage, kinetic energy, or smart meters? An interesting local example of a green product innovation is the Wi-Fi-enabled smart bulb "Qube", developed by Mr Rick Tan's Innova Technology.

As Singapore Power's launch of the *Free Electrons Global Energy Start-up Accelerator Programme* indicates, Singapore's energy market provides great opportunities for entrepreneurial energy innovators with a convincing customer value proposition and innovative business models (think smart LED lighting for smart homes or micro grids for energy cooperatives). SP teamed up with seven other power utilities to launch the programme in January. It aims to bring together utilities and start-ups to innovate and co-create ideas and clean energy solutions.

I look forward to the day when I can go to a neighbourhood shop in Ghim Moh and buy my own mobile solar power energy supply system that I can easily and safely plug into the (micro) grid in order to lower my energy costs, flexibly store energy for later use and thereby help to save the planet.

(The Straits Times, 31 March 2017)

Chapter 5

Innovation Processes

How to Make Innovation Work? Establish a Programme, Corporate Venture Fund or an Open Innovation Ecosystem that Empowers Those Who Dare to be Different

With Alex Teo Hong Hak

Ask any business leader what keeps her or him awake at night and you will hear answers ranging from concerns about the risk of supply-chain disruptions to difficulties coping with increasing business costs. Chances are they won't say, "I need to improve the quality of our innovation processes". While phrases and challenges like "blockchain-powered platform models" or "disruptive innovation" are discussed by many SME leaders, terms such as "innovation value chain" or "phase-gate model" arguably haven't quite made it into their strategic vocabulary. That is a pity because well managed innovation processes represent powerful lubricants to create and capture new value.

According to management gurus Morten T. Hansen and Julian Birkinshaw, typical innovation management challenges in "idea-poor organisations" include insufficient promotion of internal or externally-sourced ideas while "conversion-poor organisations" fail to screen or develop ideas properly which often results in the insufficient monetisation of sound ideas. In many organisations, tight budgets, risk-averse thinking, and formal bureaucratic procedures grind execution to a halt. Attempts to build a culture of innovation often amount to little more than innovation theatre, despite top management's best intentions.

Such challenges can be tackled by implementing (or enhancing existing) innovation processes. The word "process" refers to a series of steps taken in order to achieve a particular end. In our context, it is to reach strategic innovation goals in a timely manner such as incremental improvements in core products and services or truly transformational innovations. Trying to make innovation work with the same old planning, budgeting and review approaches usually doesn't do the job. Instead, adding explorative flexibility to planning and control systems by creating a new emerging business unit and providing special funds for unexpected innovation opportunities can help to drive innovation more effectively.

Innovation processes represent a core component of Enterprise Singapore's *Business Excellence Niche Standard for Innovation* (besides customers, leadership, strategy, people, knowledge and results). Examples of "excellence indicators" include: (i) the existence of a systematic process to acquire, evaluate and implement ideas that create value, (ii) improvements made to the innovation and design processes to shorten cycle time, improve design quality and reduce costs, or (iii) involving both internal and external stakeholders in the process of innovating and inventing new products, services and solutions such as staff, customers, trading partners, suppliers, and distributors.

To create an idea-rich organisation, business leaders can initiate open innovation and/or crowdsourcing processes, leveraging on both internal and external sources for ideas and resources. A corporate example is *The UBS Future of Finance Challenge* which targets start-ups and established, growing companies which are keen to change the way finance works by deploying client-centric, transformative digital technologies. Competition winners are invited to participate in a proof-of-concept or pilot program to further scale their ideas and technologies, with input and support by dedicated coaches and mentors. Another interesting case is the *Future Shapers* initiative of Oxfam, an international confederation of development NGOs. Powered by Crowdicity's idea management software platform, the initiative helped to engage Oxfam's globally dispersed people in a collaborative conversation about organisational change issues.

External sources for ideas and resources may involve non-customers, the general public or a third-party organisation such as a licensee who may develop internally generated ideas and discoveries into marketable products or services. Another approach to carry out innovation via an external route to market is the proactive sourcing of ideas or discoveries with the help of external networks such as Innoget, an *Open Innovation and Science Network* for technology, knowledge and capabilities transfer where expertise seekers can reach thousands of experts around the globe. One of Innoget's users is NIVEA manufacturer Beiersdorf, which collaborates with external innovation partners from industries and the scientific community as part of its R&D works. Imagine this scenario: your own salaried scientists need external help in developing a new skincare line for men above the age of 85. This is where the Innoget network kicks in by linking product innovation scouts with dermatology scientists, say in Japan, which is experiencing a super-aging society. Subsequently, further skincare-related development efforts may take place internally using the company's own resources.

"Good" innovation process management can help to create a conversion-rich organisation in which ideas are developed properly. One approach is to implement an effective screening process, e.g. on the basis of the so-called *Stage-Gate approach* (pioneered by Dr Robert G. Cooper), an innovation project management technique that divides the innovation initiative such as a product development process or process improvement into different phases or stages separated by decision points.[1] During these control points or "gates", the state of a particular project phase is reviewed and approved (or not). The key review purpose is to share project status information, to discuss and resolve problems as well as to review planned performance, cost and risks within a product or process (e.g. with the help of FMEA, a highly structured tool for failure analysis used in Six Sigma).

Information about how local firms have implemented such stage-gate processes can be obtained by studying the reports of Enterprise Singapore's Innovation Excellence Award winners such as Sheng Siong. Core steps of the firm's innovation process entail ideation, project planning, implementation and measurement of results. An outcome of a completed innovation project is Sheng Siong's hybrid self-checkout counter system with a cash management system which has significantly benefitted its business operations.

In many organisations, greenlighting an idea is riddled with problems such as "flawed" selection criteria (often decided by the most senior persons and/or a "committee", and not actual customer behaviour), lack

---

[1] https://www.stage-gate.com/.

of funds to pursue ideas further or disgruntled employees who do not know why their ideas were not supported. Pumping innovation ideas and staff suggestions into a dreadful organisational culture won't work.

LEGO's open innovation ecosystem exemplifies the power of "good" innovation processes. LEGO fans can offer ideas to the LEGO Ideas website by submitting pictures with self-explanatory descriptions. To convince decision-makers that the idea has merit, 10,000 supporters (votes) are required to kickstart the review process. This can be achieved by sharing ideas through Facebook or other social media. Once supporters are on board, the idea goes to the LEGO review board which then decides whether it's good enough to advance to the next stage: turning it into an official set created by LEGO (criteria include size, cost, part complexity, need for new parts, and licensing issues). While not all ideas are approved by the review board, chances are high that the winning idea will be turned into an official LEGO product once the review board has given its go ahead.

It is time to stop the innovation theatre and to achieve innovation process excellence aligned with strategy by enhancing the innovation value chain, e.g. by establishing an intrapreneurship programme, a corporate venture fund or an open innovation ecosystem that empowers those who dare to be different.

(The Business Times, 19 July 2019)

Case Study

National Library Board Singapore — World-Class Service Through Innovation and People Centricity

Thomas Menkhoff and Jochen Wirtz

The National Library Board (NLB) Singapore is a statutory board that managed to become a serial innovator. Its globally leading innovations in the library context include an award-winning radio frequency identification (RFID) system to automate check-out, returns, and sorting of books, shelf-reading robots, and even self-service libraries. NLB's consistent focus on excellent service delivery reinforced its commitment to innovation. Key levers were effective strategic leadership, a smart innovation strategy that made heavy use of technology-such as app-delivered self-service technologies and crowdsourcing as well as a people-centric staff culture. NLB managed to cocreate attractive libraries of the future together with different types of community members, such as volunteers and corporations, ushering in a new age of citizen involvement, while also preparing both the library and the population of

The authors thank Professor Kah Hin Chai for his invaluable feedback and suggestions, and Chia En Celeste for her assistance with the data collection for this case study.

Note: This is a reprint of an article originally published in J. Wirtz and C. Lovelock 2018 (eds.), *Services Marketing: People, Technology*, Strategy (8th Edition) Instructor Resources. The permission of the publisher (World Scientific Publishing) and the authors to reprint the article in this edition is gratefully acknowledged.

NLB's My Tree House: World's First Green Library for Kids

Singapore for the knowledge demands of the 21st century. This case study examines NLB's drivers of successful innovation.

National Library Board's Journey of Innovation

The National Library Board's (NLB's) vision is an ambitious one, to say the least. The vision's stated aim is to achieve "Readers for Life,

Learning Communities, and a Knowledgeable Nation". Correspondingly, it describes its mission thus: "We make knowledge come alive, spark imagination and create possibilities". Naturally, this massive endeavor could only be approached with significant and sustained innovation, and the massive deployment of technology.

NLB's Vision

The Board's innovation objectives were outlined in several master plans that envisioned the establishment of a world-class library system which sought to meet the learning needs of a rapidly developing young nation. The Board evolved through three waves of transformation, each successive wave building on what was achieved through the previous wave's master plan.

Wave 1: Library 2000

The focus of the early transformation effort in Wave 1 was to develop and expand the infrastructure of an adaptive, world-class public library system in Singapore that would be convenient, accessible, and useful. Several strategic undertakings were formulated and subsequently implemented, such as establishing a network of national reference libraries and a three-tier public library system of regional, community, and neighborhood libraries, as well as assisting in the setting up of school libraries and the development of specialized libraries for specific sectors. A coordinated national collection strategy was initiated to provide comprehensive coverage of Singapore's literary and publishing heritage. This culminated in the core collection of the Lee Kong Chian Reference Library, with more than 300,000 items featuring material in various formats (microfilms, maps, audio-visual materials, ephemera, posters, and print publications) related to the history, political, and economic history, literature, as well as social-cultural history of Singapore. As Singapore developed into a global knowledge hub offering information on regional businesses and cultures, Wave 1 laid the foundation for safeguarding the documentary heritage and intellectual memory of the country, in keeping with its aim to build a literate, informed, and participative society.

Another strategic goal was to ensure that the libraries would offer quality service through market orientation. The innovative use of radio frequency identification (RFID) technology-enabled self-service allowed customers to perform the check-out and return transactions themselves. As waiting times were minimized, customers could engage with the library more proactively. In a bid to remain relevant in an increasingly digital world, NLB launched the eLibraryHub, enabling users to access digital content easily from an online portal without having to be physically present at the libraries.

New strategic and symbiotic linkages between the government, businesses, and the general public were formed to ensure that NLB would meet the needs of Singaporeans in the 21st century. Through initiatives such as the Friends of the Library Programme, NLB involved community members, reaching out to volunteers whose personal preferences and abilities were matched with areas within its libraries. By organizing enriching programs for children from low-income families or delivering books to those unable to visit libraries, volunteers made a real difference and felt that they were a part of something greater than themselves.

Wave 2: Library 2010

Wave 2 of NLB's transformation had an even stronger focus on IT, supporting the leadership's desire to achieve higher productivity in library services. The reengineering of business processes had stretch targets in five key areas: (1) Time-to-Market, (2) Time-to-Checkout, (3) Time-to-Shelf, (4) Time-to-Information, and (5) Library Planning, Setup, and Renewal. This also included greater emphasis on user-education, so that library users could fully appreciate and explore the breadth of the collections.

The key thrusts of NLB's digital strategy included the following:

- Creation of immersive reading experiences inside physical library spaces with e-reading stations, multimedia video walls, and mobile services. The latter included the NLB Mobile app, which could be used to borrow items and bypass the queue at book-borrowing stations.
- Pushing personalized content and recommendations to encourage users to read more. This was enabled through patron analytics, smart displays, and devices.

- Increasing NLB's outreach through presence in spaces outside its libraries, such as personalized recommendations on partner platforms and spaces.
- Productivity-focused automation and self-service technology to optimize staff deployment and enhance patron convenience. For instance, thanks to reservation lockers, patrons were able to make reservations outside library opening hours.
- Data-driven library operations and collections planning allowed NLB to plan effective library services, optimize content usage, and provide relevant collections to users.

The innovative efforts by NLB to create digital libraries culminated in the OneSearch Service, an online search portal for information spread across a variety of resources, spanning NLB's libraries and archives databases, as well as the National Heritage Board's museum repository of artefacts and artworks. Through the OneSearch Service, users could conveniently retrieve a wide range of digital content (books, magazines, audio-visual materials, e-books, photographs, films, maps, etc.).

As more people were reading online, NLB's "eRead" resources offered digital and audiobooks, newspapers, and magazines from various genres and in English, Chinese, Malay, and Tamil. Capable of retrieval from a wide range of digital content including books, magazines, audio-visual materials, e-books, photographs, films, oral history interviews, and maps, NLB once again achieved service excellence with technology as an enabler.

Wave 3: Library 2020

Wave 3 was launched in 2016, with the motto "Readers for Life, Learning Communities, and a Knowledgeable Nation", to create more learning communities and inspiring spaces across Singaporean society.

To promote reading, learning, and literacy, NLB rolled out various reading programs tailored to the needs of different demographic groups. They include Early READ for children up to six years, kidsREAD for children of ages four to eight years who are from low-income families, and READ@School for students of ages seven to 17 years.

An example of NLB's concept of an "Inspiring Space" is the historical Former Ford Factory site. Once the assembly plant of the Ford Motor Company of Malaya, on February 15, 1942, it became the site where the British forces surrendered Singapore to the Japanese Imperial

Army. In early 2017, the building reopened to mark the 75th anniversary of the start of the Japanese Occupation of Singapore. It features archival records and multisensory displays to bring history to life. After a public call for donations of historical materials, such as Japanese textbooks or oral history accounts covering the years 1937 to 1954, NLB received more than 400 donated items.

As a guardian of historical knowledge, NLB's HistorySG projects, such as the Former Ford Factory, are critical for presenting Singapore's collective memory to the young and old alike. As a *Straits Times* journalist emphasized, "To entrench its place in the community, one would want the young to see the library as less a staid repository of tomes and more a throbbing hub of open minds, connecting physically and digitally over a host of ideas and creative impulses".[1]

How did a statutory board like NLB manage to become an award-winning serial innovator? Key fundamentals underpinning NLB's innovation success included: (1) an effective innovation leadership and innovation process, (2) a strong focus on (technology-enabled) service delivery, (3) an enduring culture of staff involvement and innovation, and (4) innovation through co-creation and 3 'Ps' (people, private, public sectors) engagement.

Transformational Leadership and Innovation Process

From the beginning, senior management exhibited strong, transformational, and intrapreneurial leadership as it worked with Singapore's public administration to enhance organizational efficiency, digitalization (e.g., as part of the computerization of the entire civil service) and service delivery. All levels of staff within NLB were galvanized for technological and organizational change as the Information Age was ushered in. If one looks at the innovation strategy development process as a series of cascading stages, where each stage derives from or acts upon the results of the preceding stage (see Exhibit 1), it becomes clear that NLB's leaders managed to ask the right strategic questions and followed through them decisively, step after step.

What Is Our Purpose/Where Should We Play?

NLB's mission, "We make knowledge come alive, spark imagination and create possibilities", and innovation objectives were derived from several

---

[1] Libraries as Hubs for Creative Learning, *The Straits Times*, October 12, 2015.

Shelf reading robot

Exhibit 1: Critical Aspects of a Strategic Innovation Cascade*

1. **What's Our Purpose?**

   Why innovate, and on the basis of what kind of objectives?

2. **Where to Play (Where Not to Play)?**

   Where should the innovation's focus and scope be?

3. **With What Intensity?**

   How much innovation (e.g., incremental or radical) is wanted?

4. **How to Win?**

   How should corporate innovation goals be pursued, and which unique value proposition should they be based on?

5. **With Whom to Innovate?**

   With whom should collaboration be (e.g., internal partners and/or external complementors), and where are the innovation boundaries?

6. **With What Capability Assets?**

   How can it be ensured that people in the organization are capable and motivated to make innovation work?

7. **With What Management Systems?**

   How can working relationships be structured and organized to "get things done" innovatively? What business processes need to be built in order to create and capture innovation value? How can strategic innovation matters be tracked and innovation efforts be evaluated?

---

*As an innovation strategy tool, the Strategic Innovation Cascade can point management's attention to critical questions that need to be answered to make innovation work.

master plans envisioning the establishment of a world-class library system. National development goals, such as becoming an internationally competitive nation and a cohesive society with a strong national identity, paved the way for NLB to find the right "playing field" in terms of its vision, mission, localities, product and service categories, customer segments, channels, etc. Encouraging Singaporeans to discover and celebrate the joy of reading propelled many of its nationwide reading initiatives, such as "Read! Singapore" (2005). The initiative was aimed at promoting a culture of reading fiction among Singaporeans, and a key component of the initiative was the promotion of short stories that were cross-translated. Presented in Singapore's four official languages, the initiative featured meet-the-author sessions, book club sessions, writing workshops, storytelling sessions, and book-derived workshops for children and adults. This allowed the public to be more hands-on with the library's initiatives. Important questions that NLB's leadership team had to answer concerned the *Intensity Level of Innovation Efforts* ("How much incremental or radical innovation do we want?") and the strategic approach towards pursuing innovation goals on the basis of a compelling value proposition ("how to win"). The outcomes of such strategy decisions included the deployment of RFID technology to enable self-service borrowing and returning, as well as the development of a new mobile application enabling library members to borrow materials using their mobile devices on the go (see Exhibit 4).

With Whom to Innovate?

NLB became a leader in co-creation. An example of this boundary-spanning collaboration approach was the 2013 opening of the library@chinatown, whose whole day to-day operations are fully run by volunteers. Through this kind of novel service co-creation, NLB involved community members and public organizations, such as CP1 Pte. Ltd. (the property developer for the Chinatown Point shopping center) and Kwan Im Thong Hood Cho Temple, based on the 3 'P's sector motto (People, Public, and Private). It enabled NLB to tap into the knowledge, input, and resources of the wider community, contributing to improved public service delivery.

Gradually, NLB further strengthened its customer value proposition with a focus on "non-customers", and demonstrated the ability to create and capture new demand as evidenced by its "Verging All Teens" program, rolled out in the Jurong Regional Library (the first library to hold a space created for teens by teens), and My Tree House, the world's first green library for children (created in collaboration with City Development Limited) to promote learning and reading for life, in line with the 'Library 2020' vision.The colorful indoor setting changed the perception of reading, while the decor was made of recyclable or environmentally friendly resources and completed with energy-saving furnishings. Such partnerships with private companies added to NLB's capabilities in developing and improving public libraries while serving as a touch point for these organizations to give back to the public.

With What Capability Assets?

All this would not have worked out if not for a strong foundation comprising a set of reinforcing capabilities and competency-enhancing activities, such as the Master of Science in Library Science program for library staff (developed together with the Nanyang Technological University in Singapore), embedded in a robust culture of learning and innovation.

With What Management Systems?

Besides good innovation governance and strategy execution in general, NLB established various supporting management systems (e.g., for innovative IT deployment such as the OneSearch service). Rather than focusing on traditional librarianship duties, staff across all levels were motivated to provide ideas for innovation, and engage in new initiatives such as crowdsourcing. The latter became a core component of NLB's Citizen Archivist Project, which enabled the public to contribute to the nation's intellectual memory. NLB's success in innovation was driven by numerous value-adding business processes, such as rapid prototyping and open innovation, and an integrative performance measurement approach. Recently, NLB deployed the use of geospatial analytics to better understand the borrowing behavior of library users across the island.

At the structural level, several innovation processes were implemented to create and capture innovation value. This provided a conducive environment for all ideas to be considered and then further refined for implementation (see Exhibit 2). Through the establishment of strong channels for internal communication within NLB, staff was kept informed about organizational changes and also encouraged to make suggestions for improvements.

Exhibit 2: Examples of Innovation Processes and Strategic Actions Taken by NLB

Organizations	Positioning
The organization generates, gathers, and screens creative ideas from all sources.	NLB involved its own employees in the innovation process through various initiatives. An example of its "dare to try" innovation spirit and ideation process was the BlackBox program. It consisted of (i) a call for ideas, (ii) an innovation competition, (iii) development and trial, and (iv) the presentation of findings and recommendations to senior management. While testing out technology-based ideas, NLB employed a rapid prototyping approach called proof of concept (PoC), through which NLB could safely and economically assess the viability of an idea by developing small-scale projects. By maximizing time and resources within a limited period of time, the PoC approach helped NLB to evaluate the viability of ideas and to minimize the financial risks they might pose.
The organization incorporates new developments and changing requirements into innovations.	Predictive data analytics enables NLB to forecast user demand for new and existing titles which, in turn, leads to more efficient resource management and greater servic equality.
The organization involves employees and partners in the new product and service design.	NLB proactively maintained and expanded partnerships with overseas libraries, government agencies, non-profit organizations, and private organizations, as well as communities. The library@chinatown was Singapore's first volunteer-run public library that was co-developed with and managed by the community for the community. NLB's mobile library, MOLLY, brought library services to orphanages, childrens' homes, and special education schools such as Pathlight School (a school for autistic children), in collaboration with SBS Transit Ltd. and Comfort Oelgro Pte. Ltd.

The organization has a relationship with customers to identify and address innovation opportunities.	NLB aligned itself effectively between several customer segments and its customer strategy, in line with its overall mission. An example was its engagement with seniors above the age of 60 and examining their requirements for productive leisure, mental stimulation, and social engagement. Tools deployed to understand their (future) needs included customer dialogue sessions and customer feedback channels. Customers were involved systematically in library renovation projects or when niche library spaces we redesigned for community members, via face-to-face sessions and customer relationship management (CRM)-enabled feedback loops.
The organization reviews management of innovation projects and validates them.	To ensure that innovation projects delivered the intended outcomes, NLB carefully managed the end-to-end maturation journey of an idea. Key milestones included planning, followed by business cases, project management, and post-implementation review.
The organization seeks breakthrough improvements in key business processes for value creation.	One strategic goal of NLB was to make its content discoverable with the help of digital services. NLB's Mobile app, the revamp of its Archives Online, the Oral History Interviews Portal, and the oneSearch search engine were examples of e-services that were rolled out to facilitate easy access to content on Singapore and to NLB's resources.
The organization evaluates and improves its management of innovation processes for product, service and business process innovation.	One hallmark of NLB's innovation culture was co-creation powered by the strategic belief in the importance of harnessing the power of collective wisdom via public participation.

Source: Various NLB materials, such as its Innovation Award Report.

Autonomous Bookdrop

NLB's leadership team created a strong foundation for greater inno-vativeness by putting in place systems for effective people management (e.g., training programs on ideation and innovation management) and innovation process management (e.g., idea generation approaches together with staff, customers, suppliers, and other partners). While the impetus was to adopt advanced technology to improve work processes, NLB's leadership involved all levels of staff as part of the change efforts in order to create a trustworthy and engaged work environment.

Focus on Technology-Enabled Service

Delivery to library Users

Over the years, NLB continuously rolled out numerous digital services (self-service technologies) aimed at making its content accessible. For example, in the nation with the highest mobile penetration rate in the world, the NLB Mobile app has given library users access to library infor-mation and allowed transactions, such as the loaning of library materials and e-books that can be read on the go. Users can borrow books with their mobile phones using updated RFID technology via the app, making the queuing for self-checkout machines a thing of the past.

NLB provided e-books (in all four official languages) that could also be accessed through its website. Subjects include the arts, economics, literature, history and geography, philosophy and religion, social science, politics and law, and science. These e-books were procured through major international e-books providers. To provide easy access to Singapore's archival holdings, Archives Online was revamped to enable a seamless search for information across the National Archives of Singapore's (NAS) various databases, which include photographs, maps, oral history interview samplers, and snippets of audio-visual recordings. Library users could also get online access to the Oral History collection of Singapore's National Archives, including a vast collection of stories collected from politicians to street hawkers, medical professionals to prisoners-of-war, and artists to entrepreneurs.

NLB's innovation was successful because it was both technological and non-technological. This was in line with academics' and consulting firms' findings that it was organizational strategy and innovation culture, not technology per se, that drove the success of digital transformation efforts. NLB used technological innovation not as an end goal but as a means to free up resources so that they could engage in other forms of innovation, mainly co-creation for service excellence and productivity with external parties.

Technologically enabled service innovations pioneered by NLB such as book drops, self-checkout machines, and borrower enquiry machines became standard features in new libraries. They exemplified a positive trend where innovation efforts by NLB were accompanied by the gradual evolution of citizen engagement.

As an example of innovative service co-creation, the library@ orchard won the prestigious President's Design Award for its outstanding interior design in 2015. Its space design was informed by the ideas and proposals contributed by Orchard Road "regulars" and other members of the public in collaboration with design thinking experts from Singapore Polytechnic (SP). The three development phases included (i) observing target users and understanding their needs and "pain points" via interviews, (ii) ideation based on the results of data collection efforts, and (iii) development of prototypes to obtain user reactions and to appreciate customer preferences. At the Pasir Ris Public Library, a new (volunteer-run) teen's mezzanine with comfortable multifunctional furniture and a doodle wall for self-expression and discussions was created for teenagers.

Culture of Staff Involvement and Innovation

Future-proofing the libraries and expanding the nation's learning capacity with the aid of information resources provided a purpose for many organizational members and ultimately helped NLB to achieve its strategic objectives. All librarians were encouraged to build up relevant competencies and human capital alongside the transformation of the library, aimed at reaching Level One certification from the Singapore Workforce Skills Qualifications in six months. Thus, a culture of staff involvement was built from the organization's beginning.

While public organizations elsewhere were stereotyped as being bureaucratic, NLB gave its staff the autonomy and empowerment to voice their opinions and raise suggestions. The adoption of the Staff Suggestion Scheme served as a channel for staff across all levels to share their ideas, to be evaluated by the heads of the divisions and then approved online. This was not a token exercise. For example, as early as in 1997, when the scheme was introduced, 60 percent of 2,239 suggestions received were implemented. This sent a strong signal to all levels of staff that contributions were taken seriously and that the organization was genuine about constant incremental improvements. Tools such as the BlackBox program (see below) ensured that the ideas and innovation potential of NLB's staff were fully exploited.

To sustain innovation efforts, NLB realized that it was key to invest in people. Librarians' competencies were developed over the years in line with changing customer expectations. The form in which knowledge was processed and interpreted evolved even if the core services of providing research and references services to the public remained. Traditional librarianship had to be further professionalized, moving beyond cataloguing and referencing to research, synthetization, and packaging of information. To aid in this upgrade, NLB signed a memorandum of understanding (MoU) with the Nanyang Technological University in 1998 to offer the Master of Science in Library Science degree to library staff. These formal academic qualifications helped librarians specialize in information and navigate the Information Age, serving readers all the same. Many more MoUs followed to facilitate knowledge sharing on technical systems and innovations with academics.

Other capabilities that were built for librarians included skills to develop specialized collections, including arts, multi-culture, and Singapore; the productization of information services to provide reference answers to the public on an online database, namely, Singapore Infopedia; specialized information services in business information and customized information; cataloguing and indexing newspapers on the digital space through the Dublin Core Standard; and Cybrarian services for users to communicate remotely on the eLibraryHub.

Specialization in these roles helped NLB to increase the range of services delivered to customers as well as serve a wider segment. Knowledge across different areas also helped to expand the scope for innovation.

As we know from innovation studies, trying to make innovation work with the same tight planning, budgeting, and reviews that are applied to existing businesses can create a "trap:" One remedy is to add flexibility to planning and control systems; for example, by providing special funds for new opportunities. NLB did just that. To support the passage of ideas from initial planning to post implementation review,various means and channels were instituted. The BlackBox program (held biennially) was spearheaded by the Technology and Innovation division (see Exhibit 3) and has helped to identify numerous potential innovative projects. Winning teams were provided with funds, mentors, and financial resources to conduct a six-month proof-of-concept.

One of the projects spawned out of BlackBox was Quest, a trading-card game aimed at encouraging young boys to read. Quest won the American Library Association Presidential Citation for Innovative International Projects in 2011.The continuity of the BlackBox program exemplifies NLB's strong innovation culture.

Another effective innovation management approach adopted by NLB was the involvement of staff in projects that featured cross-divisional teams. The formation of such work groups broke the functional silos and allowed staff from all levels to come together. Cross-functional project teams reduced hierarchy and bureaucracy, bringing together various domain experts to be involved as team members and manage and implement projects together. The re-opening of revamped libraries like the Pasir

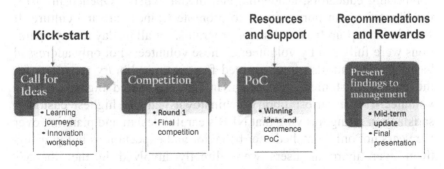

Exhibit 3: NLB's BlackBox Program

Ris Public Library in 2015 provided clear evidence of the benefits of cross-divisional collaboration between staff from the Public Library Service, Properties and Facilities Management division, and the Technology and Information division to ensure that the library provides up-to-date services across all functions on time.

Innovation through Co-Creation and 3P (People, Private, Public Sectors) Engagement

One of the first instances of public involvement with NLB beyond the traditional library usage was during the rollout of the Verging All Teens program in the Jurong Regional Library. It was the first library created for teens by teens, meant to inspire each other to read more about the creation of relevant library spaces. Thanks to youths' input, the Teens Library had unique features catered to this target group, including music, decor, stage performances, and even a graffiti wall. This section of the library was publicly run by volunteers.

NLB's co-creation approach eventually expanded beyond the daily running of operations to the very conceptualization of libraries. This was particularly important for mall libraries, because they were set apart from the regional, neighborhood, and national libraries in terms of space, location, and curated collections. The library@esplanade became Singapore's first performing arts library. Taking in feedback from the arts community, it boasted an exhibition space and performing stage alongside a niche collection of books, screenplays, and music scores.

The success of this mall library led to the co-development of library@chinatown alongside a panel of experts on Chinese culture comprising educators, academia, and media experts. Opened in 2013, the library's main purpose was to promote Chinese art and culture. It was also a step-up from volunteer programs, for all its day to-day operations were fully run by volunteers. These volunteers not only addressed basic queries but also brainstormed for engaging library programs for the public. Customer satisfaction, in fact, registered higher in these volunteer-run libraries; library@chinatown had the highest customer satisfaction rating, proving that NLB's careful design and planning over the years not only matched user behavior and expectations but gratified them even more as users were directly involved in the library's activities.

Exhibit 4: Components and Outcomes of NLB's Breakthrough Innovations

Innovation Strategy Components	NLB's Innovation Strengths
Component Citizen Engagement and Collaboration through Co-Creation	Co-creation and volunteer-delivered services have multiplied impact and reach:
Outcome: Greater social engagement of NLB's stakeholders (e.g. volunteers)	• library@orchard • library@chinatown • Pasir Ris Public library • Citizen Archivist project aimed at greater public participation in the archival process
Component: Making NLB Content Discoverable through Digital Services	Digital services facilitated easy access to content on Singapore and NLB's e-Resources:
Outcome: Effective harnessing of digital (e.g. self-service) technologies	• NLB Mobile app • Revamp of Archives Online • Oral History Interviews Portal • One Search Portal
Component Buffering Front Office Activities from the Back Office **Outcome:** Organizational efficiency gains through resource optimization	Resources saved through technologies were channeled to higher value tasks: • Auto-sorter system • Self-service reservation system • Shelf-reading robot

Co-creating with public and private organizations allowed NLB to participate in other projects beyond the library, combining its internal strengths with the business know-how of these organizations. In 2011, NLB led the Singapore Memory Project for the Singapore Government, reaching out and partnering with other institutions, which included heritage agencies and research institutions, to kick-start a memory movement. Through their shared expertise, the partnership enabled the creation of a new wave of knowledge assets in a Library 2.0 environment. The term "Library 2.0" refers to the application of interactive and collaborative (multi media) web-based technologies to library services and collections. An Add to Singapore Memory app was created through which the public could contribute their own perspectives in the form of videos, photographs, and web links to the platform, with NLB playing a key role in the curation and archiving of these assets.

The Citizen Archivist project, a crowd-sourcing portal launched in 2015, tapped the public's knowledge and wisdom for its extensive collections of archival records. This encouraged more public participation in the archival process. Citizens' involvement in the description and transcription of archival records directly contributed to the greater accessibility of Singapore's intellectual memory in the form of archives.

Another example of 3P participation was the development of NewspaperSG, a digital archive of Singaporean and Malaysian newspapers published between 1831 and 2009. With the support of Singapore Press Holdings, the leading publisher in Singapore, NLB was granted permission to digitize The Straits Times from its first issue onwards. Once again, it was the fruitful partnership with different stakeholders that allowed NLB to broaden its range of services offered to the public, maintaining its commitment to customer-centricity.

Going Forward

NLB's strong staff culture has provided a conducive environment for innovations to occur, supported by leadership, strategy, innovation culture, capacity-building, formalized processes, IT mastery, and 3P partnerships for co-creation. The adoption of both technological and non-technological innovations enabled NLB to engage stakeholders such as the public in unprecedented ways. Although innovations usually started internally within the organization, through suggestions from the staff seeking to improve customer delivery, these novel and value-creating ways of doing things eventually diffused outwards and had a far-reaching impact on the scope and depth of NLB's services.

In the era of Big Data, NLB continues to use innovations to serve its customers in line with its mission and vision. As Singapore's demographics change, NLB is well advised to harness the capabilities of data analytics and artificial intelligence for effective collection planning m order to serve the different segments of Singapore's diverse population. With transformation as a continual process rather than an end goal along with Singapore's growth as a smart nation, NLB can rely on its established innovation processes, forward-looking vision, and digital thrusts to address the ever-changing needs of readers of all ages and backgrounds. Several of NLB's current technology initiatives are aimed at figuring out how to use technology for personalization and to push out actionable information that is useful to individual users. This is just one of numerous new initiatives of NLB to future-proof itself.

Study Question

1. What are the main transformation waves NLB has gone through?
2. How did NLB manage to create a strong culture of innovation and service excellence?
3. What did NLB do in terms of staff capacity-building in order to expand the propensity for innovation?
4. What was the role of IT and digital services in transforming NLB and to improve the customer experience?
5. How did organizational strategy and culture riveNLB's digital transformation and innovation outcomes?
6. What else could NLB do to further stay ahead as a "library for life "so as to achieve its visionary goals of Readers for Life, Learning Communities, and a Knowledgeable Nation"?

Chapter 6

Knowledge & Learning

Harnessing the Benefits of Knowledge Management

The KM toolkit can help start-ups become smarter, more innovative organisations.

With Jennifer Chong

Ask a start-up founder what keeps him or her up at night and you'll hear a range of answers: "I don't know if we can make payroll" or "I need to figure out how to acquire more customers". Chances are they won't say, "I need to improve knowledge management in my organisation". In fact, they probably have never heard the term. While phrases such as "minimum viable product" (which refers to a product with a minimum set of features that allows lean start-ups to get feedback from early adopters on its vision plans) or "A/B testing" (website optimization approach) are thrown around by many tech start-up founders, knowledge management KM hasn't quite made it into their vocabulary. That's a shame because KM is a powerful tool to improve business results. Knowledge management refers to all the strategies that organisations can use to capture, share and create new knowledge. KM approaches include benchmarking, internal best practice transfer or efforts to create cultures that incentivise innovation. Singapore is home to various KM-enabled businesses.

Singapore Airlines' internationally acclaimed customer service excellence is built on rigorous data collection and analytics linked to business goals. The Health Promotion Board's Health Ambassador Network relies on robust systems of pushing health information out through volunteers, and feeding information from communities back to the board. Finally, the Infocomm Development Authority of Singapore has created a useful information repository and collaboration platform to connect CIO offices across Singapore's government.

While KM practices in such large organisations are well documented, KM in start-ups has thus far been poorly understood. Start-ups are particularly interesting because they grow rapidly and pivot their business models. This creates a constant need to quickly get new employees on board or to find different ways of engaging customers. In our research, we interviewed several start-up founders in Asia to understand to what extent KM is used in their organisations and the challenges that they face. The most immediately apparent finding was that none of them had heard of the concept.

Of course, all of them had an innate sense of what it meant — everybody is managing knowledge, but it's a matter of how, how much and whether they prioritise it. Rather than designing an overarching KM strategy, the start-ups we spoke to had implemented KM practices that were reactive, piecemeal solutions to immediate challenges that they faced. Sometimes these initiatives were successful in achieving a business goal, but often they failed due to the lack of an overarching KM strategy.

Here's an example: One of the larger start-ups that we spoke to had been expanding its ecommerce operations into several countries. Initially, they had no framework in place for the veteran country heads to share knowledge with the new country heads. Naturally, the new country operations repeated many costly mistakes that could have been avoided. Recognising how wasteful this exercise was, the regional office set up weekly conference calls among the country heads to facilitate information sharing.

What resulted, however, was that the heads rarely shared any valuable information during these calls because the right knowledge sharing culture was not in place. The heads were directly competing with each other to have the best key performance indicators, and they were not incentivised to help the other country heads, especially if they didn't like them! Instead of sharing information with all of the counterparts, they would reach out to their friends individually — outside of the structure of the weekly call — to share helpful tips. The attempt to encourage knowledge sharing was stymied by the fact that the company did not consider knowledge management holistically, as indicated by the insufficient alignment of the company's business model and knowledge management enablers such as a culture of sharing based on effective reward management approaches.

Even though they didn't have a term for "knowledge management", some start-ups utilised interesting approaches that helped them to leverage knowledge assets to improve business results. To locate and capture strategic knowledge, some used social media tools such as digital storytelling. Others used yellow pages applications, enabling employees to find staff with particular competencies, or created knowledge maps to visualise internal knowledge assets, including information bottlenecks, and knowledge brokers.

Collaborative Innovation Culture

Key to the effective sharing of explicit or tacit knowledge is the development of a collaborative innovation culture with room for experimentation, real learning and risk-taking. One of the start-ups we spoke to had built up a very spirited team culture that encouraged communication and real-time sharing with the help of a feedback gathering application called Tiny Pulse. Gathering employee feedback and prompt issue management by top management had a positive impact upon engagement levels. Others used wikis to enhance collaboration between teams to avoid "making the same mistake twice". Through a wiki, teams captured and shared important know how and lessons learned such as product launch experiences. Another start-up used idea logging "everything from customer requests to creative ideas" enabled by an issue tracking application (for example Jira).

With regard to new knowledge creation processes in start-ups, customers do take centre stage. By utilising customer relationship management systems such as SugarCRM, more established start-up teams can capture actionable customer-related information needs and feedback, which can then be analysed to improve product offerings or to change business strategy.

A powerful customer service solution is nanoRep, which provides customers with instant, self-service answers to online products inquiries. It tracks prospect traffic and quantifies the total number of buyers and non-buyers who visit a site as well as the conversion rate computed by dividing sales transactions by gross traffic counts. Results can be used to increase the number of buyers by understanding why people don't buy for example because of insufficient product information or by avoiding technical glitches during peak hours.

In the daily hustle and bustle of running a start-up, founders may be hard-pressed to find time to plan and execute a KM strategy. However, without proper strategies to leverage internal or external knowledge such as open innovation opportunities, they could be missing out on game-changing business opportunities. Start-ups would do well to explore how the KM toolkit can help them become smarter, more innovative organisations.

(The Business Times, 14 March 2014)

The Cluster Effect and Shark's fin Trade

"Find out how modern the trade in traditional products such as shark's fin is", my German professor advised when I first arrived here in 1988. I interviewed dozens of owner managers of family-based Chinese trading firms in 1988 and 1989 at Boat Quay, examining their unique business management patterns and entrepreneurial strategies. The merchants who once ran their far-flung networks from here were certainly not antiquated in their business operations.

Long before German scholar Alfred Weber discussed the phenomenon of spatial clustering in his 1929 book, *Theory of the Location of Industries*, sharks fin traders in Singapore's Boat Quay district had already congregated geographically.

Boat Quay was the historic centre of Singapore's trade and maritime commerce. For decades, bumboats transported rice, tin, rubber, and dried seafood from the ships in the sea to the shophouses and godowns along the Singapore River. Good business prospects attracted more traders and shop-keepers, until the district's decline in the early 1980s, triggered by Singapore's new container port and modern cargo facilities in Pasir Panjang.

Dried goods, including shark's fin, moved out of Boat Quay because of the massive conservation efforts of the Urban Redevelopment Authority in Boat Quay and Clarke Quay, which transformed these areas into leisure hubs with pubs and restaurants. Dried goods traders congregated at the Victoria Wholesale Centre. Today, as in the past, shark's fin traders know exactly what it takes to be profitable: trustworthiness. Without mutual trust, suppliers would send you inferior fins ("stones") instead of the requested first-grade fins, one trader said.

They were early clusterers long before Harvard's Professor Michael Porter, generally recognised as the father of the modern strategy field, came up with the notion of clusters as strategic management tools. While many businesses in North Canal Road and Tew Chew Street made way for the modernisation of the Singapore River district during the past few years, some of the old shops where I conducted my interviews long ago are still there.

I was often puzzled why all those traders set up shop in North Canal Road, like those selling quality lighting do in Balestier Road or those offering affordable garage services do in Sin Ming Road. Why do companies congregate at one place?

The answer is simple: It makes good business sense. Being close to competitors enables traders to watch price developments or new customer service arrangements.

It also helps customers to compare quality and prices. Such proximity to rival companies also allows workers to compare various employers and pay rates.

An initial concentration of firms, talent and other related businesses can attract new dependent businesses and experienced workers, creating a virtuous circle as these new clusters encourage others to join in. This, in turn, increases the cluster's efficiency and potential hub function. While rising business costs can lead to a cluster's erosion, good cluster management (by business associations) can work against such trends.

Through clustering, businesses can benefit from specialised services. For a Boat Quay shark's fin trader, that might be a Teochew restaurant where seafood is on the menu. Restaurants in that area could explain the spatial clustering of shark's fin firms there. Proximity to the Singapore River was also a key factor explaining the agglomeration of dried goods shops in this area.

In modern land-scarce Singapore, proactive and visionary government policy led to dynamic economic clusters such as the petrochemical hub on Jurong Island (formed from seven islands reclaimed over 15 years) and the offshore marine cluster in Tuas centring on Keppel Corporation.

Clustering has another advantage: It is good for innovation. Whether it is Singapore's shark's fin trading cluster near the Singapore River or the research hub Biopolis in one-north, both are what we call "knowledge clusters", that is, agglomerations of organisations where knowledge matters as input and/or output. Dense and systemically cohesive knowledge clusters have the organisational capability to drive innovations and create new products, services or entire industries.

While the shark's fin cluster appears dormant, Singapore's new WaterHub led by national water agency PUB has taken a strategic approach towards innovation. For example, it uses knowledge about the fine gill membranes of fish to push the boundaries of research on membrane technologies to purify water.

Biopolis also has research and development plans with a focus on neuro-degenerative diseases, vaccines for infectious diseases and non-invasive imaging. The more know-how, resources and connections between industry, human capital, cluster development, and governance bodies that exist both within the cluster and beyond, the higher the potential ability to create value through new knowledge and innovations.

A planner's key challenge would be to create hubs of innovation within such clusters. Our research has shown that sharing knowledge has a positive impact on brainstorming, creativity, and idea generation. While architects of hubs such as Biopolis or Fusionopolis often have grand visions of cluster "connectivity" — such as in elevated "sky bridges" — a visit to local coffee shops can show that sipping *kopi* (coffee) with a colleague or a friend is often all it takes to exchange knowledge and generate new ideas. Physical proximity enables knowledge-sharing which in turn drives learning, competitiveness and new value creation.

What some shark's fin traders arguably overlook is the power of open innovation. Industry watchers are less concerned with processing or product development innovations such as canned fins (soup) and ready-to-eat products. It is more about using outside ideas generated by stakeholders such as customers, relevant knowledge partners (scientists) or even business opponents.

Can innovation help Singapore's shark's fin traders cope with and even profit from the efforts of the "ban the fin movement"? Back in the 1980s, Japanese food-processing companies were already developing artificial shark's fin made out of gelatin. Rising prices and increasing demand in Asia for fins suggest that the trade in these "fake fins" could be very profitable provided there are no issues with regulators, and local businessmen and consumers are open to such "revolutionary" change.

This might also help those remaining in Singapore's shark's fin trading cluster to cope with the demands of environmentalists, and avoid the final stage of the cluster life cycle: decline (and going bust). This might be a wise move given the current threats to the business, including the collapse of shark populations around the world.

In a recent walk through the Boat Quay district, I counted three shops selling shark's fins and a number of seafood restaurants. As the numerous bars and hairdressing salons in this area suggest, the old maritime cluster strength is long gone. More restaurants refuse to serve shark's fin. Times are changing. The traders know this, but they need to embrace the next step of looking beyond their cluster for innovative ways to survive.

(The Straits Times, 30 May 2012)

Asean Should Have Its Own Erasmus

It needs a bold vision and mindful leadership to enhance connectivity and innovation through collaborative knowledge hubs.

If all goes well, Asean will be turning into a single economic bloc by 2015. Despite challenges ahead such as development gaps, infrastructural bottlenecks or the issue of the South China Sea, there is one opportunity with great potential which can be easily realised: pan-Asean mobility of students and educators. While it is envisaged that Asean will eventually become something like a eurozone entity with no trade barriers, a common visa system, and possibly even a single currency, the further expansion of pan-Asean learning opportunities can be a quick win.

A possible role model is the European Erasmus programme, a backronym for the *European Community Action Scheme for the Mobility of University Students*. Named after the Dutch philosopher and theologian Desiderius Erasmus of Rotterdam (1466–1536) who sought wisdom in many countries, the Europe-wide Erasmus programme has enabled more than 2.2 million students (including thousands of higher education faculty and staff) to learn across Europe since it was established in 1987.

In 1989, I spent a term at the reputable London School of Oriental and African Studies (SOAS), a college of the University of London, to learn more about the People's Republic of China. While exploring other places of interest such as London's East Asia docks or the famous Marquee Club — once the most important place for the jazz and rhythm & blues scenes in London, I rubbed shoulders with some of the most influential East Asia scholars in those days such as professor Elizabeth Croll who contributed greatly to the development of SOAS as one of the most reputable think tanks specialising in the study of Asia, Africa and the near and Middle East. Like thousands of other students, I benefited enormously from this temporary migration in terms of knowledge gains, maturity and social network ties to knowledge centres in East and Southeast Asia, including Singapore.

As the global knowledge tide is increasingly shifting towards Asia, Asean's traditional knowledge hubs such as Bandung Institute of Technology (ITB) in Indonesia or Universiti Sains Malaysia (USM) in Penang, Malaysia, are becoming important both as catalysts of knowledge-centric development processes in their own countries and interesting places of learning for pan-Asean students and educators.

One of USM's strengths, for example, is in sustainable green and healthcare technology with a focus on those who live in poverty. A recent invention from USM is FruitPlast, a biodegradable plastic film made from tropical fruit waste which won a gold medal at the International Trade Fair ideas-InventionsNew Product (IENA, 2011) in Germany. Examples of potentially interesting ITB courses include geophysical engineering (Bandung's most famous tourist volcano, Mount Tangkuban Perahu, is located 28 km north of the city), Indonesian architecture or ancient Indonesian art.

A key challenge is to further promote these centres with their local knowledge assets through, say, study grants among Asean students and scholars who often prefer to study in Europe or the US. Not only will this help the Asean community to appreciate the region's rich diversity in terms of culture, biodiversity or doing business, it will also create a new generation of knowledgeable pan-Asean brand ambassadors supportive of Asean's vision.

Just as in Europe where universities are part and parcel of the triple helix of higher educational institutions, government bodies and industry, an increasing number of Asean's academic knowledge hubs are firmly embedded in local and international networks of research & development (R&D) in support of indigenous development processes. However, the average citizen of an Asean country arguably knows very little about the core competencies of urban or rural universities in other Asean member countries. Dedicated and well-funded pan-Asean exchange programmes can change all that.

Within South-east Asia, Singapore has taken the lead in developing a knowledge-based economy with various sustainable knowledge hubs such as the marine cluster, comprising more than 5,000 establishments in three sectors: ship repair and conversion, shipbuilding and offshore. Since its creation in the 1960s, this cluster has played a significant role in Singapore's economy in terms of job creation and value added. In 2008, it provided 70,000 jobs of which 12,000 were skilled workers with an output in 2009 of S$16.83 billion. The most important role, providing 55 per cent of total industry earnings, is played by the offshore sector. Respective cluster companies are situated in close proximity to one another in the south-western region of Singapore called Tuas.

With 70% of the global market share of floating production storage offloading (FPSO) vessel conversion, 70% of world market share for jack-up rig building and 20% of world market share for ship repair, Singapore's marine cluster continues to thrive due to good knowledge governance at the national level and effective human capital management at the micro levels of both the hub and within participating firms.

A key corporate actor within the Singapore marine cluster with over 300 years of combined experience is the Keppel group of companies, comprising Keppel Fels, Keppel Shipyard and Keppel Singmarine. Keppel Offshore & Marine's companies and yards are situated relatively close to one another within the cluster which facilitates knowledge sharing and creation, arguably key success factors in this business. In terms of product innovations, Keppel Offshore & Marine is well known for its ultra deepwater solutions such as semisubmersibles or compact drill ships. It also built the first pair of icebreakers in the hot Asian tropic region destined for customers in the West.

Institutional cluster actors which helped to create, maintain and expand the sector include Singapore's Economic Development Board (EDB), the Maritime and Port Authority (MPA) and the Centre for Offshore Research & Engineering (Core) in the Faculty of Engineering at the National University of Singapore (NUS) with its endowed Keppel Professorship in Ocean, Offshore and Marine Technology. Core and Keppel's research & development units represent important knowledge-centric nodes in Singapore's offshore marine hub. Historically speaking, the hub's successful evolution also benefited from technical assistance provided by several European countries, including Germany's German-Singapore Institute (GSI), in the area of precision engineering know-how.

Singapore's knowledge cluster creation know-how indirectly points to the great potential of Asean's knowledge hubs as drivers of inclusive growth which need to be further built up and nurtured through target-oriented development measures. An important element of such efforts must be the creation of an Asean higher education area which will help to foster peace and innovation throughout South-east Asia, just as it did in Europe.

Besides regular exchanges to enhance transnational mobility within Asean and beyond, specific measures need to be initiated to connect Asean's higher education institutions and to kick-start intra-regional, collaborative research programmes, actionable knowledge networks and multilateral learning projects, for example, with a focus on science & technology for sustainable development. As in Europe where the Erasmus programme led to the modernisation of higher education institutions and systems, Asean needs a bold vision and mindful leadership to enhance connectivity and innovation through collaborative knowledge hubs.

(The Business Times, 17 January 2012)

Playing the Medici Trick to Innovate

Intersection innovation combines concepts between multiple fields, generating ideas that leap in new directions.

Policymakers in Singapore continue to push ahead with the mission of strengthening the country's research and development (R&D) capabilities and encouraging greater innovation. One manifestation is the establishment of innovation funds in local universities to support technology incubators aimed at achieving the successful commercialisation of ideas and innovations.

An underutilised opportunity to drive innovation is the strategic management of intersectional innovation. Today, there are many innovation challenges which cannot be solved by one scientific discipline alone. Many questions relating to health, energy, climate change and others require thinking across different fields.

Learning to step into an intersection of fields, disciplines and cultures can generate a large number of extraordinary ideas for innovation. While this sounds good in theory, practising it can be a challenge for those responsible for making innovation work. One reason is the difficulty to motivate smart-knowledge workers to become more innovative.

One simple approach to introduce smart people to the mindset and logic of innovation potential at intersections is the Medici Board Game, based on the bestselling book *The Medici Effect* published by Harvard Business School Press a couple of years ago.

It was developed in cooperation with its author, Frans Johansson, and helps to explore confluences that occur when different ideas are combined to create insights which may lead to new strategies, products and services. Such confluences can be brought about coincidentally as well as systematically. Creating an environment for innovation is about creating the conditions for organisations in which intersectional learning and confluences can happen more easily.

The Medici Game (developed by a Swedish learning tool developer) engages participants in discussions that lead them to challenge their beliefs and assumptions around good — or not so good — management practices for fostering innovation-friendly conditions and a creative environment. On the basis of small group discussions and with the help of engaging innovation cards, participants explore the intersections between different disciplines and fields of science.

Warm-up questions include: What are potential fields for intersectional innovation between ICT (infocomm technology) and medicine? How can biology inspire the automotive industry? How can people with different backgrounds and specialisations be innovative?

Intersections are places where ideas from different fields and cultures meet, leading (potentially) to an explosion of ideas and possibilities. What are the forces that are creating it and why is this type of innovation growing in importance? Innovation management experts distinguish between incremental and disruptive, intersectional ones.

According to Mr Johansson, combining concepts within a particular field can generate interesting ideas but that represents a somehow narrow approach because they evolve along a particular direction. Contrary to such "directional ideas", stepping into the intersection enables the combination of concepts between multiple fields, generating "intersectional ideas that leap in new directions".

Examples with commercial potential include electronic healthcare services (based on the interdisciplinary collaboration between biomedical and infocomm technologies), such as Singapore's electronic health records initiative, Volvo's vision to develop a collision safety system for cars based on the African grasshopper's ability to not collide when it flies in swarms or the ongoing efforts by urban planners, ICT experts and futurists to come up with smart city models where all city-wide subsystems are interconnected via a communicative network of sensors, data and smart devices, enabling stakeholders to access real-time information on traffic conditions or faulty streetlights.

We can think of intersections as physical and mental spaces of innovation. Innovation is increasingly seen as a recursive process instead of the old view of innovation as commercialised invention based on technological or scientific knowledge. The recursive innovation model stresses the versatile feedback mechanisms and interactive relationships involving producer companies, product users, scientific and technical research, development activities and supporting infrastructure. It is a model of continuous learning in which the actors in different fields learn from one another in interactive innovation processes.

Unfortunately, smart people sometimes refuse to learn and to explore innovation potential as evidenced by numerous research studies conducted by learning organisation experts. In many knowledge-intensive organisations, learning is often "single-looped" (a term coined by Harvard Business School professor emeritus Chris Argyris) qua improvements that rest on unchallenged, implicit assumptions. Attempts to identify and question underlying assumptions (Professor Argyris refers to this as "double-loop learning") and to debate alternatives, for example to the traditional approach of doing business, are often thwarted by organisational antibodies that can ultimately defeat innovation efforts.

One way of fostering a robust culture of learning and innovation is to initiate a novel approach towards effective communication on the basis of a structured dialogue, for example with the help of the Medici Board Game. Participants discover by themselves rather than being told intersectional innovation opportunities, which can lead to increased motivation and the willingness to change and to execute on innovation-related insights gained during the game phase (chances to do so increase when both leaders and followers regard this as a real strategic necessity: another requirement is the alignment of performance indicators and rewards).

Singapore continues to invest heavily into innovative forms of smart urban environments driven by a strong cross-disciplinary spirit. Examples include *Fusionopolis* (a megascience facility aimed at stimulating multidisciplinary knowledge creation between bioinformatics, molecular design, chemical engineering and ICT research) or the new *Campus for Research Excellence and Technological Enterprise* established by the National Research Foundation in collaboration with world-class research universities and corporate labs to nurture an "inventive, innovative and entrepreneurial economy".

Within these concrete structures and their diverse talent pools, value added innovation does not just happen. It has to be effectively managed. The Medici experience can help to prepare professionals to see opportunities in intersections more clearly, thus creating more buy-in and increasing the capacity for effective innovation.

(The Business Times, 2 October 2013)

Harnessing the Benefits of Knowledge Management in Higher Education Institutions

Ask any University President what keeps her or him awake at night and you will hear answers ranging from: "I don't know whether the jobs that we are preparing our students for will still be there when they graduate" to "How do I know that the research at my university is making impact to society?". Chances are they will not say, "I need to improve the quality of *knowledge management (KM)* in my organisation". In fact, some of them probably are not very familiar with what KM really is at the core or how it helps with achieving strategic goals. While phrases and disruptive challenges like "Massive Open On-Line Courses" ("MOOCs" refer to courses made available over the Internet to a large group of people — at times without a fee) or creating an "entrepreneurial university" (which requires a truly multidisciplinary mindset and academic instructors who are also successful in business and entrepreneurship) are discussed by many leaders of higher education institutions (HEIs), KM hasn't quite made it into their strategic vocabulary even though the popular use of the KM term is more than two decades old. That is a pity because KM is such a powerful tool to combat the "ivory tower" mentality. "Practical" KM approaches include documenting lessons learned (e.g. about successful strategies to create the next unicorn), internal "best practice" transfer (e.g. about publishing success in top journals) or efforts to create cultures that incentivise innovation (e.g. through innovation jams).

Knowledge management refers to the totality of strategies that organisations can use to locate, capture, share and create new knowledge. In short, it ensures that *organizational knowledge assets* are effectively utilized to enhance organizational performance. Singapore is home to various award-winning, KM-enabled organizations such as Singapore Airlines with its internationally-acclaimed customer service excellence built on rigorous data collection and analytics linked to business goals. Singapore's Inland Revenue Authority (IRAS) achieved quantum leaps in organisational excellence through KM. Both organisations have a strong business case for investing time and resources on KM: unrivalled customer service (SIA) and hassle-free tax payment/collection (IRAS).

Although the positive impact of KM practices in large organisations is well documented, KM in (knowledge-centric) universities is akin to a black box. In the context of higher educational institutions, the role of KM is to harness the collective knowledge from both internal and external sources to create meaningful impact through education, research and service. That's a challenging task. Many HEIs are loosely-coupled systems comprising various partially connected, often separate units eager to maintain their autonomy despite "shared" values and grand vision statements. Some typical issues include emphasis on solo-authored articles which often deters collaboration, ignorance pertaining ongoing research works across campus, duplication of effort (e.g. developing "good" assessment rubrics) or lack of "really nice" places where faculty, administrators, staff, and students can jointly share informal knowledge and assist each other.

In our research, we focused on understanding how leaders in higher education can successfully harness the benefits of Knowledge Management vis-à-vis the possible challenges in making KM work. A review of recent journal articles on KM for HEIs matters suggest that most university leaders should be familiar with the term "KM". In fact, most university staff we communicated with had an innate sense of what it means — everybody manages knowledge, but it's a matter of knowing *why* and *what* (identifying KM goals and priorities), *how* (determining the "right" management approach and suitable KM tools), *how much* (effort intensity/pilot project), *where* (gap analysis/knowledge audit), *how well* (degree of KM readiness/impact measurement), and scaling up. Which steps have to be taken to achieve KM sustainability?

1. To make KM work, it is imperative that the KM team has the support of a KM Champion such as a member of the top management team. What follows is usually a discussion about strategic KM opportunities and the definition of visionary goals, e.g. the identification of new areas of *growth* (and revenues) by translating relevant mega trends into attractive new programme offerings in case of increasing resource constraints. Other strategic KM goals may include maintaining and

enhancing organisational quality systems (Lean-Six Sigma), enterprise risk management, securing financial sustainability, or innovation.

2. Once the overall strategic knowledge area is determined and aligned with the sponsor's needs and aspirations, the KM team needs to design the "right" KM intervention by determining the most effective KM approach, e.g. by comparing actual vs. target performance in priority knowledge areas. One outcome of this step could be the identification of knowledge gaps such as blocked knowledge flows that prevent internal collaborations between organizational units (who could otherwise co-create a novel, multi-disciplinary teaching & learning initiative in case connecting "deep smarts" across their own units is deemed to be important) or closer university-industry collaboration on the basis of a new cooperative work-study programme. Another result of this step might be the initiation of a pilot crowd-sourcing project to apply existing knowledge of faculty and graduate students to human problems in underserved communities (as part of efforts to identify critical knowledge it already possesses).

Ideally, strategic KM aspirations, project initiatives and expected outcomes are codified in a knowledge management strategy plan so that they are properly aligned with the overall vision and business drivers as indicated in Table 1. Rather than pursuing reactive, piece-meal KM solutions to immediate challenges faced, a strategic, future-oriented KM approach will ensure better outcomes.

3. After the broad strategic KM direction has been established and there is initial buy-in, a (hopefully impactful) pilot initiative can be rolled out to demonstrate the value added of the proposed KM strategy. This could entail licensing internally generated intellectual property to another company or nurturing greater collaboration between staff across discipline boundaries to enhance teaching and research on the basis of a newly formed and well-funded community of practice (COP).

4. Once the KM initiative has demonstrated its impact, it can be scaled up to other units, business lines or client segments. To be successful, KM practices must be driven by a well-governed KM system with effective KM processes. To locate and capture strategic knowledge such as lessons learned, some universities utilise social media tools such as digital story-telling. Others use "Yellow Pages" type of applications, enabling employees to quickly find staff with particular competencies, or create knowledge maps to visualise hidden internal

Table 1: Components of a KM Strategy Plan

KM Planning/Steps	Key Goal-Oriented Activities	Outcomes	Drivers
1. Planning Formation of KM planning team and identification of KM champion in top management team	Identification of KM goals and priorities (e.g. greater knowledge sharing amongst faculty and collaboration across organisational boundaries in priority areas)	KM buy-in, support and resources Development of innovative course offerings spanning several disciplines that help to future-proof students and meet urgent needs	Deep knowledge of faculty Optimised use of resources
2. Designing the "right" KM intervention	Determining the "right" approach by comparing actual vs. target performance in priority areas to enable better knowledge flows (e.g. stronger university-industry collaboration qua balanced work-study programmes) Develop measures of success and action plan Performance management system to be tweaked to include KPIs on the number of cross-faculty collaborations	University branded as producing "workplace-ready" graduates who can hit the ground running High graduate employment rates Admin buy-in	Employability of (workplace-ready) graduates Brand (i.e. the stuff that makes the organization stand out from all the other HEIs)
3. Implementation	Launch of a pilot measure (e.g. creating fora for the exchange of tacit knowledge and experiences related to on-the-job training activities comprising students, employers, faculty and admin) Publicizing success stories	University is well-known for its innovative (dual) educational efforts Value creation	Innovation
4. Scale-Up	Realigning strategy with university objectives Scale-up to other organizational units	Achieving desired state of performance in terms of vision & mission	Key inputs and activities (knowledge)

knowledge assets, including information bottlenecks and knowledge brokers. A popular technical KM tool is the knowledge portal, a web-based computer program that enables a single point of access to (hopefully) actionable organizational knowledge, strategic knowledge repositories, expert directories and collaboration tools. Wikis and after action reviews can enhance collaboration between teams to capture and share important know how to avoid making the same mistake twice or to repeat success.

Key for the effective sharing of tacit and explicit knowledge (e.g. to turn experience-based knowledge such as lessons learned into a database/ intranet with adequate use) is the development of a collaborative innovation culture with room for experimentation, real learning and risk-taking. One of the HEIs we spoke to had built up a very spirited team culture with open and transparent committees that encouraged real-time communication via a digital feedback gathering application and a voice for interested non-members so that outputs created by committee members could be shared before they were codified. Gathering employee feedback and timely issue management by top management had a positive impact on engagement levels.

Through knowledge sharing ("even" with competitors), employees gain access to valuable information. In some countries this type of "coopetition" (defined as collaboration between business competitors, in the hope of mutually beneficial results) is well institutionalised. To encourage knowledge sharing, leaders need to consider KM holistically by aligning the organisation's performance measurements and KM enablers such as strategic plans of action and a culture of sharing based on effective reward management approaches and suitable KM tools.

A very important knowledge process is *new knowledge creation*. Imagine what might happen if innovative ideas (e.g. for new-growth efforts) that bubble up within the organization do not get sufficient attention by senior management. What happens if internal (staff, students, faculty) and external (employers, suppliers, alumni, etc.) stakeholders are ignored as sources of insight and innovation? Important KM and innovation process steps include idea generation, evaluating innovative ideas, pilot testing "good" ideas, prototyping, roll-out, etc. If nobody takes charge of this process and innovation champs are not empowered, the organization will forego important benefits.

To keep an eye on important knowledge matters, leaders of HEIs are well advised to develop KM-infused dashboards that can help to organize and monitor critical performance metrics/KPIs into a single, real-time, at-a-glance control panel. A customised dashboard displays key strategic data points to evaluate the "health" of a particular organisational unit such as a Department and important performance areas such as the number and quality of research outputs, alumni engagement sessions, teaching quality, student satisfaction, placement success, innovation outcomes, and so on.

Dashboards are also very useful as instruments to manage strategic risks (e.g. with regard to the need to maintain high academic standards in research and teaching), operational risks (e.g. importance of students complying with rules of conduct), financial risks (e.g. significance of having sufficient funds for long-term operations) and legal & compliance risks (e.g. compliance with personal data protection legislation).

University Provosts are often considered to be the Chief Knowledge Officers of HEIs. In the daily hustle and bustle of running a university, some leaders may be hard-pressed to find time to plan and execute a KM strategy. However, without a proper strategy to leverage internal and external knowledge by seizing open innovation opportunities (i.e. utilising the ideas of other companies and "the crowd") or conducting online brainstorming sessions, they could be missing out on game-changing innovation opportunities. Universities would do well to explore how the KM toolkit can help them to become (even) smarter and more innovative organisations. They should also walk the talk when it comes to the formal appointment of (tertiary-educated) knowledge and innovation managers to help prepare students for success in the job market and to creating an environment for research and innovation to flourish.

(Perspectives@SMU, September 2020)

Drones, AI and Getting Undergrads Ready for Great Disruption

With Kan Siew Ning and Eugene K. B. Tan

There are many things which keep us lecturers awake at night: overdue research paper submissions, unrealistic grade expectations by students, concerns about the future employability of our graduates in a VUCA (volatility, uncertainty, complexity, ambiguity) era and so forth. A related and very exciting challenge is the endeavour to keep the curriculum relevant, attractive and future-ready as we enter the defining stage of what has been termed as "big bang disruption" (coined by Mr Larry Downes and Mr Paul Nunes in their 2013 Harvard Business Review article).

While this is easier said than done, institutions of higher learning are stepping up efforts to create new learning opportunities and experiences to support the next generation in achieving their full potential.

Against this backdrop, we recently launched an inter-disciplinary course on emerging technology at the Singapore Management University, focusing on unmanned aerial vehicles (UAV or drones), robotics, and artificial intelligence (AI). One key learning outcome is to enable students to appreciate, in a multi-disciplinary setting, the huge business potential of emerging technology in diverse areas — such as logistics, supply chain management, transportation, search and rescue, military, and scientific studies. Another is to sensitise learners to the regulatory and ethical-moral issues associated with new technologies.

Estimates by consulting firms suggest that the global market for commercial drone technology applications alone, which currently stands at about US$2 billion (S$2.8 billion), will increase to about US$120 billion by 2020 as a result of regulatory progress for UAV operations, effective legislation, lower costs as well as new, innovative business models.

In September 2014, an unmanned Deutsche Post DHL parcelcopter made headlines by successfully flying (outside of the pilot's field of vision) from the city of Norddeich in the north of Germany to the North Sea island of Juist — to deliver some urgently needed goods, such as medications. In December last year, Amazon successfully delivered items to a customer in the English countryside near Cambridge (in a drone test-flight zone) shortly after it had received the online order.

Other drone applications include aerial photography and filming, 3D imagery, surveying/mapping, crop control, inspections of offshore systems, pipelines, wind towers, buildings, and verifying insurance claims. Similarly, new technology consulting firms have emerged specialising in market research and analytics for drones.

A drone was used as part of an inter-agency effort to inspect construction sites in February last year. Other examples of the use of such vehicles in Singapore include the Urban Redevelopment Authority's use of drones to capture aerial images and videos of Jurong Lake District and the Rail Corridor for better visualisation and planning.

Drones are also boosters for the tourism industry. Last year, Dubai hosted the first World Drone Prix, a drone race with US$1 million in prize money. Later this year, the 2nd Commercial UAV Expo will take place in Las Vegas, with more than 100 exhibitors.

The headlong rush to exploit emerging technology tends to result in ethical and regulatory issues being given short shrift. The prototypes of driverless cars built by Google, Tesla, BMW and others have enough built-in AI to free drivers from routine tasks like cruise control, keeping in lane, and braking when the car gets too close to the vehicle in front. But what happens when there is an accident involving a driverless car, or when drones violate privacy rights? That is where ethicists, insurers, lawyers, policymakers, transport specialists and business planners need to offer their collaborative expertise.

Sensitivity to these technology-related issues can help ensure that stakeholders' interests and concerns are adequately dealt with, ensuring their receptivity to emerging technologies.

Examples of drone applications in Singapore include:

(i)   The research-driven, multi-data approach by the Future Cities Laboratory of the Singapore-ETH Centre to create reality-based 3D models of very high quality, using drone photogrammetry;

(ii)   Efforts by the Urban Redevelopment Authority to capture aerial images and videos of Jurong Lake District and the Rail Corridor so that stakeholders can better visualise and assess future development plans;

(iii) Safer and more efficient fire-fighting approaches by the Singapore Civil Defence Force;

(iv)   The use of aerial and terrestrial drones as waiters in restaurants;

(v)   Commercial photography and recreation; and

(vi)   Environmental monitoring and infrastructure inspection, for example in the oil and gas sector.

Besides goods, drones can autonomously transport people. The possibilities are immense. Could Singapore become a hub for socially innovative "Drones for Good" competitions?

The history of industrial robots goes back several decades, with the first robotics patent granted in 1961. Today, robots are used in assembly lines to manufacture all types of products. Robots have also found their way into homes as autonomous vacuum cleaners, or in the form of companion (love) robots.

Although AI earlier failed to meet its grand promises in the 1960s and 1970s, it has since grown by leaps and bounds. Rudimentary autopilot features in aircraft made their appearance as early as 1912. In 1997, IBM's Deep Blue supercomputer beat chess grandmaster Gary Kasparov at a match — the first time a machine beat a world champion chess player. This year, *Libratus*, an AI system built by researchers from Carnegie Mellon University, played in a poker tournament against four of the world's top professionals — and won. Perhaps a group of undergraduates from our universities could write AI software to play mahjong against the world's best players?

The nexus of inspiring technology and smart engineering, innovative business approaches, as well as robust law and regulatory policies, will have to be adroitly managed and synthesised if emerging technologies are to be successfully test-bedded in Singapore. Trust is a vital substratum if emerging technologies are to be embraced by stakeholders and become a part of our lives. This technological ecosystem of the future, comprising hardware, software and mindset, is necessary if Singapore's innovation economy is to be taken to a higher plane.

One challenge in exploiting the commercial opportunities of emerging technologies is the development of innovative business models to monetise UAV technology or smart robotics/AI applications. After initial euphoria from the triumph of machines over the best human players, technology still needs to be brought to market, and business leaders need to strategise how best to go-to-market with such a "game-playing" technology. While we educators facilitate this by utilising tools such as the business model canvas, deep learning requires various complementary skills.

In the areas of unmanned aerial vehicles, robotics and AI, there is a lot of scope for interdisciplinary collaboration and mixed teams. Social science students can provide the background on how "social" a robot needs to be. Engineering students can build the mechanical movements controlled by electrical signals and AI with speech- recognition software developed by information technology students. Business management students can find creative ways to market new types of robots, for example, social robots, after first learning to appreciate the technical details, market opportunities and societal concerns about a novel technology. Having a mixed group of students representing different disciplines can help to avoid blind spots such as difficulties in realistically assessing the (future) commercial value of this new technology in view of current weaknesses and threats, such as regulations, fear of (technology) failure, and inadequate attention to ethical concerns.

In line with Singapore's quest to become an innovation-led country, current talent gaps need to be closed. Using new technologies such as UAV technology or robotics as examples, we posit that more collaborative partnerships need to be formed between experts and novices with and within institutions of higher learning, technology/IT, business, ethics and law to ensure that learning outcomes are needs-based and aligned with the country's long-term innovation agenda, a key feature in the Committee on the Future Economy's report.

At his National Day Rally speech last year, Prime Minister Lee Hsien Loong noted that disruption is the "defining" challenge to the economy. And as Finance Minister Heng Swee Keat stressed during the Government's Budget statement earlier this week: "These deep shifts around the world will create new challenges but also open up new opportunities for many years to come. We must understand these shifts and do our best to adapt and thrive". One of the items highlighted in the Budget 2017 speech is the "Attach and Train" programme, which will help workers find jobs in new growth sectors through training or internships in industries with growth potential, but where companies may not be ready to hire yet. What is clear is that a collective effort is required to nurture resilient individuals and companies, enhancing their relevance as well as the economy's.

There is tremendous scope for Singapore to enhance its innovation capabilities and promote entrepreneurship. To do this, not only do our universities need to be rewired, Singapore's societal norms also need to shift. Such massive mindset changes do not fall neatly into just one domain. The combined expertise of engineering/IT, strategic business management, social sciences, ethics, organisational psychology and law is required to make our students future-ready.

(The Straits Times, 22 February 2017)

Asia's Mobile Learning Tsunami

Regional educators and policymakers must respond strategically to the revolutionary changes the phenomenon entails.

As the number of mobile device users owning a smartphone is rapidly increasing across Asia, more learners are making use of their cellphones, laptops and tablets in and outside classrooms to source for new knowledge — for example, by downloading YouTube videos to better appreciate abstract concepts taught in class by instructors (who may or may not appreciate their students' subversive behaviour).

New trends such as ubiquitous (omnipresent) computing and the hassle-free availability of wireless, mobile and networked technologies in combination with smart search engines point to revolutionary changes in business and society to which both Asian educators and policymakers need to respond strategically.

The term mobile learning refers to the use of ubiquitous handheld hardware, wireless networking and mobile telephony to facilitate, support, enhance and extend the reach of teaching and learning. Both the mobility of the learner and the context generated by a learner or learners with the help of mobile devices are important because communications in social spaces and/or reflections on the move" (with the help of others or in interaction with multimedia resources) can create new "food for thought".

Answers to context-based queries in turn often give rise to valuable new insights, enabling learning processes in solitude, with an instructor, through conversations with one's powers or within large online community. To support lifelong learning, mobile technologies must be portable (so that users can learn wherever they are), unobtrusive (i.e. without the technology obtruding on the particular learning situation), needs-based, and easy to use.

There are numerous good practice examples such as HUB in Kenya, which promotes software literacy; MAMA (Mobile Alliance for Maternal Action), which uses short text messages (SMS) to enable mothers expand their knowledge about pregnancy and childbirth, and the MIND (Mobile Technology Initiative for Non-Formal Distance Education) project, a joint initiative of the Philippines-based Molave Development Foundation and the Health Sciences University of Mongolia in Ulaanbaatar to develop SMS learning packs for delivering non-formal distance learning to different social groups. These suggest that mobile learning can support knowledge based development processes if it is deployed wisely.

To make this work in developing Asia with its internal knowledge gaps, both leaders and educators have first to accept the fact that mobile learning is indeed revolutionising regional educational landscapes due to its continuous character, technological leapfrogging potential and its ability to empower special demographic segments such as disaffected learners who face difficulties in succeeding in the education system.

Within Asean, Singapore continues to roll out higher-end mobile learning innovations based on the policy guideline to enable students to learn anywhere". Examples include Singapore Management University's (SMU) Twitter-enabled, interactive in-class feedback loop which allows students to deliver instant feedback to classmates and lecturer; the Centre for Educational Research and Application (Cera) established by a local primary school; the National Institute of Education's NIE effort to develop useful pedagogical methods for handheld devices, and the MyCLOUD (My Chinese Language ubiquitous learning Days) project.

This last one is a collaboration between Microsoft Singapore and several educational institutions to enhance the teaching and learning of the Chinese language via a multi-faceted interactive platform. The Singapore case contains an important lesson for latecomers in the knowledge race: the need to align educational strategies with national development goals based on good knowledge governance through a supportive national information and communication policy, and expanding broadband connectivity Research evidence suggests that mobile learning engages learners and that it can play an important catalysing role in the process of economic development with a strategic focus on English proficiency, vocational training, education for specific target groups such as young girls and STEM science, technology, engineering and mathematics) in general.

Philippines Open University offers regular formal SMS-based mobile courses in English, mathematics and the sciences, providing new development opportunities for rural youth in poor and remote areas.

While mobile STEM learning approaches can help to motivate students interest in STEM subjects and to increase their proficiency, more needs to be done at policy level to implement rigorous K-12 mathematics and science standards, to provide more qualified teaching staff, and to ensure a solid alignment between STEM job demands and the structure of national post-secondary STEM system.

Other issues which need to be tackled in order to fully leverage on mobile learning include insufficient awareness among (educational) leaders, shortage of competent support staff and lack of funds for the development of mobile learning solutions.

Essential ingredients for an effective governance system aimed at leveraging on mobile learning approaches for development at national level include senior political sponsorship at the highest levels, broad national engagement involving government, industry, academia and civil society; continuous education and talent development, as well as telecommunications affordability and maximum bandwidth.

While there is evidence that mobile data connectivity creates significant knowledge and other benefits, many Asean countries have yet to acknowledge mobile learning opportunities for development (ML4D) in their strategy documents and to implement concrete strategic mobile learning measures through handheld devices in order to realise Asean's 2015 connectivity vision.

The European Union experience in mobile learning offers useful insights in this respect, which needs to be analysed to ascertain its transferability to Asia such as institutionalised exchange (mobility) programmes for students and faculty or the set-up and systematic funding of special European research interest groups on mobile learning under the Leonardo Da Vinci Programme. Germany's Federal Institute for Vocational Education & Training (BBB) continues to conduct applied research projects to document and develop useful blended mobile learning systems in support of vocational qualification processes within the retail or electrical trades.

The "smart" competency development of skilled craftsmen is crucial for development and can be greatly enhanced through blended mobile learning suites and customised applications. While there is a bit of hype about mobile learning (for example, the promotion of SMS-management coaching by consulting firms), research suggests that it is indeed a new mega trend which will continue to change the nature of learning and learning delivery in Asia.

(The Business Times, 10 January 2013)

A Kaleidoscope of Technology Innovation

By Kan Siew Ning

Since the dawn of history, new inventions have improved the lives of human beings, enabling them to do things better and faster; many medical inventions have contributed to increased people's longevity. From the invention of the wheel to the light bulb, to the first Kitty Hawk flight, to personal computers, and to mobile phones, technology innovations have a few things in common.

Firstly, there is usually no existing market to rely on to forecast future demand because the product or service is totally new. When the affordable-cost hair salon, QB House, first started its business, it was practically operating in a Blue Ocean because the high-end salon haircuts cost three times more while the lower-end shops, although lower priced, were not as clean and comfortable. However, QB House was unable to predict the market demand as there was no compatible service to compare with.

Secondly, for every new technology breakthrough, the legal and ethical issues lag behind the technology advancements during the initial go-to-market phase. A case in point is the invention of the artificial respirator (a mechanical breathing machine) almost a century ago; the machine keeps deep-coma patients alive by helping them breathe. When the product was first sold to hospitals, the patients' relatives initially cheered because they didn't have to say goodbye to their loved ones immediately and they were harboring hopes that the patient would eventually recover. When the patient was hooked to the machine for one week to one month to a year, the medical costs of keeping the patient tethered started piling up and threatened to beggar the family members. At that time, there was no legal construct that allowed family members to decide to switch off the machine because only the patient was allowed to do so; but coma patients were unable to do so. The laws that were initially enacted eventually evolved and matured into the advanced medical directives that we have today.

Apply this to self-driving cars, and one can easily see that it is not current AV (Autonomous Vehicle) technology that fails to gain traction; but rather insurance policies, ethics of the algorithms, and laws pertaining to litigation after traffic accidents involving AVs that are still at the infancy stages. The thorniest of these issues has to do with the ethical framework used to implement the emergency management functions of the AV software; for example, if the brakes of an AV fails, and the car is on a collision course on a busy pedestrian street, how would the software choose between knocking down an elderly pedestrian or a teenage pedestrian? This and all the other governance areas need more time and much more work to evolve and mature before AVs can become ubiquitous.

Thirdly, new technologies largely follow the S-Curve framework where initial improvements are slow; this phase is then followed by a steep upward curve of fast improvements; and eventually tapering off to reach a plateau when incremental improvements reach the natural physical limit of the technology beyond which the technological design is unable to overcome. An example would be the music industry: not too long ago we used to listen to music on LP vinyl records which reached the S-Curve plateau due to the LPs' physical size and the method of encoding the analogue music. Vinyl was replaced by cassette tapes which improved from 30 minutes of music storage to more than 120 minutes. This was followed by the next generation of Compact Discs and later by MP3 players.

Fourthly, most technology inventions need supporting infrastructure. After Thomas Edison invented the light bulb in 1879, he soon discovered that meaningful sales of the new product could not take off without electricity generation. So, in 1882, Edison had to start a new power generation service located at the Pearl Street Station that served an initial load of 400 lamps for 82 customers. Without the infrastructure of electricity supply, light bulbs would merely have been ornamental decorative items that served no practical purpose. Fast forward to 2020 and we see the supporting infrastructures of fast Internet access and public Wifi services fueling the exponential growth of social media. In the domain of motorcars, petrol (gas) stations are (still) much more widespread than electric charging stations which hampers the purchase of electric cars. There is a need for a better EV infrastructure that covers both big cities and smaller towns because range anxiety among electric car owners is a very real concern.

Fifthly, technology innovations require the good work of deep technical experts. Business managers need to first understand the geeky idiosyncrasies of their deep smarts, and then know how to properly motivate them to put their best foot forward. Most geeks see their work to be akin to works of art which require inspiration; they don't like managers to be constantly looking over their shoulders and asking for regular progress updates. Pushing the R&D envelope is very unlike quarterly sales where progress reports is a common and effective management tool; apply this same reporting tool to R&D geeks and you would risk irritating them because weeks or months can go by when R&D progress is infinitesimal — especially at the beginning stages of the technology S-Curve. In the management of R&D work and the R&D scientists, a fair amount of patience is needed.

Geeks working in research laboratories also prefer to have more free time to do mental somersaults as a process of achieving technological breakthroughs. Hence, companies like 3M and Google have implemented a fixed percentage of unallocated time (15% to 20%) to encourage geeks and other innovators to spend time doing "blue-sky thinking and brainstorming". A lot of these geeks would claim that without inspiration (the proverbial light bulb above their heads), working overtime hours would be futile in trying to achieve good R&D results.

Geeks also prefer a lot of autonomy and dislike red tape; business managers cannot and should not make them jump through hoops to secure the R&D budgets and resources they need to "work their magic". Geeks also need to be properly "fed" — if they are deemed to be valuable (and oftentimes the most valuable) employees in the company, their remuneration has to come close to that of C-suite officers. Towards this end, large MNCs have put in place a variety of dual-career ladder HR schemes where the valuable geeks are promoted along the technical career path; this path typically requires much more technical prowess and much less management skills than the C-suite career path.

Until and unless the above-mentioned "colors" of the technology innovation kaleidoscope are effectively put in place, the lofty heights of phenomenal business success powered by technological excellence would be difficult to reach.

Chapter 7

Innovation Governance

Innovation Does Not Happen by Chance, Innovation Governance is Needed

With Ong Geok Chwee

One approach to encourage more innovation in business and beyond is to effectively govern it. While most business leaders would appreciate the importance of good corporate governance, for many, the term innovation governance falls into the category of "words with difficult-to-remember meanings".

In contrast to the word "innovation" which refers to the implementation of a new or significantly improved product, service or process that creates real value, the term "governance" is a bit more complex due to its connotations of authority, control and influence. The word itself derives from the Greek word kubernáo with the connotation of steering a ship (metaphorically, it refers to the challenges of steering Men).

Broadly speaking, governance is about the nature of authority relationships in a country or an organization as well as the degree of formality of associated rules, norms, and actionable procedures — which can vary widely. While knowledge governance is concerned with the institutional framework that enables the creation, absorption and dissemination of new knowledge; corporate innovation governance can be defined as a systematic approach to "align goals, allocate resources and assign decision-making authority for innovation, across the company and with external parties". According to IMD Professor Jean-Philippe Deschamps who has written extensively about the topic, innovation governance is a "top management responsibility and preserve that cannot be delegated to any single function or to lower levels of an organization".

Corporate innovation contexts are characterized by uncertainty (How will our customers react?); complexity (How best to manage diverse groups of internal and external knowledge experts from different disciplines?); low degree of predictability (Who might disrupt us and what changes will occur within our organization when we develop a new innovation strategy); and creativity (How to nurture a climate where creativity can flourish?). Therefore, business leaders need governance frameworks, tools and techniques to effectively strategise innovation efforts with a clear focus and a balanced portfolio of innovation initiatives to make innovation work.

While many would agree that winning firms are characterized by strong innovation governance approaches, empirical research about this topic in Singapore is rather poor. Anecdotal evidence suggests that there are many organizations here where formal innovation governance systems are completely lacking. But there are also a couple of real champions where innovation is effectively governed via solid innovation management frameworks, top leadership support and capable managers aimed at creating sustainable business and societal value. Examples include DSTA, Sheng Siong Group and Biosensors Interventional Technologies Pte Ltd — who recently won Innovation Excellence Awards. Their summary reports are available on the website of Enterprise Singapore and provide valuable insights into key components of innovation governance systems such as a compelling strategic innovation vision and mission (to determine the goals of innovation efforts), a system of supportive values, "the right" sources of innovation, innovation process-related details and so forth. In the case of DSTA, for example, regular strategic workshops help to surface novel ideas across the organization which is implemented as innovation and productivity initiatives via annual business plans. The Chief Executive himself is categorized as the "Chief Innovation Officer" (CIO) who provides innovation leadership in collaboration with innovation champions (Programme Centre Heads), technology innovators (Deputy Directors) and their teams. There is also a special innovation fund, an integrated project management team environment, a "reducing red tape task force" etc. — all noteworthy indicators that innovation is "imbued" in DSTA's organizational culture, values and behaviors.

A good innovation governance system not only clearly states the vision and intended goals of the innovation efforts. It also helps to clearly define roles and responsibilities related to the innovation process, including decision power lines (e.g. with regard to innovation budgets) and the nature of relationships to both internal and external collaborators (e.g. in the context of open innovation). It sheds light on the desired innovation culture and specifies how the organization intends to create and sustain a climate in which new ideas are encouraged and rewarded (and where failure is indeed an option and not a shameful defeat). Innovation governance ensures that the right innovation metrics (e.g. ratio of incremental to game-changing innovation in the portfolio, measured in the number of initiatives and/or expenditures) are used, and it establishes proper management routines regarding innovation project management, info sharing and timely decisions with reference to the stages of the product innovation process such as "Go to Development", "Go to Testing" and "Go to Launch". Without a well-balanced portfolio of incremental and radical innovation initiatives organizations may become too product centric and/or too revenue impatient.

Think of innovation governance as conducting an orchestra. According to German composer, theatre director, and conductor Richard Wagner (1813–1883), "the whole duty of a conductor is comprised in his ability always to indicate the right tempo". Besides the ability to re-imagine old music pieces anew and being a "lightening rod of listening", inspiring innovation leadership is required. Whether it's an orchestra of individualistic, unrestrained star musicians or a group of corporate "deep smarts" and innovative knowledge workers, people want to feel fully realized. If the "person up on the podium" is unable to give them a "collective focus", they might feel deprived and unhappy (and some will look for greener pastures elsewhere). Such a scenario is one of nine "innovation governance models" put forward by Professor Deschamps: nobody is in charge of innovation because it is perceived as less important by top management, and therefore no specific responsibilities are allocated. If that is the case, the organization might end up being a rudderless ship running aground to come back to Plato's term kubernáo. Innovation will not happen quasi automatically; good innovation governance is paramount.

(The Business Times, 21 December 2016)

Making Innovation a Priority at Board Level

Boards which do not promote innovation might end up destroying value rather than creating it.

With Ong Geok Chwee

Should boards hold themselves accountable for making innovation work? According to IMD Professor Jean-Philippe Deschamps, innovation needs to be part of a board's governance mission. For him, innovation governance is a "top management responsibility and preserve that cannot be delegated to any single function or to lower levels of an organisation".

Boards which do not promote innovation might end up destroying value rather than creating it. This risk is indirectly echoed by experts such as the EY Centre for Board Matters which has argued: "To stay ahead of the competition, it's important to focus on innovation".

Who wouldn't agree? One of the top priorities for board members is digital transformation (besides corporate compliance, tax risk or geopolitical risks). EY's "Five key questions for boards" under the category of digital transformation (for example, "Does your board have a designated digital expert who focuses on technology issues?") are highly relevant for business leaders in East and West. In Asian firms, in particular, the chairpersons of boards should ensure that board members and audit committees make a conscious effort to make innovation work for long-term success and continued viability.

To stay in business and to be ahead of the competition, it's important to realign business models with the new opportunities that digitalisation has created. This is easier said than done as the disruptive phenomenon of combinatorial innovation demonstrates.

An early example of combinatorial innovation is the invention of the printing press by German blacksmith, goldsmith, printer and publisher Johannes Gutenberg based on recombining existing and new components such as the screw press (originally designed for making wine), movable metal types with punch, matrix and mould as well as oil-based ink for printing books. His mechanical movable type printing innovation triggered a printing revolution in medieval Europe, disrupting the existing system of monks writing out books by hand in monasteries. Gutenberg's invention played an important role in Martin Luther's Reformation and catalysed the scientific revolution.

Modern examples of combinatorial innovation include the self-driving car capability of Tesla cars (enabled by digital mapping, GPS and artificial intelligence), Dyson's 360 Eye robot vacuum cleaner or IOT-enabled connected homes powered by Schneider Electric.

How prepared are our boards to deal with the challenge and opportunities of combinatorial innovation? A "good" strategic response would depend on deep knowledge about how best new digital technologies can be combined to create more valuable offerings for stakeholders.

Applying "digital lipstick" is certainly insufficient. How many board members are trained and educated in the science of innovation and knowledge management, and governance (i.e. determining the who, what, where, when, how of knowledge creation and innovation efforts), AI or edge computing?

Empirical research on the role of boards with regard to value creation through innovation in Asia is hard to come by. Anecdotal evidence suggests that some boards are rather antiquated and that the wisdom of *digital natives* (who know a thing or two about hackathons) is not utilised due to the valence of hierarchical relationships (reverse mentoring might help!), face or lack of intergenerational trust.

Furthermore, it is questionable that the board's own connectivity to the ground (and thereby access to first-hand knowledge about bottom-up activities of "innovation champs") is high due to "more important" priorities, lack of time or ignorance on the part of the CEO who could arrange for novel "Staff Meet Board events".

While consulting firms do offer specialised advisory services for Asian boards, for example, with reference to innovation governance, there is a possibility that the conceptual frameworks on which these services are based such as "agency theory" or "the resource-based view of the firm" are not fully aligned with the institutional logic of the Asian family enterprise with its greater emphasis on "trusted insiders". Whether there will be a rapid convergence of Asian and non-Asian corporate (innovation) governance approaches as proclaimed by some observers is everyone's guess.

We believe that there is indeed something unique about "good" and "bad" innovation governance in local businesses which has yet to be unearthed. A shared view among several interviewees we talked to recently in the context of an ongoing study on boards and innovation is that while innovation is deemed of great importance for the sustainable growth of an organisation, the boards of directors are not actively driving innovation governance.

Key reasons behind the lack in focus at board level with regard to innovation governance include: (i) lack of clarity of board's roles in driving innovation, (ii) insufficient number of board members with expertise and/or experience in driving innovation, and (iii) lack of motivation at board level to drive innovation that is deemed as more "risky" and difficult to measure.

A beacon for many Asian companies keen to innovate is DBS, whose board decided in 2013 to move decisively into a digital future. As CEO Piyush Gupta emphasised in an interview with McKinsey senior partner Joydeep Sengupta (which makes great reading for any business leader interested in the mechanics of making innovation work): "We felt that if we didn't lead the charge, frankly, we might die".

Cultural Challenges

The key challenges of innovating are usually cultural — can board members and the CEO create an organisational culture that is adaptable and nimble, and where employees are truly passionate about the change imperative and the intrapreneurial, more innovative way forward?

Building a solid foundation for being continually innovative requires numerous pillars. One is to encourage employees to try and to accept that they can make mistakes, according to Kenny Yap, CEO of integrated ornamental fish service provider Qian Hu. In a radio interview about innovation, failure and the pressure of being number one, he said: "If you can have a culture of people making mistakes with the intention of learning, you have to encourage them. You cannot punish them".

While there is very little empirical knowledge about the innovation management and governance specifics discussed in the boardrooms of Asian family-based companies — whether big or small — both CEOs interviewed in that radio programme sent an important message to latecomers in the innovation governance journey: "There is a very urgent need to embrace and master innovation!" Whether (more) boards here will take heed remains to be seen.

(The Business Times, 22 March 2018)

Innovation Governance in Chinese Family Business: A Case Study

With Ong Geok Chwee

What Is Innovation Governance and Why Does It Matter?

One approach to encourage more innovation in business and beyond is to effectively govern it. In contrast to the word innovation which refers to the implementation of a new or significantly improved product, service or process that creates real value (Dong *et al.*, 2003; Crossan & Apaydin, 2010), the term governance is a bit more complex due to its connotations of authority, control and influence. The word itself derives from the Greek word kubernáo with the connotation of steering a ship (metaphorically, it refers to the challenges of steering Men).

Broadly speaking, governance is about the nature of authority relationships in a country or an organisation as well as the degree of formality of associated rules, norms, and actionable procedures — which can vary widely (Deschamps, 2013, 2014, 2015). Corporate innovation governance can be defined as a systematic approach to "align goals, allocate resources and assign decision-making authority for innovation, across the company and with external parties". Innovation governance is a "top management responsibility" that cannot be delegated to any single function or to lower levels of an organisation (Deschamps, 2008).

Corporate innovation contexts are characterised by uncertainty (How will our customers react?); complexity (How best to manage diverse groups of internal and external knowledge experts from different disciplines?); low degree of predictability (Who might disrupt us and what changes will occur within our organisation when we develop a new innovation strategy); and creativity (How to nurture a climate where creativity can flourish?). Therefore, business leaders need governance frameworks, tools and techniques to effectively strategise innovation efforts with a clear focus and a balanced portfolio of innovation initiatives to make innovation work (Adams *et al.*, 2010).

While many would agree that winning firms are characterised by strong innovation governance approaches, empirical research about this topic in Asia is rather poor. Anecdotal evidence suggests that there are many organisations here where formal innovation governance systems are completely lacking. But there are also a couple of real champions where innovation is effectively governed via solid innovation management frameworks, top leadership support and capable managers aimed at creating sustainable business and societal value. Examples include Defence Science Technology Agency (DSTA), Sheng Siong Group and Biosensors Interventional Technologies Pte Ltd — all of which recently won the SPRING Innovation Excellence Awards. Their summary reports are available on the website of Enterprise Singapore and provide valuable insights into key components of innovation governance systems such as a compelling strategic innovation vision and mission (to determine the goals of innovation efforts), a system of supportive values, "the right" sources of innovation, innovation process-related details and so forth.

A good innovation governance system not only clearly states the vision and intended goals of innovation efforts, it also helps to clearly define roles and responsibilities related to the innovation process, including decision power lines (e.g. with regard to innovation budgets) and the nature of relationships with both internal and external collaborators, e.g. in the context of open innovation. It sheds light on the desired innovation culture and specifies how the organisation intends to create and sustain a climate in where new ideas are encouraged and rewarded, and where failure is indeed an option and not a shameful defeat.

Innovation governance ensures that the right innovation metrics (e.g. ratio of incremental to game-changing innovation in the portfolio, measured in the number of initiatives and/or expenditures) are used (Adams *et al.*, 2006), and it establishes proper management routines regarding innovation project management, information sharing and timely decisions with reference to the stages of the product innovation process, such as "Go to Development", "Go to Testing" and "Go to Launch" (Cormican & O'Sullivan, 2004). Without a well-balanced portfolio of incremental and radical innovation initiatives, organisations may become too product centric and/or too revenue impatient.

Enterprise Singapore's Business Excellence Framework

A useful tool to develop a governance system for innovation is Enterprise Singapore's business excellence framework. Enterprise Singapore is a government agency championing enterprise development[1] under the Ministry of Trade and Industry. Its Business Excellence Framework helps companies build their business capabilities, improve their organisational strengths

---

[1] https://www.enterprisesg.gov.sg.

and identify areas for improvement. The Business Excellence (BE) initiative was launched in Singapore in 1994 to help organisations assess which stage they are at on the excellence journey and what they need to do to achieve a higher level of performance. This is done by an assessment of organisational performance against the requirements of the BE framework which provides a holistic standard that covers all critical drivers and results for business excellence. It illustrates the cause and effect relationships between the drivers of performance, what the organisation does, and the results it achieves. It covers the following areas (see Figure 1).

The organisational profile sets the context for the way the organisation operates and serves as an overarching guide for how the framework is applied. So-called "attributes of excellence" describe key characteristics of high performing organisations and are embedded throughout all critical drivers of the framework. These are: 1. Leading with Vision and Integrity, 2. Creating Value for Customers, 3. Driving Innovation and Productivity, 4. Developing Organisational Capability, 5. Valuing People and Partners, 6. Managing with Agility, 7. Sustaining Outstanding Results, 8. Adopting an Integrated Perspective, and 9. Anticipating the Future.

Together, the organisational profile and the attributes of excellence form the context and foundation that encapsulate the entire framework as shown in the diagram below. To achieve excellence, an organisation needs strong leadership to drive the mind-set of excellence and to set a clear

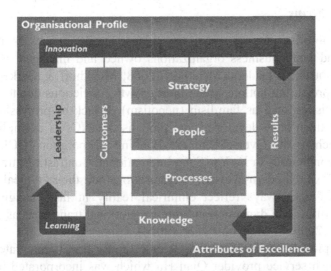

Figure 1:   Areas Covered by the Business Excellence Framework

strategic direction. Customer-centricity is positioned after leadership to demonstrate the focus on anticipating customer needs and creating value for them. Strategy is developed based on understanding internal and external stakeholder requirements to guide people and process capabilities required to drive desired results. To sustain excellent performance, organisations need to continually learn, improve and innovate. Continuous learning and innovation is demonstrated through acquiring knowledge from the lessons learned and the measurement of results, and using them in a closed feedback loop to support decision-making and drive improvements.

The so-called Singapore Innovation Class is one of four standards and certification programmes based on the BE framework interested companies can choose from (based on the same seven dimensions of excellence, namely, Leadership, Planning, Information, People, Processes, Customers, and Results). Singapore Innovation Class (I-Class) offers certification for business excellence in innovation aimed at helping organisations to develop their innovation management capabilities. There were 107 I-Class certified organisations as of October 2016.

Launched in 2001, the Innovation Excellence Award (I-Award) recognises organisations for outstanding innovation management capabilities resulting in breakthrough or impactful innovations observed in areas such as business models, processes, and products and services (Mcgrath, 2010).

Managerial and Organizational Features of Chinese Family Firms

Asian enterprises are dominated by Chinese family businesses, i.e. both small and large business organizations owned and managed by ethnic Chinese business leaders (Menkhoff, 2008; Menkhoff & Gerke, 2004). Despite prevailing notions about their growth restrictions due to cultural characteristics such as familism (nepotism) or lack of professionalism, many of them have developed into globalised MNCs as exemplified by firms such as the Oversea-Chinese Banking Corporation (OCBC), the Hong Leong Group or Eu Yan Sang International. Contrasting "traditional Chinese" vs. "modern Western" organisations and their "typical" attributes does not always reflect empirical reality in fast changing Asia because of growth dynamics and intergenerational transitions as stressed by Fock (2009) or Menkhoff *et al.* (2014).

A typical example of a local Chinese family firm is integrated ornamental fish service provider Qian Hu which was incorporated in 1998.

Since 2000, it is listed on the Singapore Exchange. The firm's business activities include the breeding of Dragon Fish as well as farming, importing, exporting, and distributing of over 1,000 species and varieties of ornamental fish. The company under the leadership of Kenny Yap also produces and distributes several aquarium and pet accessories.[2] In 2013, Qian Hu won the Innovation Excellence Award (I-Award).

Comment on Research Method

In the following, we will present selected insights from an ongoing study on the innovation governance specifics of Asian family firms based on the grounded theory (Glaser & Strauss, 1967; Urquhart, 2013) and case study approach (Yin, 2014; Bernard, 2000) to uncover what makes innovation tick in Asian enterprise.

Innovation Governance at Qian Hu

Visionary Innovation Leadership

According to Kenny Yap, innovation is extremely important in the changing business environment, especially in Singapore with its continuous emphasis on improving productivity:

> "How do you increase your productivity? It's only through innovation. There's no other way. You say "you save a little bit here and there". That's not significant. You've got to create some significant and impactful kind of productivity increase. You have to go for innovation because innovation is about finding new things to do, which you can do to increase the value added ... It's extremely important for any company, especially for SMBs, because the impact of the disruptions of technology is going to make them die faster than the bigger company".

The CEO "must be the key driver" of innovation efforts because the management staff may not always have the complete picture about finance and other resources:

> "If the CEO does not have the heart and the belief in making innovation work, I don't think that the organization can do that. Who are those

---

[2] http://www.qianhu.com/about-qian-hu/corporate-profile.

groups of people that are heavily involved? Usually all the top management members … and then you have to empower all the other people to try, you know, to come up with new things. This is why I say innovation is broad-based. Of course, you have to have a certain kind of hierarchy and chain of command. But basically, I want to involve everybody. Every project small or big must make a difference".

Strategy as Driver of Customer Satisfaction, Innovation and Productivity

Since its ISO 9002 certification in 1996, Qian Hu has put emphasis on value creation through quality products and processes. Through Qian Hu's new e-shop, for example, customers have easy access to the firm's quality products at competitive prices. Qian Hu started to innovate internal processes in 1997 by semi-automating their packing processes while most of the other fish farms still relied on manual processes: "But we semi-automated. We also integrated the weighting machine, computers, and all these to generate packing orders or the invoice. We started the whole thing back in 1997. There was a government agency called Productivity Board which helped us".

In 2009, a strategically integrated R&D division was formed to spearhead the firm's research and development efforts. For Kenny technology is a key innovation driver:

"No matter what kind of new things you do, you have to involve technology. So technology is something that I wanted to put in. Before I retire, I want people to call Qian Hu a technology company. Not a fish company because, regardless of what we do, we use technology to enable what we are doing".

Over the years, Qian Hu has implemented numerous innovative projects, automated processes and increased efficiency, for example, by developing a new filtration system called HydroPure as part of its R&D driven technology innovation efforts:

"Conventionally we used filter material but now we use current electrolytes to break down the things that we don't want like ammonia. We retain all the minerals. So that's new. Of course, we have to spend a lot of money on it. During the past few years, Qian Hu was not doing too well but is profitable — not as profitable as before. I always tell my shareholders, 'if I stop doing innovative projects or invest in R&D, I can show you the numbers; but Qian Hu will die after I leave the company'. So this is why I always say, 'a CEO's job is to think beyond the current generation kind of business'".

R&D is critical for further differentiating Qian Hu from its competitors. Recently, the firm has moved into edible fish:

"Innovation helps us to diversify into other things. This is why it is extremely important for Qian Hu. We have been doing a lot of innovative things, and we invested a lot in R&D. We are able to diversify quite smoothly. The learning process of going into edible fish is slightly shorter than any of the things that we attempted before".

To ensure business continuity and successful strategy execution, a long-term business perspective is important. A short-term business perspective based on quarterly reporting can hurt the business quite badly:

"I'm lucky because nobody can fire me because my family owns the business so I can think long term. Just imagine an employed CEO, the bonus tied to annual results and he not being ethical, the company will collapse. So I say, 'sometimes I do not know what shareholders want'… When they buy a share today, they expect that it appreciates by 10% the next day. They never have the heart, and so I say, 'I will care for my employee more than you. Because I'm the bigger shareholder. I know how to take care of the shareholders already. You are the short term ones. I'm the long term one. And my employees actually create value for you'. This is the truth but nobody wants to say that. But I dare to tell my shareholders that. I say, 'whether you like it or not, it's a free market, free will, you can always sell Qian Hu share'".

With regard to the importance of formalizing innovation strategy per se, Kenny has a dualistic view. On the one hand, Qian Hu has implemented a strategic, formalised approach towards innovation based on a 5-year plan which has helped the firm to clinch the SPRING innovation award:

"We have all the systems of doing innovative things. The whole process is being audited and we got the Singapore SQA award. We are also a people excellence award winner. We also got the innovations award. We have the whole systems of getting all the people involved in place".

But on the other hand, Qian Hu's boss believes that it is important to maintain a more organic, less structured approach towards innovation management driven by an innovation-friendly environment:

"Structuring innovation is so unreal. I remember in the army we had these work improvement teams, a structured work improvement approach. The HQ forced us to come up with an innovation and then, if you did not, you had issues. You know innovative ideas can just suddenly appear. So we give our staff a good environment — whenever they have a good idea, when they propose it to us, and we think its good, we will implement it, and we'll recognize them by giving them a plaque or a monetary award. So we have this system of asking all the people, the ground people, to be innovative. And, of course, during top management meetings we always talk about the new things that we do that can create an impactful outcome".

With regard to budget-driven, strategic R&D management approaches, a flexible approach works better according to Qian Hu's leader:

"Budgeting R&D does not really make sense because you never know when a good idea comes out. Between 2011 and 2017, our expenditures for R&D were higher than our annual net profit. The R&D budget fluctuates. Besides my revenues, it's based on what kind of good ideas come up every year. You don't wait or say, 'oh, I don't have a budget — let's wait. No, no, no'. This year I have three projects on hand. I know it's going to eat into a lot of my expenses and all that. But I say, 'do it now'. I mean, like, why do I have to schedule it. Just do it. Unless you say you can't because you do not have the right people".

Differentiation and Impact: Criteria for Project-Related R&D Decisions

Asked how he determines and decides whether a project is worth investing into, Kenny stressed that important criteria include its impact and whether it helps Qian Hu to further differentiate itself from other companies. At the moment the firm is doing a project with NUS (National University of Singapore) to produce high value fish albino. It involves two Ph.D. researchers: "We had to sponsor them for four years. Their Ph.D. projects focus on this technology. Later, I might employ them if I think they are good and if they can strengthen my R&D".

Sometimes he uses his gut feelings when it comes to decisions about innovative R&D projects:

> "You can not always put numbers on the paper and do all the changes because those really stifle your decision making process. You have to look at a person. Can I trust you? Yes, I think I can. Because the way you talk. Okay, anyway, I know this professor X for several years already. So I know his character. All these kinds of things will come together and help to form my opinion to say 'yes we'll do this project'".

Minor decisions about potential new projects are delegated to his Deputy Directors and the MDs of the firm's subsidiaries:

> "Only when it comes to major ones involving millions of dollars or half a million or so that are going to drag down profit, they have to inform me. And then I will approve or not. Minor ones, you know, as long as they are below hundred thousand Singapore dollars they can go and do that so they don't go bothering me".

Valuing and Rewarding People

Kenny puts great emphasis on building a robust culture of innovation:

> "You must have a culture of doing these kinds of things. It's all about culture anyway. The identity of any company is determined by the culture and the behaviour of the upper management". One way of endorsing this is to put it into the mission statement so that employees know that the company tries to be different.

In terms of staff participation and innovation efforts, management tries to involve everyone by making people "a little bit more creative" and by creating an environment to try things without getting penalized when mistakes are made:

> "Making a mistake twice is a stupid mistake. They must learn from the first mistake. How do people get wisdom? You make a lot of mistakes. You have a lot of experiences, and when you come to a certain age you

become wiser because of these experiences. Without all the mistakes do you think you can have the experience? I don't think so".

As Kenny pointed out, responsible employees do care about the survival of the company and its sustainability:

"If the company can survive, they will bring good things to other people. Responsibility is a must. The other thing is attitude. The attitude towards life and towards what is right and what is wrong also determines how you want to run the company. Try to bring good things to other people. When I employ an employee, we look at attitude first of all".

Qian Hu has a system to reward staff for suggesting good ideas:

"Every month or any week, staff can come up with some things that we think are fantastic, and immediately we will reward them during that month rather than drag it to the end of the year ... Innovation things cannot have KPIs. Innovation is a feel. Innovation is a behavioural thing. Creativity is about certain daily behaviors and certain actions that define certain kinds of outcomes. You don't go and measure this. When they do all the things right, eventually the outcomes will show. You don't have to specifically reward certain types of ideas because you stifle the way you come up with new ideas ... Let them try everything. Think outside the box".

To generate innovative ideas through external collaborations Qian Hu has recently invested into a start-up:

"We have one project which is a start-up. A few years ago it was struggling but I really believe they have a good product, and they have knowledge that we need ... We might want to acquire the company. I think the best way to assess that is to do a project first and then see whether the management people are comfortable with it. If we are, then we might acquire the company. We have attempted to do that before, e.g. acquiring medical plant-based formula. You know, we tried to go into aquaculture but we refused to use antibiotics. But we must have some things to treat them when they get sick, right? We do acquire herbal formula or other kind of things because it would take us years to develop that on our own".

Innovation Governance at Board Level

Asked about the role of the board in the area of innovation (Zahra & Pearce, 1990; Liang *et al.*, 2013; Zhou & Li, 2016), Kenny stressed that this is contingent upon the stage of business development, the importance of technology as innovation lever and the required expertise. Board members may change according to the needs of the company:

"Initially we only had lawyers, accountants or consultants. Some of my ex-consultants became my board members. The IPO lawyer became my board member. A few years ago I started replacing some of the board members or added in new board members with more emphasis on innovations or technology. Two or three years ago I asked a retired AVA expert, head of fisheries with a Ph.D. in fish disease and other things, to become a board member. I believe that if NUS has no problem with the lecturer, after the albino project I might invite him to become my board member. So I develop board members according to the needs of the company".

Kenny doesn't want to have "all the politics" which are typical for larger organizations:

"A small company can be controlled by me or by my family. I know exactly what the company needs. We hate politics. I told my people 'if you want to play politics, become a politician. Don't become a Qian Hu family member. We don't do this'. If you have anything, put it on the table. Address it. Move on. Life should be like that. Life should not, you know, be about back stabbing or having grievances or grudges against someone. Just be a happy ... I want Qian Hu to be a happy company, and in a happy company employees are happy ... Not happy in terms of financial results but whether I'm also doing some things that are beneficial to other people. One of the greatest things I told my brothers, my friends and during some other open occasions, the greatest satisfaction for me is not because I'm the CEO of Qian Hu, it's because when I look at my brothers and I look at my employees, Qian Hu has made many millionaires over the years. If they know how to save and if they don't spend it all".

Family Matters

Most of Qian Hu's shares are owned by the Yap family (over 50% according to Kenny). Top management comprises 30% family members while 70% are outside professionals. Kenny puts strong emphasis on family values:

> "Actually, you know, when I created Qian Hu, when we listed the company, I was aware of the importance of corporate culture and values. So this is why you have to put in something to tell people what we believe in and what we care about. So the kind of behavior dictates our attitude. How do I come up with all these kinds of things? It's because I pick and choose from my Yap family values and culture and I just put it there and I said, 'we call it Qian Hu family members' so there are family elements of all the people involving in this entity. This is what you see right now, whatever you can sense in terms of culture and values, its part of the Qian Hu family values. Regardless of race, sexual preferences, gender, you know, religion and all that, if you concur with my values and you agree with my culture, right, you're part of the Qian Hu family. So we expanded the definition of the Qian Hu Family".

Kenny is proud that the Qian Hu business has helped its staff to provide their families with a brighter future:

> "We came from a poor family ... Maybe I have helped society to keep certain families well-off by working. That's one of the biggest incentives for me to come to work, rather than anything else. I think maybe Qian Hu has created something good in the broader sense of it".

Conclusion and Implications

In this Chapter, we provided insights into the innovation management philosophy of Kenny Yap, the leader of a Chinese family-based enterprise (Qian Hu) in Singapore with reference to innovation governance. The term corporate innovation governance refers to a systematic approach to align goals, allocate resources and assign decision-making authority for innovation, across the company and with external parties (March, 1991; Waldman & Bass, 1991; Schmidt & Brauer, 2006; Deschamps, 2008). Key capabilities include Kenny Yap's visionary and values-based innovation leadership cum strategic innovation approach as exemplified by the emphasis on family continuity, value creation through R&D and product innovations beyond existing ones such as the Lumi-Q fish tank. Qian Hu's innovation governance approach can be described as both explorative and exploitative. "Yap family values" serve as guidance system for managing both people and partners while business processes are optimised through IT and strategic L&D approaches with a view towards achieving greater business results. Table 1 summarizes key components of Qian Hu's innovation governance capabilities.

Not surprising perhaps if one scans the literature on Chinese family firms and innovation (e.g. Roed, 2016), the study revealed that the innovation governance at Qian Hu corporation is driven by the Executive Chairman himself (rather than other people appointed by him or the Board). "Family involvement" in Qian Hu's board seems to strengthen the relationship between R&D investment and the firm's innovation

Table 1: Features of Qian Hu's Innovation Management Capabilities

Leading with Vision and Integrity	• Values-based leadership with a focus on quality, innovation, technology and productivity improvements combined with bottom-up staff participation (e.g. based on the "creating value from mistakes" approach)
Creating Value for Customers	• Value creation through quality products and processes • Improved customer satisfaction index • Fast(er) on-time delivery
Strategy as Driver of Innovation and Productivity	• 5-year product and process innovation plan • Technology and business model innovation
Valuing People and Partners	• Staff dialogues, open channels, project teams, career development • Increasing support for innovation learning • Improved staff innovation index and length of service
Managing Processes with Agility	• Harvesting creative ideas and implementing them to create value for the organization • Use of patented HydroPure technology to provide optimum healthy water conditions for the fish • Leveraging IT to increase process efficiency, e.g. zero error in shipments • E-shop (e-commerce)
Knowledge and Learning	• KM system and strategic human capital development
Sustaining Outstanding Results	• Improved sales turnover for innovative, patented accessories, trademarks, R&D investments vs. sales, operational improvements (e.g. lobster quarantine), patents

performance. The role of Qian Hu's Board in innovation governance turned out to be skewed towards providing expertise that the firm needs (again, that seems to be directed by "the boss" as well) while Kenny himself stands out as the company's "Innovation Czar". Decisions about major innovation investments are mainly made by Kenny himself while smaller ones are delegated to those managers who are responsible for the business units. As a result, innovation governance in this dynamic Chinese family firm is arguably very different compared with large, non-family owned organisations (Hendry & Kiel, 2004) and the premises of the Anglo-American corporate governance model.

Besides this key hypothesis, the interview data point to a couple of other important components such as proactive innovation leadership with a clear vision towards innovation and productivity improvements, a robust organisational culture and inclusive family values beyond the immediate family as drivers of intra-organizational innovation efforts as well as disdain for a codified (rigid) innovation strategy. The entire management approach at Qian Hu comes across as being organic and contingent rather than inorganic-mechanistic which arguably is well aligned with the current VUCA environment.

Challenges ahead include the search for novel business model components beyond ornamental fish, accessories, plastics and e-retail (in a bearish operating environment) as well as continuous technology innovation in order to create and capture new value.

References

Adams, R., Bessant, J. & Phelps, R. (2006). Innovation management measurement: A review. *International Journal of Management Reviews, 8*(1), 21–47.

Adams, R.B., Hermalin, B.E. & Weisbach, M.S. (2010). The role of boards of directors in corporate governance: A conceptual framework and survey. *Journal of Economic Literature, 48*, 58–107.

Bernard, R. (2000). *Social Research Methods: Qualitative and Quantitative Approaches*. Thousand Oaks, CA: Sage Publications.

Cormican, K. & O'Sullivan, D. (2004). Auditing best practice for effective product innovation management, *Technovation, 24*(10), 819–829.

Crossan, M. & Apaydin, M. (2010). A multi-dimensional framework of organizational innovation: A systematic review of the literature. *Journal of Management Studies, 47*(6), 1154–1191.

Deschamps, J.-P. (2008). *Innovation Leaders: How Senior Executives Stimulate, Steer and Sustain Innovation*. Chichester: Wiley/Jossey-Bass.

Deschamps, J.-P. (2013): What is innovation governance? — Definition and scope, Organization & Culture, May 3.

Deschamps, J.-P. (2014). *Innovation Governance: How Top Management Organizes and Mobilizes for Innovation* (co-authored with Beebe Nelson). Wiley/Jossey-Bass — April 2014.

Deschamps, J.-P. (2015). Innovation governance: How proactive is your board? *Asian Management Insights, 2*(2), 74–77.

Dong I. Jung, Chee W. Chow & Anne Wu (2003). The role of transformational leadership in enhancing organizational innovation: Hypotheses and some preliminary findings. *The Leadership Quarterly, 14*, 525–544.

Fock, S.T. (2009). *Dynamics of Family Business: The Chinese Way*. Singapore: Cengage Learning.

Glaser, B.G. & Strauss, A. (1967). *The Discovery of Grounded Theory: Strategies for Qualitative Research*. New York: Aldine Publishing Co.

Hendry, K. & Kiel, G. (2004). The role of the board in firm strategy: Integrating agency and organisational control perspectives. *Corporate Governance: An International Review, 12*(4), 500–520.

Liang, Q., Li, Xinchun, Yang, X., Lin, D. & Zheng, D. (2013). How does family involvement affect innovation in China? *Asia Pacific Journal of Management, 30*(3), 677–695.

March, J.G. (1991). Exploration and exploitation in organizational learning. *Organization Science, 2*, 71–86.

Mcgrath, R.G. (2010). Business models: A discovery driven approach. *Long Range Planning, 43*(2–3), 247–261.

Menkhoff, T. & Gerke, S. (2004). *Chinese Entrepreneurship and Asian Business Networks*, London and New York: RoutledgeCurzon.

Menkhoff, T. (2008). Case Study Knowledge Management at Qian Hu Corporation Limited, Asia Productivity Organization (APO), Knowledge Management in Asia: Experience and Lessons. Report of the APO Survey on the Status of Knowledge Management in Member Countries. Tokyo: APO, 2008, pp. 177–192 (ISBN: 92-833-2382-3).

Menkhoff, T., Chay, Y.W., Evers, H.-D. & Hoon, C.Y. (eds.) (2014). *Catalyst for Change: Chinese Business in Asia*. World Scientific Publishing.

Roed, I. (2016). Disentangling the family firm's innovation process: A systematic review. *Journal of Family Business Strategy, 7*, 185–201.

Schmidt, S. & Brauer, M. (2006). Strategic governance: How to assess board effectiveness in guiding strategy execution. *Corporate Governance: An International Review, 14*(1), 13–22.

Urquhart, C. (2013). *Grounded Theory for Qualitative Research: A Practical Guide*, Los Angeles, CA. London: SAGE Publications.

Waldman, D.A. & Bass, B.M. (1991). Transformational leadership at different phases of the innovation process. *The Journal of High Technology Management Research, 2*(2), 169–180.

Wong, R. (ed.) (2008). A New Breed of Chinese Entrepreneurs? Critical Reflections, in: *Chinese Entrepreneurship in Global Era*. London: Routledge, pp. 3–22.

Yin, R.K. (2014). *Case Study Research: Design and Methods* (5th Edition). Los Angeles, CA: SAGE Publications.

Zahra, S.A. & Pearce, J.A. (1990). Determinants of board directors' strategic involvement. *European Management Journal, 8*(2), 164–173.

Zhou, T. & Li, W. (2016). Board governance and managerial risk taking: Dynamic analysis. *The Chinese Economy, 49*(2), 60–80.

Chapter 8

Sustainable Smart City

Sensors Alone Don't Make a City Smart — People Do

Smart sensors are part of what makes a city smart. But recent visits to Berlin and Barcelona suggest that ground-up, collaborative efforts by citizens and entrepreneurs are the essential ingredients to turn a smart city into a truly compelling place to call home.

On a first glance, Berlin (capital of Germany), Singapore and Barcelona (capital of the Catalonia region in northeastern Spain) do not seem to have a lot in common. After taking a second look, however, it becomes apparent that all three cities aspire to become smart cities in order to increase the quality of urban life. This was confirmed during a study trip to Germany and Spain that 28 Singapore Management University (SMU) undergraduates and I went on this month.

I had themed the trip "Living in Smart Cities: Innovation and Sustainability in Berlin (Germany) and Barcelona (Spain)". The key objective was to expose Singapore youth to selected smart city concepts and practice approaches in two great European cities with reference to smart city dimensions such as the economy, governance, people, living, mobility, and the environment.

Smart cities use information and communication technologies so as to become more intelligent and efficient in the use of resources with more efficient services for their citizens and a higher quality of life. They aspire to significantly reduce their environmental footprint via a sustainable built

185

environment, zero carbon strategies, intelligent mobility systems and renewable energy supply.

Participation of Urban Society in Berlin

Rather than starting off by scrutinizing Berlin's smart city achievements and ambition towards becoming a "sensorized" city, we began our journey with a long walk on the runway of Berlin's former Tempelhof Airport (built at the beginning of the 1920s) on a sunny afternoon. The goal was to appreciate the importance of participatory urban development in turning this site (which became famous during the Berlin Blockade of 1948–1949 when the allied forces responded to Russian attempts to take over all of Berlin with the so-called Airlift Berlin) into a public park. In seeking to create a smart(er) city, Berlin's administration is in the process of further digitising business processes and to roll out more e-government projects. Accordingly, a novel e-participation project was conducted with several stages, such as brainstorming, dialogue, and "call for ideas" (including several airport events, workshops, open councils, etc.) to build a broad consensus regarding the use of the land of the former Tempelhof airport which was closed in 2008. The project contributes to the vision of Berlin as a climate-neutral city. With 386-hectare, it is now one of the world's largest, centrally located open spaces for public use, featuring a six-kilometre cycling, skating and jogging trail, a BBQ area, a huge communal garden, a dog-walking field, and picnic sites for visitors. Tempelhof also houses refugees from Syria, Afghanistan, Iraq, and elsewhere.

No Smart Economy Without Smart Energy

The importance of creating "locations for the future" as part of the smart economy dimension of a Smart City became obvious when we visited the 5.5-hectare EUREF (EURopean Energy Forum) Campus in Berlin-Schöneberg, a forward-looking "model project" on a former industrial site which has been redeveloped into a business, research and education hub. EUREF hosts a variety of clean-energy related companies and organisations such as the "Green Garage", a cleantech accelerator that helps start-ups to turn the climate challenge into a business opportunity. Another tenant is Schneider-Electric, a globally operating specialist in the field of energy management and automation which provides integrated solutions for energy and infrastructure, industrial processes, data networks and buildings. At their showroom ZeeMo.base, the students gained deeper insights into the importance of zero emission energy (i.e. energy that emits no waste products that could be harmful for the environment or the climate) and smart electricity distribution systems. Via a micro smart grid demonstrator, they were exposed to different energy management scenarios while watching real-time monitors displaying varied consumption patterns and energy flows of both renewable and non-renewable energy sources ranging from solar to nuclear energy. The visit was instrumental to appreciate the reasons behind Germany's so-called "Energiewende" (= energy transition) policy, i.e. the transition to a low carbon, environmentally sound, reliable, and affordable energy supply.

At Berlin's Adlershof Science City, the students continued to explore what it takes in terms of research and innovation to become an energy efficient city. The science park (one of the most successful high-technology sites in Germany) is home to 1,013 companies and scientific institutions. About 16,000 people work here on an area of 4.2 km² plus ca. 6,500 students. As coal-fired generators and nuclear power plants are phased out, Germany continues to push forward the change towards renewable energy sources such as wind, photovoltaics, and biomass. Ambitious goals include greenhouse gas (GHG) reductions of 80–95% by 2050 and a renewable energy target of 60% by 2050. Adlershof's expertise in the area of energy efficiency is a powerful driver of this mega change. It also supports start-ups in the field of smart energy and IOT such as "ICE GATEWAY" whose business model leverages the "connected city" concept by exploiting new possibilities to connect information and communications systems, buildings, and (wireless) infrastructural elements such as smart lighting systems.

Innovation Districts and Maker Spaces

Innovation districts such as Adlershof play an important role in a "smart" city. A famous Spanish example is 22@Barcelona (or Districte De La Innovació), an urban renewal area in Barcelona's formerly industrial area of Poblenou (historians refer to it as the "Catalonian Manchester"). Its massive transformation into an urban technological and innovation district with leisure and residential spaces was triggered by the Olympic Games in 1992 and subsequently accelerated in 2000 by a new urban planning ordinance approved by the Barcelona City Council. As explained during a meeting with Mr Antoni Vives, former Deputy Mayor of Barcelona, Barcelona's Smart City Strategy contains 22 integrated "habitat" programmes in areas such as data-driven water and waste management, smart mobility, innovative healthcare, and so forth.

An interesting example of a ground-up, community-based and citizen-centric smart city project is Barcelona's so-called Fab Ateneus Network which offers spaces for "creating collaborative, socially innovative outcomes that help to manage to transform peoples' urban surroundings in a sustainable manner". The network's mission is to nurture an "Innovate and Create Culture" in different boroughs of Barcelona based on collective creation, innovation, and participatory bottom-up initiatives. La Fàbrica del Sol, a facility for environmental education supported by the Ecology, Urban Planning and Mobility Department of the Barcelona City Council, has a similar socially innovative co-creation vision. The renovated building has various environmentally-friendly features such as a pergola for solar collectors and photovoltaic panels. Equipped with 3D printers, laser cutting and stitching machines, powertools, computers etc. La Fàbrica del Sol represents an organic space for the exchange of ideas, joint learning and making things with a view towards meeting both the challenges of sustainability and needs of the immediate neighbourhood.

Visits of CaixaBank (one of Spain's most innovative banks and an early fintech pioneer) and the Center for Innovation in Cities at ESTADE Business School (Professor Esteve Almirall) concluded the formal visit programme in Barcelona.

Conclusion

The smart city movement in Berlin and Barcelona turned out to be very diverse, alive and kicking, with Barcelona (arguably) being the more attractive urban destination not least because of its rich cultural sites such as Gaudi's Familia Sagrada, authentic urban street life and mediterranean climate. "Open urban innovation", "Internet of Things", "open data", "the maker movement", "sharing economy", "politics of space", "travel on demand" and the "use of empty city plots by civil collectives as smart platforms to create community gardens and to share books or tools" emerged as topical concerns of smart city experts and citizens we spoke to.

What impressed me the most? In Berlin it was the collective determination and practical capacity of start-ups to fight climate change and to monetise that agenda on the basis of very smart business models (we also noticed while exploring the former Tempelhof airport runway that Berliners seemingly do not use their smart phones during their leisure pursuits). In Barcelona, we enjoyed the city's walkability which — in combination with a very pleasant environment — represents an essential component of smart urban (integrated) mobility systems. It also enhances quality of life and one's health provided its safe, pollution-free and age-friendly. At times we also pondered about the question whether it would make sense to integrate communal maker spaces ala La Fàbrica del Sol into Singapore's HDB heartlands.

(The Straits Times, 2 November 2016)

The Lessons We Learned from a Smart Nation: Germany

With Jonas Schorr

A study trip to Germany by a group of Singapore Management University students offers insights into how this European nation has built its cities sustainably and innovatively.

Germany and Singapore have many commonalities, such as their strategic interests in creating liveable cities, nurturing start-ups and entrepreneurship, as well as value creation through innovation. This was confirmed during our study trip to Germany with 25 Singapore Management University (SMU) undergraduates last month; the theme for the trip was "Living in Smart Cities: Innovation, Sustainability and Start-Ups in Germany".

Besides examining general aspects of business management and innovative entrepreneurship in Berlin and Stuttgart (Baden-Wuerttemberg), a key objective was to expose Singapore youth to one of the "secrets" of Germany's economic success: the country's operational (engineering) excellence, which enables German export-oriented multi-nationals such as BMW or Daimler Benz, as well as Mittelstand firms such as Mann+Hummel, to maintain and expand their global market leadership.

Germany's New Start-up Hub

In 2014, Berlin adopted its official Smart City Strategy, aimed at becoming one of Europe's leading smart cities. With an emphasis on quality of life, climate projection and citizen participation, it has become a booming centre of innovation for solutions in future urban mobility, renewable energy, and circular economies.

Many of these projects are pilots driven by the city's strong research community and funded as a combination of public grants from Germany's federal ministries and the European Union (Horizon 2020, Climate-KIC, EIT Digital), and complemented by third-party, private funding.

But there is also innovation coming from ordinary Berliners, who have launched successful petitions to lobby for a better bicycle infrastructure and a new mobility law; they have also won a public referendum to keep the site of the former Tempelhof airport to be kept open as a public park and ecological conservation area.

A visible result of Berlin's smart-city aspirations is the large number of start-ups there. One of the Top 100 start-ups (in terms of funding) in the city is SoundCloud, a social networking service for music established in 2007 with a user base of about 175 million active music fans.

One location where start-up founders have access to an inspiring work environment, networking events and knowledge creation opportunities is The Factory. Located near the site of the former Berlin Wall, its campus in Berlin Mitte was inaugurated by Google chairman Eric Schmidt and Berlin mayor Klaus Wowereit in 2014.

Like Singapore, Berlin has attracted several international accelerators such as NUMA (located in Paris, France), which builds future-proof tech start-ups and supports both corporates and public institutions on their innovation journey. NUMA's innovative DataCity programme matches the entrepreneurial passion of start-ups with the know-how of established companies to better manage urban challenges, such as in the area of mobility through the promotion of green(er) modes of transport such as cargo bikes.

An interesting smart mobility initiative is Berlin's Radbahn (Cycle Track) Project. The goal of its founders, a society called paperplanes eV, is to transform the unutilised space below Berlin's famous U1 elevated subway line into a major urban cycling path. They recently launched a competition for innovative ideas around their U1 track vision "to make Berlin's urban spaces more people-oriented and environmentally friendly".

Berlin's 5.5 ha Euref (European Energy Forum) campus (a business, research and education hub built on a former industrial site) hosts several clean-energy-related companies and organisations such as the Green Garage, a cleantech accelerator that helps start-ups turn the climate challenge into a business opportunity.

Another Euref tenant is InfraLab Berlin, a long-term co-working project of leading infrastructure and energy companies such as waste management firm BSR (Berliner Stadtreinigung), BVG (Berlin's main public transport company) and Vattenfall (a major power company), to develop innovative smart-city solutions.

One project under discussion is aimed at upgrading BVG's public bus fleet with moving sensors that scan the environment for necessary maintenance works in order to avoid costly spillovers of man holes after heavy rainfall. It is a pilot measure of Greenbox Global Holding GmbH[1] aimed at creating innovative value in the areas of environmental protection, infrastructure, energy supply, and digitalisation. With Berlin as a reference case, there are already talks ongoing to export the InfraLab approach to cities in Asia.

The Berlin leg of our journey also included a visit to ECF Aquaponic Farm Systems, which has built Europe's largest urban aquaponic farm in the city, producing fish, and high-quality vegetables.

ECF stands for efficient city farming. Its aquaponic farm systems ensure efficient food production because the water is used for both fish cultivation and subsequent vegetable production. Waste products from fish fertilise the plants in the greenhouses, and due to ECF's closed water cycle and its location, emissions from transportation, and cooling chains are minimised.

The increasing importance of low-emission and market-driven, sustainable mobility of the future became obvious during our company visits in Stuttgart, capital of the state of Baden-Wuerttemberg (hub of Germany's innovative automotive firms such as Porsche and Daimler-Benz). Despite increasing competition among local and international car makers, leaders in business and government work hand in hand to advance electric mobility and fuel-cell technology.

One driver in terms of cluster governance and cooperative competition is e-mobil, an innovation agency of the state of Baden-Wuerttemberg. It coordinates the cluster "Electric Mobility South-West" (within the Karlsruhe-Mannheim-Stuttgart-Ulm region) to leverage the expertise of large, medium-size, and small enterprises in vehicle construction, energy

---

[1] https://www.greenbox.global/.

engineering, information and communication technology, and the interdisciplinary field of production engineering with local research institutes.

Collaborative R&D projects for enhanced interlinked mobility or wireless charging are funded by the High-Tech Strategy 2020 of the Federal Ministry of Education and Research, BMBF.

While in Stuttgart, we also took a closer look at the strategic business and innovation management systems of the Mann+Hummel Group. The company produces various filter elements for the local and international automotive and mechanical engineering industries.

Due to the entry of new types of electronics into the engine compartments in cars and respective space requirements, there is a need to adapt air filter systems to this new trend. The firm employs hundreds of research-and-development experts to ensure that it can respond to changing installation conditions and future electromobility trends with novel product solutions.

One major current concern is the need to develop cleaner solutions for both people and machines to combat the high levels of air pollution in cities, in particular pollution caused by particulates.

The World Health Organisation says that particulates are responsible for the deaths of around 47,000 people every year in Germany. Besides the usual culprits such as nitrogen dioxide and nitrogen oxides (NOX), sulfur oxides (SOX), carbon dioxide (CO_2), carbon monoxide (CO), ammonia (NH_3), volatile organic compounds (VOC), and ozone (O_3), research is focused on understanding small particulates, which are fine enough to penetrate deep into human lungs, causing chronic lung, and heart diseases.

Particulate vehicle emissions come not only from the exhaust but also from braking and tyre and road abrasion.

Electric vehicles are not entirely pollution-free, although they are often labelled as zero emission vehicles. Mann+Hummel's so-called "Fine Dust (Feinstaub') Eater" project, with test vehicles operating in the airpolluted city of Stuttgart is a response to this threat. One commercial challenge is to figure out how to monetise fine dust-related data collected via test cars and stationary particulate matter filtration stations.

"Dual Training"

At the Mercedes-Benz Training Centre in Esslingen-Bruehl, we gained deeper insights into Daimler's "dual" training and higher education approach. A key feature of the German dual system of vocational training is the close integration of both companies and educational institutions in teaching and training, so that apprentices can apply newly acquired competencies within their companies.

As we saw during a tour of the Mercedes Benz plant in Sindelfingen, the success of the German automotive cluster and participating firms depends on the country's high-quality technical and vocational training system. Trainees are well paid and acquire core skills in an environment conducive to learning through highly skilled master craftsmen and on the basis of systematic training plans.

One of the outcomes is a high-performance work culture (a hallmark of Germany's Mittelstand), which acknowledges the wisdom of older employees and the need to respond to automation and digitalised (Factory 4.0) production systems trends with a "human" work regime. This in turn provides fertile ground for both greater production efficiency and technology innovation as we observed during plant visits in Stuttgart and Berlin.

The study tour was instrumental in appreciating the reasons behind Germany's transition to a low-carbon, environmentally sound, reliable and affordable energy supply. The focus on renewables has become an important driver behind the success of "Berlin Valley" as an increasingly dynamic hub for digital entrepreneurs and start-ups driven by deep smarts, low rents and a vibrant alternative innovation culture.

Besides a better understanding of the roots of Germany's economic success, the importance of engineering excellence as a source of national wealth creation and competitive challenges ahead, such as the rise of the autonomous vehicle, the Stuttgart visit reminded us that there can be no smart city without clean air.

It is perhaps ironic that the authorities in this traditional automotive hub are increasingly forced to trigger fine dust ("Feinstaub") alerts when pollution is particularly high, nudging commuters to use public transport, car pools, or electric taxis. Here, we note that how fine dust affects Singaporeans has yet been studied.

We were further humbled by Germany's deposit and return system for non-refillable beverage containers, a core element towards a truly zero-waste country where all discarded materials are resources for others to use.

(Business Times, 13 April 2018)

Lessons from Germany's "Hidden Champions"

While Singapore SMEs tend to lag behind in innovation, the Mittelstand firms' are at the cutting edge, despite a lack of heft.

Germany and Singapore have many things in common, such as their strategic interests in value creation through innovation, and they continue to develop their strong partnership for mutual benefit. This was confirmed during a study trip to Germany that 28 Singapore Management University (SMU) undergraduates and I went on last month I had themed the trip Germany's "Hidden Champions" — Global Market Leadership through Innovation". Besides examining general aspects of business management and innovative entrepreneurship in several German states (Bundeslaender), the objective was to expose Singapore youth to the business logic of Germany's "Mittelstand firms", from which many lessons can be learnt. The "German Mittelstand" refers to world-class, export-oriented small and medium-sized enterprises (SMEs). There are similarities between the German Mittelstand and Singapore's SME sector: German Mittelstand make up more than 99% of all German firms, contribute almost 52% of the country's total economic output, and employ about 60% of the workforce. Over 1.300 of these Mittelstand firms are regarded as "Hidden Champions", a term coined by Professor Hermann Simon to categorise these mostly family-run private companies which are among the top three in the global market with revenues below €3billion (S$4.6 billion). "Hidden Champions" are extremely ambitious, growth-oriented and determined to maintain and further expand their global market leadership role. One of their "secrets" is operational excellence in (large) global market niches and the entrepreneurial ability to create real sustainable value for their customers.

Science-Driven

The importance of science-driven, innovative entrepreneurship became obvious during our visit to Heraeus Holding GmbH, a global engineering group headquartered in Hanau near Frankfurt. This leading international family-owned company was founded in 1851 and has over 12,000 employees worldwide in more than 100 subsidiaries in 38 countries. It leverages its deep material expertise and innovative technological know-how in business areas such as the environment, energy, health, mobility, and industrial applications. Its new "3D start-up" (with its own laser and electron beam printers) is in the process of creating high-strength components for thrusters on navigation satellites made of precious metal powder for 3D printing. Strategic innovation and R&D capabilities are at the core of what makes Germany's "Hidden Champions" tick. In Baden-Wuerttemberg, my students took a closer look at the strategic business and innovation management systems of Duerr AG and the Mann+Hummel Group to appreciate what it takes to create value through innovation management and to gain insights into the inner workings of Germany's (networked) automotive cluster, One example of Duerr's innovation efforts is its "Eco-Paintshop" which offers customers in the automotive industry around the world a paint shop with optimised energy utilisation, better environmental compatibility, paint cost savings and lower unit costs. Mann+Hummel produces various filter elements for the international automotive and mechanical engineering industries, As engine compartments in cars require more space for new types of electronics, air filter systems must adapt to this trend in line with changing installation conditions, The firm's research and development specialists ensure that the company responds to this new development with innovative product solutions, At the Mercedes-Benz Training Centre in Esslingen-Bruhl, the students gained deeper insights into Daimler's "dual" training and higher education approach. A key feature of the German dual system of vocational training is the close integration of both companies and educational institutions in teaching and training so that apprentices can apply newly acquired competencies within their companies.

Singapore continues to learn from the German experience as exemplified by the foundation of the German-Singapore Institute (now part of Nanyang Polytechnic) in the 1980s, an early pioneer of the Teaching Factory concept with its emphasis on a realistic, practice oriented learning environment with a focus on problem-solving and productive employability. The recently implemented collaborative Dual Studies industry Sponsorship Pioneer Programme, comprising local polytechnics, Singapore Institute of Technology, German firms (which sponsor local polytechnic graduates who complete their university degrees in Germany) and Singapore's Economic Development Board is a more recent example A value-creating economy requires well-trained, loyal and highly qualified employees. The success of the German automotive cluster and participating firms such as Mann+Hummel or Daimler depends on a high quality technical and vocational training system. Trainees are well paid and acquire core competencies in an environment conducive to learning through highly skilled master craftsmen. One of the outcomes is a high performance work culture (another hallmark of Germany's "Hidden Champions"). This in turn provides a fertile ground for technology innovation and greater production efficiency as we observed during a visit to the Mercedes-Benz plant in Berlin (established in 1902) and a tour of the BMW factory in Regensburg (Bavaria) where robots work right next to autoworkers.

Innovation Hubs

Lightweight construction, digitalised (Factory 4.0) production systems, new materials, processes or the abolishment of the assembly line and the need to further reduce the harmful environmental impacts of mobility in general represent some of the challenges for R&D specialists in Germany's automotive cluster and beyond. DLR's (German Aerospace Centre) Institute of Transport Research which we visited in Berlin, for example, is involved in various innovative research projects on mobility and traffic with special focus on developing a "smart" inner-urban, sustainable cycling infrastructure, car and bike sharing, and electro-mobility. Closeness to customers was a common pattern in all firms we visited. Not only do they go the extra mile to reach out to customers in order to be of value and to further enhance their business models, but they also increasingly support the establishment of networked innovation hubs such as the new German Tech Entrepreneurship Centre (GTEC) at the European School of Management and Technology in Berlin. GTEC is Germany's first open campus to unite technology-based start-ups, international corporations, academic institutions, accelerators, venture capital funds and business angels in one location. "Berlin Valley" has become a dynamic hub for digital entrepreneurs and start-ups driven by smart people, low rents and a vibrant alternative innovation culture. At BMW's new Research and Technology House in Garching (near Munich), we could observe a similar trend. Like in many other German firms, the gates are wide open at BMW for external ideas. Through its BMW Start-up Garage, automotive start-ups (which target exclusively the automotive industry) and start-ups from other industries (with value-added technologies for the automotive industry) can enter into a co-development partnership with the BMW Group aimed at further improving BMW vehicles and customer experiences. Innovation turned out to be very well governed in the firms visited via effective innovation management frameworks, top leadership support and capable managers. Besides relentless efforts to innovate with the objective of creating sustainable business and societal value driven by the need for better environmental compatibility and cost savings, "coopetition" (cooperative competition) emerged as a powerful driver of Germany's export-oriented automotive cluster.

While the government provides leadership and resources, it is the visionary business community which takes charge because it has realised that cooperation with other cluster firms, universities and research institutions deep into and across the value chain pays, as they are able to reach a higher level of value creation by jointly pushing the frontiers of new knowledge creation and R&D.

Singapore's vibrant SME sector would do well to learn from Germany's Mittelstand in going regional and global. Successful scaling requires the existence of international customers delighted about new products and services.

Besides a better understanding of the story of Germany's entrepreneurial innovators, we were humbled by the green hospitality of our hosts. All of them provided us with returnable water or juice glass bottles rather than non-returnable plastic bottles, a hallmark of the German recycling system.

(The Straits Times, 18 November 2015)

Lessons from Two Smart Nations: Germany & Estonia

Innovation and entrepreneurship help strengthen ties between Singapore, Germany, and Estonia.

Cooperation links between Singapore, Germany, and Estonia continue to grow steadily marked by several commonalities, such as successful start-ups, an open business environment, as well as strategic value creation through entrepreneurial innovation.

This impression was confirmed during a recent study trip to the capitals of Germany (Berlin) and Estonia (Tallinn) with 27 Singapore Management University (SMU) undergraduates last month with the theme

"Coping with Digital Transformation". Besides examining general aspects of business management and digital change, a key objective was to expose Singapore youth to some of the secrets of Germany's and Estonia's economic dynamism: Germany's operational (engineering) excellence and sustainable mobility solutions, which enables export-oriented multinationals such Daimler Benz to continue their global market leadership role in the automotive sector; and Estonia's digital leadership in the area of government e-initiatives and cyber security.

Berlin: Germany's New Start-up Hub

Like Singapore and Barcelona, Berlin is determined to become one of Europe's leading carbon-neutral "Smart Cities". Propelled by the transition to a low carbon, environmentally sound, reliable and affordable energy supply, and a vibrant technology ecosystem, Germany's capital has become a hub for ground-up initiatives in the areas of urban mobility, renewable energy and digital economy to develop intelligent solutions for the city of tomorrow.

One driver is the Berlin Agency for Electromobility eMO, the central point of contact for smart mobility in the German capital region. Its "Pole Position project" features a self-driving shuttle called "EZ 10" which is running on Berlin's 5.5 ha futuristic EUREF (European Energy Forum) campus that will be upgraded for fully automated inductive charging and on-demand use. The EUREF campus is a business, research and education hub built on a former industrial site. It serves as test bed and showcase platform for regulators, transport operators, airports, corporations, business parks, and universities who wish to experience new autonomous mobility solutions. While the self-driving shuttle EZ 10 is ideal for last-mile transportation, experts from global testing, certification, inspection and training provider TÜV SÜD have assessed the EZ10 for open road usage.

The EUREF campus hosts clean-energy-related companies and organisations such as the Green Garage, a cleantech accelerator that helps start-ups turn the climate challenge into a business opportunity. Another example is SirPlus founded by food activist Raphael Fellmer and his team. Its mission is to curb food wastage, a huge problem in Europe as 50% of edible food is being wasted (which in turn adds to the problem of CO_2 pollution). SirPlus manages to save tons of food from landing in the bin by selling surplus food in their own food outlet store, via their same-day delivery service in Berlin, and also online with delivery across Germany.

I also noted in Berlin several bottom-up initiatives towards a more citizen-focused smart city. For instance, the Flussbad project which is aimed at transforming the Spree Canal in downtown Berlin into a river pool to allow public swimming. Citizens were also instrumental in turning the former Tempelhof airport (built at the beginning of the 1920s) into one of the world's largest, centrally located open spaces for public use, comprising a six kilometre cycling, skating and jogging trail, a barbecue area, a huge communal garden, and picnic sites.

The increasing importance of low-emission, sustainable mobility of the future became obvious during our visit to the Mercedes-Benz plant in Berlin-Marienfelde. The plant is a key component of the company's global powertrain production network with over 2,500 employees (the term "powertrain" refers to the engine, transmission, and drivetrain). The hi-tech plant produces the innovative valve timing system CAMTRONIC which cuts fuel consumption and helps to minimise CO_2 emissions. Our group also gained deeper insights into Daimler's dual training and higher education approach characterised by the close integration of both on-the-job and off-the-job training.

The future success of the German automotive cluster and participating firms increasingly depends on the mastery of the digital transformation and electric drive technology. Like other big firms, Daimler aspires to digitise the entire value chain.

It has implemented new formats for digital transformation, such as Digital Life Campus hackathons, where the most creative and passionate coders from around the world come together to build ground-breaking prototypes and new A.I. powered software solutions during one weekend. Its new smart Pop-up Store in Berlin's central boulevard Unter den Linden educates mall-goers and millennial shoppers about the Mercedes brand and the smart (brand) portfolio, such as the electric Smart ForFour city car.

Innovation Oriented and Ready for Business: The City of Tallinn

The study trip to Estonia was a first for SMU. Just like Berlin, Tallinn, Estonia's capital, has become home to numerous start-ups, such as cloud-based CAD collaboration solution provider GrabCAD, Pipedrive (a cloud-based sales software company), and cyber security expert CybExer.

The smart Baltic state was part of the German-led Hanseatic League formed around the middle of the 12th century by German and Scandinavian seafaring merchants. It borders the Baltic Sea and the Gulf of Finland between Latvia and Russia. Its population of 1.3 million people comprises Estonians (68.7%), Russians (24.8%), Ukrainians (1.7%), Belarusians (1%), Finns (0.6%), and others (3.2%). While covered to a large extent by forests, Estonia has produced famous unicorns like SKYPE, and continues to create digital innovations ranging from e-Government to smart agriculture. Estonia regained independence from the Soviet Union in 1991, and has been a member of the EU since 2004. It joined the Euro Zone (a monetary union of 19 of the 28 European Union member states) in 2011, adopted the euro as its currency and became a member of NATO.

Estonians are very tech savvy (even our tour bus had wi-fi). 98% of Estonians possess a catch-all ID card that is used to securely access various e-services ranging from voting and tax declarations to disaster response or getting doctors' prescriptions. In 2014, Estonia pioneered the novel e-Residency Identity Card which enables non-Estonians such as digital nomads, start-ups, free lancers or EU companies to utilise Estonian services such as registering a company, finance, processing payments, and settling tax matters. Since its launch, thousands of e-residents have enjoyed the benefits of the Estonian ID card to start location-independent businesses, sign contracts, etc.

One of the firms we visited in Tallinn was the money transfer firm, TransferWise. The company was started by Taavet Hinrikus and Kristo Käärmann in London in 2011 to enable transfers between the British pound and euro. Its competitive strengths include favourable exchange rates, transfer speed and its easy-to-use website.

Estonia's home-grown challenges include migration dependence as a result of negative natural population increase vis-à-vis decreasing emigration, socio-economic issues arising from the existence of two large Estonian-speaking and Russian-speaking language groups, the rural-urban divide and its small domestic market. Overall, we found Estonia's digitised society and smart e-Governance approach exemplary for both digital latecomers and the leaders of "smart" nations.

While both Germany and Estonia are confronted with an increasingly volatile and uncertain environment characterised by cyber warfare (e.g. to hobble competitors), a large number of non-citizens (with associated growing anti-immigrant sentiments in the German case) and a trend towards national introspection, the visits confirmed that digitalisation continues to create a swell of change that needs to be managed sustainably.

(The Business Times, 1 December 2018)

How Sending E-mails Compares with Carbon Emission of Car Use

Digital natives can reduce their carbon footprint by being conscious about Internet usage.

Ever wondered how your emails may contribute to your personal carbon footprint? According to estimates published in Phys.org, sending a short email adds about four grammes of CO_2 equivalent (gCO_2e) to the atmosphere (an email with a long attachment has a 10-fold carbon footprint, i.e. 50 gCO_2e!).

The carbon output of 65 emails is comparable to driving a mid-sized sedan passenger (petrol) car for about one kilometre. After five workdays, your 325 emails would have pumped out at least 1.3 kilogramme of CO_2 into the atmosphere. Over a year, your emails would have contributed quite drastically to the global greenhouse effect and indirectly to global warming.

This is indeed "An Inconvenient Truth", as explained in the 2006 Oscar-winning environmental documentary film by Davis Guggenheim featuring former US Vice President Al Gore who triggered a global movement against the climate crisis.

As citizens of a "smart nation" undergoing digital transformation, and as consumers of digital products and services, are we knowledgeable about what is at stake?

According to Singapore's National Climate Change Secretariat, Singapore's "business-as-usual emissions" are estimated to amount to 77.2 million tonnes (MT) in 2020 (Singapore contributes around 0.11% of global emissions).

Climate change affects Singapore through rising annual mean temperatures — from 26.6°C in 1972 to 27.7°C in 2014. In addition, there is an increased mean sea level in the Straits of Singapore at the rate of 1.2 mm to 1.7 mm per year between 1975 and 2009, and an uptrend in annual average rainfall from 2192 mm in 1980 to 2727 mm in 2014. Not surprisingly, residents have noticed increased episodes of flash floods, all exemplifying some of the effects of climate change on this island nation.

From 2019, the Ministry of Finance will introduce a new carbon tax to steer Singapore's transformation towards a low-carbon economy.

Facilities emitting 25,000 tCO_2e or more of GHG emissions annually will be taxed at $5/$tCO_2e$ (beyond 2023, the tax may be doubled to $10/$tCO_2e$).

The first carbon tax payment will be due in 2020, based on emissions in 2019. It will be interesting to see how effective the new policy will be in convincing private and public organisations that digital products are neither "carbon light" nor "low-impact", and that we are all accountable for the emissions.

Whether new carbon cost-related financial regulations or a formal ISO 14064 Carbon Emission Reduction Validation programme will effectively nudge stakeholders to adopt greener energy sources remains to be seen.

An interesting challenge for educators is to create buy-in for the concept of digital sustainability among a generation of digital natives who contribute quite significantly to the problem of "Internet pollution".

Sending short messages, using photo and video-sharing social networking services and searching the internet requires electrical energy which in turn causes a negative environmental impact. According to BBC's Science Focus, the internet is responsible for roughly one billion tonne of greenhouse gases a year, or around two per cent of world emissions. In 2017, Facebook (which has made a long-term commitment to be 100% renewably powered), with a total of 2.2 billion social network users, registered 979,000 metric tons of carbon dioxide equivalent (MT CO_2e).

What about streaming videos? Netflix itself also said in 2014 that in delivering its service, its average customer had a carbon footprint of 300g per year. It has since made its service carbon neutral; however, this does not factor in the power used by the devices when content is consumed. The carbon challenge of social media will no doubt further intensify with the rising number of users, which is expected to exceed 3 billion by 2021.

Powered by big data centres that house computing, server and networking equipment, the rapidly increasing volume of digital transactions is arguably not sustainable given their large carbon footprint.

While there is a trend towards reducing the energy usage in data centres and evaluating their energy sources in favour of green(er) cloud-based hosting solutions, it requires more thinking to find ways to nudge individuals into concrete behavioural change to reduce carbon emissions as much as possible, and offset as much carbon pollution as they emit.

One classroom approach is to use social norms to alter behaviour. Research has shown that informing people about their own energy use as compared to nearby residents (and how they can decrease energy consumption) can lead to significant long-term reduction in energy consumption to more sustainable levels. Imagine the behavioural and public relations impact if we begin to rank organisations by their carbon emissions.

Another educational strategy is to use a carbon footprint calculator to estimate one's own GHG emission level in comparison to one's peers. Better still if that can calculate emissions generated as a result of activities like watching YouTube, driving Mum's car to school or using Scoot for a weekend trip to Bali, and can tell users what it takes in terms of tree planting or financial contributions to carbon-offsetting foundations to effectively offset them.

Yet another tactic to obtain buy-in is to refer back to the early (and visibly very successful) tree-planting initiative of Singapore's founding prime minister, the late Mr Lee Kuan Yew, which began with him planting a mempat tree in Farrer Circus in 1963 that catalysed Singapore becoming a green "City in a Garden".

Any discussion about digital sustainability must go beyond meeting the digital needs of the contemporary generation. In order not to compromise the ability of future generations to meet their own needs, we need to act now and reduce the greenhouse effect which is warming Planet Earth.

Start small — change your email habits by unsubscribing from all the financial market news that you do not read, and skip that non-essential internet search (0.2 gCO_2e on an energy-efficient laptop and 4.5 gCO_2e on an old desktop computer).

Or be bolder — calculate your personal carbon footprint and plant a tree. A Poplar tree, for example, can absorb about 300kg of CO_2 and offset 1,000 air miles.

As the proverb goes — "The best time to plant a tree was 20 years ago. The second best time is now".

(The Straits Times, 15 November 2018)

The AI Way to Cleaner Air for Smart Cities

The use of deep technology and innovation such as AI for cleaner, greener environments is one area where Singapore can excel.

With Kan Siew Ning and Eugene K. B. Tan

The prospects look promising for the deployment of artificial intelligence (AI) in the quest for a clean and liveable environment in urban settings. The use of deep technology and innovation such as AI is one area where Singapore can excel while also being the ideal test bed for such experimentation.

One of the salient points in Finance Minister Heng Swee Keat's recent Budget 2019 speech was the emphasis on a smart, green and liveable city. In particular, the Budget makes specific reference to "emissions abatement".

The government expects to collect carbon tax revenues of nearly S$1 billion in the first five years of its implementation. But, and more importantly, it is also prepared to spend an amount more than tax revenue collected "to support worthwhile projects which deliver the necessary abatement in emissions".

This fiscal nudge is timely because reducing emissions intensity and volume will lower particulate air pollution and simultaneously create beneficial health risk reductions.

Particulate matter (PM), many of which are hazardous, refers to the sum of all solid and liquid particles suspended in air. This includes organic and inorganic particles, such as dust, pollen, soot ("black carbon"), smoke, and liquid droplets.

PM-induced pollution can result in chronic bronchitis or asthma and premature deaths as a result of cardiovascular problems or a stroke. PM2.5, for example, are inhalable pollutant particles measuring 2.5 microns and smaller in diameter — about a 30th the diameter of a human hair. These ultrafine particles are perilous because they can lead to a variety of health issues such as reduced lung function. Some may even be absorbed into the bloodstream.

The economic cost of particulate air pollution on health in Singapore is substantial. An earlier study conducted by economists Euston Quah and Wai-Mun Chia estimated the total health costs associated with particulate matter in the air at US$3.75 billion or about 2.04% of Singapore's GDP in 2009.

Vehicles represent a major source of particulate matter besides carbon dioxide and other tailpipe pollutants, such as carbon monoxide, hydrocarbons and nitrogen oxides. According to data by the World Health Organisation, 92% of the world's population live in places where air quality levels exceed WHO limits, resulting in millions of deaths every year. In 2012, 6.5 million deaths (or 11.6% of all global deaths) were associated with indoor and outdoor air pollution according to WHO estimates.

While more cities are now vigorously monitoring air pollution, comprehensive and actionable baseline data for monitoring progress in combatting it are not always available. Measurements are often done selectively based on a limited number of measurement stations.

This makes it difficult to get reliable and valid environmental data, for example, about the sources of contaminants that could inform better policy-making for greener cities on the basis of real 24/7 insights. Reducing harmful emissions and clean air predictions require precise, intelligent and actionable measurement systems.

This is a pain point that can be addressed by harnessing the power of sensor technologies, Internet of things (IoT) and artificial intelligence. Through the computation of real-time IoT sensor data (with detailed spatial and temporal pollutant measurements) obtained from various sources such as ground-based sensor units and commercial satellites, user-friendly air quality heat maps and executive dashboards can be created (such as with the help of machine learning algorithms for predictive modelling) to determine the most severe pollution hotspots in order to take proactive steps towards further decarbonising the economy.

Examples of important use cases include tackling specific areas with higher concentrations of pollutants or leveraging (anonymous) crowdsourced sensor data from cell phones to localise parts of the city which are harmful, with the aim of reducing one's own exposure to PM. Entrepreneurs keen to monetise air pollution data are well advised to do so on the basis of a digitalised business model that uses AI algorithms for creating green(er) and (more) liveable cities with better air quality via real-time assessment and management of outdoor air.

To stay ahead in the smart city race in an era of AI-enabled smart (urban) solutions, civil engineers, planners, regulators and green start-ups keen to fight against air pollution should possess basic AI know-how and know-why, over and above their expertise and experience in developing land use plans, revitalising urban precincts, making infrastructure services more accessible to disadvantaged segments of the population or creating a scalable business model.

Smart city development programmes will have to be quickly rebooted with an AI advantage in order to leverage new digital technologies, big-data analytics, and cloud computing for cleaner air and better public health. AI is arguably the new frontier of instrumented, environmentally friendly smart city initiatives.

AI-powered computer vision analytics with facial detection systems, in combination with environmental sensors mounted on smart lamp posts, for example, could enable authorities to identify in real time where exactly air pollution occurs, who is causing it, and where remedial and preventive action is required.

As these systems are able to index faces to determine gender, race and age, as well as perform facial matching against databases, rule violations may become a thing of the past provided the ethics of such surveillance is feasible, guaranteed, and accepted.

Current technological advances in the area of AI-enabled smart city systems suggest that intelligent air quality management systems may soon become fully autonomous in making decisions, for example, remotely turning off the (combustion) engine of a self-driving car which is polluting the environment.

The possibilities of smart, AI-enabled "emissions abatements" are indeed endless. Singapore should seek a first-mover advantage through large-scale deployment. The demand for clean, green, and liveable cities is growing in tandem with the deep concern over climate change and how it intimately affects the health of people and the living environment.

Emission abatements will require companies to respond to this massive societal challenge in a purposeful manner. It is also the ethical and socially responsible thing to do with significant benefits beyond the health outcomes and economic well-being. Companies have to reduce their environmental footprint, with governments and consumers requiring they do more to account for the negative externalities their business activities generate.

AI-powered emissions abatement can be a powerful lever towards an empirically-based targeted approach to dealing with environmental pollution and better public health. Singapore can and should exploit this window of opportunity to be a policy- and thought-leader in emissions abatement while spawning technological innovations to power the environmental drive.

(Business Times, 6 March 2019)

"Are We Ready for Climate Change?": Learning from Sustainable Universities

By Sarah Woon, Natasha Lian, Alex Koh, Seah Yi Shan and Jacie Lim

Climate change has been and continues to be a pressing issue for countries around the world. Its implications are pervasive and greatly threatens the livelihood and safety of humanity. Recognizing the depth that these problems could pose to Singapore, the Government has put in place several initiatives to combat climate change. Working through six broad segments — transport, industry, waste and water, households, buildings, and power — specific initiatives have been introduced to work collectively toward building a more planet-friendly Singapore. Under "Transport", for instance, there have been plans to double the network of cycling paths by 2030 and phase out combustion vehicles by 2040.

As a result, Singapore ranks one of the lowest in carbon dioxide emissions per dollar of economic output. Singaporeans also seemingly display a strong willingness (78.2% of respondents) to play their part towards offsetting their carbon emission contributions, according to the National Climate Change Secretariat (NCCS).

While many local universities have committed to and made progress in achieving their sustainability goals, these commitments, however, largely remain at an institutional level. On the ground, greater efforts can definitely be made towards encouraging behavioural changes that espouse sustainable practices. For this to be possible, taking stronger climate action needs to also be seen as an individual responsibility rather than just an institutional one.

The Singapore Management University (SMU) for instance, has achieved a 30% decrease in energy consumption and 18% decrease in water usage despite its student population doubling between 2006 and 2017. The university's dedication to its sustainability goals was also recognised as a recipient of the Building and Construction Authority (BCA) Green Mark Platinum status, one of the highest attainable levels. While this sets SMU on track to meet its sustainability goals of a 40% and 30% reduction in energy intensity and water usage respectively, climate action on an individual level remains limited.

One need only look to some of the world's leading schools to see how climate-conscious practices can be systematically ingrained into a school's culture and values.

Oxford University, having received several sustainability accreditations, is highly recognised for its climate change schemes. The college provides robust coverage of its environmental policies and performance on its Sustainability website, which is host to extensive reports on carbon emissions, food wastage and more. Students are actively encouraged to participate in the school's climate change efforts through a whole slew of creative initiatives: *Green Impact*, for example, is an engagement program which groom students into ambassadors for sustainable living. Oxford also runs *Student Switch Off*, an inter-college competition which encourages energy reduction and recycling habits. Community collaboration is similarly promoted through platforms such as the *Waste Action Reuse Portal* (WARPit!), an online resource-redistribution network allowing students and staff to upload images of unwanted school resources for other departments to claim.

Indeed, the key to the success of green initiatives appears to lie in the active engagement of the student body. UC Davis, an exemplar for campus sustainability, often hosts collaborative student-led green initiatives that weave sustainability efforts into the fabric of the student's overall university education. The university offers diverse internship opportunities to students interested in spearheading innovative sustainability initiatives in the school. Through working with the university's in-house Energy & Engineering team, students are given the liberty to choose a variety of roles ranging from communications to engineering and building-design. UC Davis also commits to nurturing and empowering students to become sustainability leaders: the Green Initiative Fund, for example, was elected to offer financial support to the UC Davis community to develop and launch initiatives benefiting the campus or neighbouring vicinities. These efforts have had a positive influence on the student body, hence, it is no wonder that UC Davis boasts a leading position in the world, and in the US, for campus sustainability.

Looking back to current local practices, there is still much that local universities can draw from our international counterparts. Indeed, many of our local practices are limited to the infrastructure of the campus. At best, they consist of ad-hoc activities that only engage students who are already interested and invested in contributing to environmental sustainability. However, stronger action must be taken across the board to reap tangible benefits from these efforts through education, engagement, and empowerment.

Firstly, students must be educated about the importance of environmental efforts and persuaded to be involved in such efforts. Once they have been educated, the school can then engage them through consistent initiatives and activities. This way, environmental efforts can become a sustainable part of the students' lives, and students will also buy into this vision. Finally, once they are invested and involved in the cause, students must be empowered to champion the cause themselves by running their own projects and initiatives.

Apart from the students, universities should also involve the faculty and staff, who comprise a significant portion of stakeholders. This can encourage environmentally-friendly behaviour in using university resources, and also more environmentally-conscious usage of campus facilities.

Having established potential areas for growth in the current approach, it is clear that there is still much to be done in sustainability efforts by local universities. With a more holistic approach to encouraging climate action, universities will also be able to build a generation of leaders who see the value of protecting the environment and her resources for many more generations to come. With this, efforts will not only be more tangible and effective, but forward-looking and enduring as well.

Drones over Singaporean Heritage Sites: Exploring the Potential of Small UAVs (Drones) for Educational Smart City Projects and Heritage Preservation

Project Background and Key Activities

Due to rapid technological developments in the area of unmanned aerial vehicles (UAVs), the application of UAVs is becoming increasingly popular in heritage management projects. Examples include the visual documentation and inspection of standing monuments such as lighthouses or the detection of subsurface archaeological remains (e.g. Deng, 2018).

While Asian countries arguably lag behind the UK or the USA in leveraging UAVs for such purposes, more and more local government agencies are tapping into unmanned aerial vehicles (UAVs) for various purposes. In Singapore, for example, authorities such as MPA & PSA are experimenting with water spider drones to assess oil spills; the Singapore Civil Defence Force is utilising drones for developing safer and more efficient fire-fighting approaches; Singapore's National Environment Agency is exploring how this technology can be used for monitoring mosquito breeding grounds. Local institutions of higher learning have also started to utilize drones as "pedagogical tools" both in the classroom and outdoors as exemplified by NUS' (National University of Singapore) drone delivery test bed co-funded by Airbus.

A central element of our initiatives is to conduct effective teaching and learning projects (Brown, 2006) with low altitude drones (Birtchnell and Gibson, 2015; Church, 2015; Graves, 2016; Mirot and Klein, 2014; Wolpert-Gawron, 2015; Zuger, 2016; Menkhoff et al., 2017) aimed at integrating aerial images of selected heritage sites and identity nodes captured through a small (DJI Spark) drone and its camera in addition to Google earth maps, historical pictures and maps in an attractive "before-and-after" media format for students.

Drones over Singaporean Heritage Sites — Core Project Activities

- Examining the potential of small drones for educational smart city capstone projects at tertiary level aimed at supporting students in appreciating the importance of Singapore's built heritage and identity nodes;
- Conducting teaching experiments with low altitude drones aimed at integrating aerial images captured through the drone's camera and other types of media via pedagogical capstone projects in order to motivate more students to appreciate their own "urban" heritage and acknowledge the necessity for active heritage preservation;
- Supporting Singapore's (heritage-related) smart nation aspirations by conducting learning projects with emphasis on "historical place evolution" on the basis of images taken by drones, Google earth maps, old pictures/maps etc. (and transforming these visuals into novel and effective "historical place evolution templates" aimed at contributing to building Singaporeans' sense of belonging and identity).

We believe that newly created ("before-and-after") visuals (different from and better than existing resources due to their time-dynamic nature covering the past, current era and future) arising from the project will motivate students to appreciate and safeguard Singapore's urban heritage since they have been actively involved in their creation.

The teaching and learning media (time-lapse) outcomes created by the projects with the help of MapKnitter (a free, open source tool for combining and positioning images into a composite image map, a process known as "orthorectification" or "georectification"), Adobe Photoshop, Adobe Movie Maker, Gawker, etc. will enable students to explain both the historical and policy dimensions of (smart) place making vis-à-vis the stages of Singapore's nation-building and development process (Kong, 2009; Lee Beard, 2011).

Project activities center around a "before-and-after" visualisation approach so that learners can acknowledge the role of active heritage preservation with regard to area conservation or revitalisation of "old" places as means to enrich "the character of places where we live, work, and play". By knitting and overlaying various materials from different eras, students can internalise how places changed over time which in turn helps them to acknowledge the necessity for active heritage (Kohn, 2017) preservation in a "smart" city.

Project Sites

- Tanjung Rhu
- SMU at Bras Basah (incl. Fort Canning Hill)
- Lorong Halus Wetland, a former landfill in the eastern part of Singapore
- Bidadari Estate (a former burial site)

Project Tasks and Plans

- Documental and pictorial research in NLB/National Archives and on site (selected heritage sites and identity nodes)
- Drone photography (e.g. with Spark Drone)
- Use of MapKnitting with MapKnitter software[2]
- Media integration with Photoshop, etc.

---

[2]https://mapknitter.org/.

By integrating aerial images of these sites taken by drones and historical images cum old maps and future designs, the project will result in "historical place evolution templates" to be used in various SMU course initiatives in support of Singapore's smart nation and national heritage management thrusts. Through drone and maps-enabled georectification processes and before-and-after visualizations, students will appreciate the historical evolution of sites and places over time and draw conclusions with regard to the various stages of Singapore's development and respective place cum urban development concerns.

The end product are media-based "historical place evolution templates", i.e. new types of "before-and-after" teaching media that can be used in various course initiatives at tertiary level in support of Singapore's smart nation and national heritage management thrusts. A related learning outcome is that students as "digital natives" (Bennett *et al.*, 2007) internalise and explain how heritage contributes to building a sense of belonging and that "smart" urban planning is a key enabler for that.

> *Places of national heritage and our national monuments are central to the nation's identity and collective memory. However, as feelings of belonging and social identity can also be found in local and everyday places, more effort will be made to showcase vernacular heritage within our towns. Elements of local history and heritage will be woven into the design and development of the built environment, helping to preserve and enhance local identity, allowing future generations to learn and understand the local histories of their neighbourhoods (URA*).*[3]

Future-Proofing University Students with "Drones for 'Smart' City Projects"

Drones are unmanned, multi-purpose tools (Ball, 2015). Their history can be traced back to World War I when the US army experimented with unmanned aerial torpedos. Nowadays, drone technology belongs to the military arsenal of many nations. Drones serve many purposes (intelligence, surveillance, reconnaissance, traffic, and crowed management, etc.), and they can be deadly. In business and society, drones are utilised

---

[3] https://www.ura.gov.sg/Corporate/Planning/Master-Plan/Key-Focuses/Identity/Local-Identity.

to capture images of people and/or buildings, to monitor agricultural conditions, to take pictures from (or of) hard to reach places, to assess the impact of climate change on rainforests, to film events, to deliver parcels, to survey real estate, to deliver help to heart attack victims in remote areas via a flying defibrillator or to fly life-saving kits to swimmers in emergency situations.

In view of their increasing importance in terms of commercial value creation, R&D (it is estimated that about US$6.4 billion is spent annually for R&D on drones), job creation, innovation (e.g. Internet of Things), new forms of warfare as well as legal/moral-ethical/regulatory concerns, it is imperative that students learn to critically appreciate the multiple and often conflicting implications and consequences of this technology for business and society. Estimates by consulting firms suggest that the global market for commercial drone technology applications alone (which currently stands at about US$2 billion) will increase to about US$120 billion by 2020 as a result of regulatory progress for UAV operations, effective legislation, lower costs and new, innovative business models.

Research on how drones could be used for communication and audience building/engagement by heritage institutions is scarce as this PhD research call by University College London (Institute for Sustainable Heritage) suggests.[4]

Looking forward, it is planned to show on the basis of the proposed project activities how drones can be used in support of selected smart city dimensions (Taylor *et al.*, 2015; Foo and Pan, 2016). Table 1 presents some application examples (Mohammed *et al.*, 2014) based on the dimensions of the European smart city model.

One of the basic premises of the smart city discourse (Menkhoff *et al.* eds., 2018) is the notion that "smart cities" can and should use information and communication technologies so as to become more intelligent and efficient in the use of resources with more efficient services for their citizens and a higher quality of life. Examples of applied drone pilot projects in Singapore include (i) the research-driven, multi-data approach by the Future Cities Laboratory (FCL) of the Singapore-ETH Centre to create reality-based 3D models of very high quality, using drone photogrammetry; (ii) efforts by the URA to capture aerial images and videos of Jurong Lake District and the Rail Corridor so that stakeholders can better visualise and assess future development plans; (iii) safer and more

---

[4]https://www.findaphd.com/search/projectdetails.aspx?PJID=95888.

Table 1:   Drones for Smart Cities — Application Examples

Smart City Dimensions	
Economy	**Mobility**
• Track food crops (precision vertical agriculture)	• Ensuring railway safety
• Survey landscapes for risk assessment (insurance)	• Traffic and crowd management
• Building maintenance (construction industry)	• Delivery of medical or logistical supplies (e.g. to secluded areas)
Environment	**People**
• Aerial mapping and nature monitoring	• Urban security (medical, search & rescue, firefighting)
• Natural disaster control and monitoring	• Geospatial activities/aerial photography (urban planning, media)
• Assessing impact of environmental disasters	• Drone racing (entertainment, tourism)
Living	**Governance**
• Provision of internet access to rural areas	• "Test-bedding" a safe drone test flight zone
• Energy provision for secluded areas	• Monitor traffic congestion
• Leisure activities	• Public safety and border control

efficient fire-fighting approaches by the Singapore Civil Defence Force; (iv) the use of aerial and terrestrial drones as waiters in restaurants; (v) commercial photography and recreation, and (vi) environmental monitoring and infrastructure inspection, e.g. in the oil & gas sector.

Acquisition of Multidisciplinary Skills through "Drones for a Smart City Project"

In an earlier paper, we have reported multidisciplinary teaching and learning experiences made during the implementation of two newly developed courses entitled "Innovations for Asia's Smart Cities" and "Understanding Drone & Robotics Technology — History, Usage, Ethics & Legal Issues" taught at an Asian university (Menkhoff *et al.*, 2017). Feedback by students enrolled in these course (comments: "interesting", "fun drone flying lesson", "more activities outdoor and less in class teaching", "too many essays to cover", "thinking out of the box and making things happen") as well as their final project presentations in class suggest that an integrated, multidisciplinary teaching and learning approach in conjunction with interesting expert presentations, site visits and relevant project assignments do indeed enable a deep(er) learning experience, e.g. when it comes to appreciating the impact of new technologies on business and society in general and smart cities in particular (Table 2).

In the areas of unmanned aerial vehicles, robotics, and A.I., there is a lot of scope for inter-disciplinary collaboration and mixed teams (Morris, 2015; Menkhoff *et al.*, 2018). Social science students can provide the background on how "social" a robot needs to be. Engineering students can build the mechanical movements controlled by electrical signals and A.I. with speech recognition software developed by information technology students. Business management students can find creative ways to market new types of robots (e.g. social robots) but having to first appreciate the technical details, market opportunities and societal concerns with a novel technology. Having a mixed group of students representing different disciplines can help to avoid blind spots such as difficulties to realistically assess the (future) commercial value of this new technology in view of current weaknesses and threats such as regulations, fear of (technology) failure, and inadequate attention to ethical concerns. A similar case could be made for the strengths of inter-disciplinary collaboration and mixed teams in a course with a focus on heritage preservation (Lawson and Holton, 2016).

By spending considerable time writing individual (course topic related) essays, getting exposure to the knowledge needs of "real" clients out there such as NHB or URA as well as R&D activities in the field of robotics or interacting with drone entrepreneurs as part of their project works, students (i) learn to connect the dots, (ii) have a good learning experience, (iii) are able to assess future tech trends and their impact on business and society more deeply, (iv) gain confidence in their own coping abilities cum competencies, and (v) manage to contextualize the respective course topics and how they are embedded in the wider sociotechnical context locally and globally.

Appreciating the Impact of Past "Place-making" Endeavors of Singapore Agencies on Urban Development through Educational UAV Projects

The novel didactical approach of creating aerial photographs and utilizing old/contemporary maps cum historical photographs of "heritage sites"

Table 2:   Strategic Work Skills Acquisition through a "Drones for a Smart City" Project

Future Work Skills	Multidisciplinarity	Novel & Adaptive Thinking Skills	Real Work Exposure	Managing Collaboration with Industry Partners
Drone — enabled aerial photography of the annual Thaipusam event when participants carry "kavadis" along a processional route as part of a penance to Lord Murugan	The collaboration between students from the social sciences, business and technology & design schools in preparing the flight path and post-procession analysis of images can result in a win-win situation with tangible, multi-disciplinary knowledge and competency gains for all participants.	"Good" aerial photography with hi-tech cameras mounted on drones represents a new and increasingly popular technological trend. Mastering the theory and practice of this requires innovative and adaptive thinking skills in order to anticipate how best to create real value for "consumers" such as the National Heritage Board, urban planners or the police.	"Mastering" drone-enabled aerial photography of the annual Thaipusam event would help students to appreciate the challenges urban authorities are facing in planning, approving and monitoring such (ethnic) crowd events, incl. the importance of guaranteeing urban security of big public events vis-à-vis the importance of city branding.	Potential collaboration partners include National Heritage Board, Land Transport Authority, Singapore Police Force etc.

(seamlessly integrated through "MapKnitting" and other types of software like Adobe Photoshop) produces new sorts of "before-and-after" pedagogical visualization templates that enable students to reconstruct "place evolution" from the past to the contemporary era.

An example is the transformation of Singapore's Tanjong Rhu shipyards into a private residential area with waterfront condominiums such as the Water Place or Pebble Bay which served as place-making project assignment for student groups in a recent drone course supplemented by the sourcing of historical photographs from the Singapore's National Library Board (NLB).

Post course evaluations and informal discussions with students suggest that such projects give students a better understanding and appreciation of past urban redevelopment projects. Without such a UAV project, students would not have taken the time to reflect on urban developments but simply take the progress of the area (nation) at face value. UAV projects support students in achieving a greater understanding of the sheer scale of past redevelopment projects via aerial elements. On a more critical note, it arguably may make sense to ask learners to document physical planning induced changes over a longer time span so as to visualise Singapore's modernization and rapid change from Third to First world.

Another interesting case site is the former Lorong Halus dumping ground. Until its closure in 1999, it was a smelly dump. A part of the area has been developed into "man-made wildlife sanctuary", the Lorong Halus Wetland. Despite the obvious signs of human intervention, the area (including that beyond the sanctuary) does have an aesthetic value from a natural environment (albeit man made) perspective, and offers that escape that can be hard to find in an island overgrown with too much concrete".[5]

It is envisaged that students who will produce and watch the drone-enabled media story about the "evolution" of Lorong Halus Wetland will not only acknowledge past place-making endeavours of Singapore agencies but also develop (more) empathy towards the challenges Singaporeans are facing with regard to the appreciation of sustainability issues in general and the "preservation of sites" in particular by agencies such as URA or NHB in a rapidly modernizing and developing nation.

---

[5] https://thelongnwindingroad.wordpress.com/tag/lorong-halus-landfill/.

Besides document-related research, recce visits of heritage sites and identity nodes as well as the actual drone-based project implementation, students conduct evaluative research qua interviews with various stakeholders in support of the course objectives.

A similar approach will be adopted to enable students to appreciate the interesting story of the Bidadari Cemetery vis-à-vis selected heritage and identity aspects of "Singaporean life" from its early beginnings to HDB's current housing projects.

Conclusion

In this chapter, we reported experiences gained in ongoing smart city-related teaching and learning projects at SMU that utilize small drones (UAVs) aimed at enabling students to appreciate the importance of Singapore's urban heritage in general and past urban planning efforts in particular. The project idea was triggered by various questions such as:

(i) To what extent can research and teaching experiments with low altitude drones aimed at integrating aerial images captured through the drone's camera and other types of media via pedagogical projects motivate more students to appreciate their own "urban" heritage and acknowledge the necessity for active heritage preservation?

(ii) How can aerial images collected by small drones in combination with other "before-and-after" visuals (e.g. contemporary Google maps or old images of sites kept at the National Archives) support Singapore's smart nation aspirations with emphasis on appreciating national heritage sites and urban redevelopment efforts?

(iii) To what extent does students' active involvement in a technology-rich learning environment (featuring small drones) with a historical place-making component qua Map-Knitting software, Adobe Movie Maker, etc. enable them to acknowledge the importance of heritage in building a sense of belonging and identity as well as the outcomes of past physical development efforts?

By integrating aerial images of selected urban sites taken by drones and overlaying them with historical images cum old maps and present/

future designs, the projects can be instrumental in creating novel "historical place evolution templates" that can be used in higher educational courses to impart critical (future ready) work skills into students in support of "smart city" and national heritage development cum management thrusts. Examples of acquired competencies include multidisciplinarity, novel & adaptive thinking skills as well as collaboration skills.

Capturing and analyzing aerial images of "real" sites with UAVs can help learners to appreciate the importance of nature monitoring and urban (spatial) change by comparing the results with old maps/pics. We posit that students' active involvement in a technology-rich learning environment with a historical place-making component helps them to acknowledge how critical heritage and "good" urban planning are in building a sense of belonging in a "smart", livable city.

Informal student feedback suggests that drone-centric courses with focus on urban development issues add value as the UAV technology is "still not really understood by many". Project outcomes suggest that course content and class discussions contributed to a better understanding and grasp of the "UAVs for urban development" topic.

Small UAV projects ensure that students appreciate past urban redevelopment efforts because they are forced to reconstruct the evolution of sites from the 1960s to the current era with the help of various media. Without such a aerial-historical component, they would not have taken the time to reflect on past urban development initiatives but simply take the nation's progress for granted.

While the overall teaching and learning experiences in our ongoing course initiatives have been positive, it should be highlighted that continuous skills upgrading with regard to technology-enhanced learning and teaching (Hare *et al.*, 2011; Gan *et al.*, 2015) is indispensable, especially for more or less tech-savvy instructors who belong to the baby boomer generation.

Obtaining funding for the purchase of "real" drones for outdoor (e.g. smart city-related) class activities, to obtain "flight permission" for UAV flights in a high-rise environment and to establish collaborative ties to lecturers from other disciplines to ensure deep (e.g. UAV tech) learning are other issues. The combined expertise of engineering/IT, strategic business management, social sciences, ethics, organisational psychology, and law on the basis of a multi-disciplinary teaching and learning agenda are required to make our students future-ready.

References

Ball, L. (2015). Rise of the machines: Can drones change the face of air logistics? *Air Cargo World, 18*(8), 32–34, 40. Retrieved from http://libproxy.smu.edu.sg/login?url=http://search.proquest.com/docview/1732269 305?accountid=28662.

Bennett, S., Maton, K. & L. Kervin (2007). The "digital natives" debate: A critical review of the evidence. *British Journal of Educational Technology, 39*(5), 775–786.

Birtchnell, T. & Gibson, C. (2015). Less talk more drone: Social research with UAVs. *Journal of Geography in Higher Education, 39*(1), 182–189 DOI:10.1080/03098265.2014.1003799. Retrieved from http://dx.doi.org. libproxy.smu.edu.sg/10.1080/03098265.2014.1003799.

Brown, J. S. (2006). New learning environments for the 21st century: Exploring the edge. *Change, 38*(5), 18–24.

Church, J. (2015). A Bird's Eye View: Photogrammetric Documentation using Drones. Retrieved from https://www.ncptt.nps.gov/blog/a-birds-eye-view-photogrammetric-documentation-using-drones/.

Deng, I. (2018). China's crumbling Great Wall is getting some hi-tech conservation help from drones. http://www.scmp.com/tech/enterprises/article/2144222/chinas-crumbling-great-wall-getting-some-hi-tech-conservation-help.

Foo, S. L. & G. Pan (2016). Singapore's vision of a smart nation. *Asian Management Insights, 3*(1), 76–82.

Gan, B., Menkhoff, T. & R. Smith (2015). Enhancing students' learning process through interactive digital media: New opportunities for collaborative learning. *Computers in Human Behavior, 51*, 652–663.

Graves, B. (2016). Miniature drone takes teaching code to new heights. *San Diego Business Journal, 37*(12), 4. Retrieved from http://libproxy.smu.edu.sg/login?url=http://search.proquest.com/docview/1784163513?accountid=28662.

Hare, J. C., Ault, M. & C. Niileksela (2011). The influence of technology-rich learning environments: A classroom-based observation study. *Technology and Teacher Education Annual, 8*, 4304–4311.

Kohn, J. (2017). Drone Preservation of Cultural Heritage Architecture in Texas. Retrieved from https://www.linkedin.com/pulse/drone-preservation-cultural-heritage-architecture-texas-jonathan-kohn.

Kong, L. (2009). Making sustainable creative/cultural space in Shanghai and Singapore. *Geographical Review, 99*(1), 1–22.

Lawson, S. & A. Holton (2016). Collaboration and Innovation: Welcoming Drones and Emerging Technology into Higher Education [YouTube Video]: Keynote Address given at 2016 Symposium on Emerging Technology Trends in Higher Education. Retrieved from https://youtu.be/kOidMylmTPo.

Lee Beard, D. (2011). Creating Time Lapse Videos and Converting for PowerPoint Ep.144. Retrieved from https://www.youtube.com/watch?v=MR3FcePQ1u0.

Menkhoff, T., Tan, E., Kan S. N., Tan, G. H. & Pan, G. (2017). Tapping Drone Technology to Acquire 21st Century Skills: A Smart City Approach. Paper presented at the 1st IEEE International Conference on Smart City Innovations (IEEE SCI 2017), August 4–8, 2017, San Francisco, USA.

Menkhoff, T. *et al.* (2017). Drones, AI and getting undergrads ready for great disruption. The Straits Times, 22 February 2017, p. A20.

Menkhoff, T. *et al.* (2018). *Living in Smart Cities: Innovation and Sustainability.* World Scientific Publishing.

Menkhoff, T., Tan, E., Kan S. N., Tan, G. H. & Pan, G. (2018). Strategic 21st Century Work Skills Acquisition through Smart City and Drone Technology: An Exploratory Perspective, In Thomas Menkhoff, Kan Siew Ning, Hans-Dieter Evers and Chay Yue Wah (eds.), *Living in Smart Cities: Innovation and Sustainability*, World Scientific Publishing, 2018, pp. 281–301.

Mirot, A. & Klein, J. (2014). Using the AR.drone to implement model-based learning. *Journal of Applied Learning Technology*, *4*(2), 34–39. Retrieved from http://search.ebscohost.com.libproxy.smu.edu.sg/login.aspx?direct=true&db=ehh&AN=97479499&site=ehost-live&scope=site.

Mohammed, F., Idries, A., Mohamed, N. & Jawhar, I. (2014). UAVs for Smart Cities: Opportunities and Challenges. Paper presented at the 2014 International Conference on Unmanned Aircraft Systems (ICUAS), May 27–30, Orlando, Florida. Retrieved from https://www.researchgate.net/publication/269299864_UAVs_for_smart_cities_Opportunities_and_challenges.

Morris, L. (2015). On or coming to your campus soon: Drones. *Innovative Higher Education*, *40*(3), 187–189. Retrieved from http://link.springer.com.libproxy.smu.edu.sg/article/10.1007/s10755-015-9323-x.

Taylor, S., Zook, M. & A. Wiig (2015). The "actually existing smart city". *Cambridge Journal of Regions, Economy and Society*, *8*, 13–25.

Wolpert-Gawron, H. (2015). Drones Can Be Fun — and Educational/Check out a variety of ways schools might use drones as a teaching. Retrieved from https://www.edutopia.org/blog/7-ways-use-drones-classroom-heather-wolpert-gawron.

Zuger, S. (2016). Drones: These Classes Fly By. *Technology & Learning*, *36*(10), 39–40. Retrieved from http://www.techlearning.com/resources/0003/drones-these-classes-fly-by/70018.

Enabling Singapore's Youths to Adapt in an Era of Climate Change

With Mark Chong and Benjamin Kok Siew Gan

Nudging them towards more eco-friendly behavioural habits is arguably a feasible approach to build greater climate resilience

In its 2020 government budget, Singapore committed close to S$1 billion for climate change mitigation and adaptation efforts. Key strategic measures to build a low-carbon economy include quadrupling solar energy production by 2025; phasing out internal combustion engine vehicles by 2040; actively investing in low-carbon solutions; and promoting green financing through a US$2 billion Green Investments Programme.

The climate matter is of utmost importance not least because Singapore is heating up twice as fast as the rest of the world — at 0.25 degrees Celsius per decade — according to the Meteorological Service Singapore (MSS). Projections by the Centre for Climate Research Singapore suggest that the city-state could experience an increase in daily mean temperature of 1.4C to 4.6C towards the end of this century.

Climate researchers have attributed Singapore's rising temperatures to both global warming and the Urban Heat Island (UHI) effect. Asphalt and concrete from urban development have replaced greenery and waterways, trapping more heat. The UHI effect (Singapore's Central Region has the highest mean UHI intensity according to research) increases energy costs due to a higher usage of air conditioning, which in turn contributes to air pollution triggered by increased electricity consumption.

The UHI phenomenon reduces thermal comfort and discourages walking or cycling. Besides heat-related illnesses, other climate-related concerns include flash floods and sea level rise. As a low-lying coastal island, Singapore's mean sea level rise is estimated to be up to 1 metre by 2100. MSS data suggest that the average sea level around the island today is 14cm above pre-1970 levels. In view of these challenges, "good" climate education plays an important role in imparting climate resilience to our youths. At SMU, all undergraduates get some exposure to sustainability issues in the course of their university education, particularly via the Core Curriculum's Big Questions and Ethics course, various sustainability-related course initiatives (e.g. SMU's Lee Kong Chian School of Business offers a second major in Sustainability), or the DBS-SMU Sustainability Initiative.

Vision-driven learning outcomes in our own courses on communication, information systems, and smart city management include effective climate change communication so that students understand climate change risks (and *act* on climate change); prototyping mobile applications (Apps) to calculate (and *reduce*) one's carbon footprint or food/water wastage in line with the five R's methodology (refuse, reduce, reuse, repurpose, recycle); and designing (*executing*) appropriate responses to protect oneself from negative climate change consequences.

Through guided educational trips to one of Singapore's waste-to-energy plants (with their huge waste storage bunkers), students see for themselves how the incineration process works with real-time exposure to national waste management issues such as the plastic pollution crisis. Without *actionable climate literacy*, climate change risk perceptions will remain low, and pro-environmental behaviours of students will run into the void.

Moral Persuasion Doesn't Always Work

While our students are generally very obliging and eager to comply with actionable assignments such as measuring the total amount of greenhouse gases that are generated by their actions or explaining the role of carbon pricing for sustaining a green environment, translating concrete offsetting ideas — such as planting trees or mangroves — into reality is tough. Moral persuasion does not always work. Some of the barriers we have come across include competing priorities such as GPA concerns, no real acknowledgement that the climate catastrophe is indeed "real" (it seems inconceivable that the perennial Arctic ice cap has shrunk by more than a million square miles over the past half century), strong system trust in the ability of the government to take care of combatting urban warming, and lack of deep knowledge of local climate impacts and solutions.

Key climate change messages about the risk of global warming (even those formulated by expert panels) don't always work as intended for a number of reasons: First of all, humans suffer from confirmation bias, which is the tendency to seek out and interpret information in a way that confirms our pre-existing opinions, values, and beliefs — it is one of the strongest biases we hold. Conversely, we have a tendency to disregard or ignore information that contradicts or challenges our opinions, values, and beliefs. Another challenge is that our mental models have narrow temporal boundaries and focus on the short term. This short-term focus leads to judgment errors and biases in situations where the consequences of our actions span swathes of space and time.

What then can be done to enable students to better understand what lies ahead in an era of climate change, appreciate the limits of growth, and effect constructive change? Nudging our youths towards more eco-friendly behavioural habits (using fans rather than air-con, walking rather than driving, composting organic waste, harvesting of rainwater, reducing consumption, decreasing social media consumption, etc.) is arguably a feasible approach to build greater climate resilience.

Since Thaler and Sunstein's 2008 publication of *Nudge: Improving Decisions About Health, Wealth, and Happiness*, there has been great interest across public policy domains in what drives the behaviour and decision-making logic of individuals or groups. Instead of traditional compliance methods such as education, legislation, or enforcement, nudging puts emphasis on reinforcement and indirect suggestions as influence strategies.

According to Thaler and Sunstein, a nudge is "any aspect of the choice architecture that alters people's behaviour in a predictable way without forbidding any options or significantly changing their economic incentives". Examples of nudges are the deterrent disease pictures on cigarette packs encouraging smokers to reduce cigarette consumption through emotional responses or the rumble strip on highways that let drivers know if they are drifting out of the lane.

In the context of urban climate change mitigation, nudging can be used to become carbon neutral in support of sustainability and liveability goals, e.g. by influencing commuters so that they modify transport-related choices aimed at minimizing carbon emissions and congestion on the basis of personalised "active" push notifications that nudge them to optimise individual personal (green) routes without getting stuck in traffic.

To be sustainable, successful climate education must be embedded into science-based, experiential teaching and learning approaches on site. Two useful preparatory resources are Al Gore's documentary film *An Inconvenient Truth* (2006) and the author videos featuring Dennis Meadows (emeritus professor of systems policy and social science research at the University of New Hampshire), co-author of the 1972 book *The Limits to Growth* with his concerns for the declining availability of energy, rising disruptions from climate change, falling agricultural yields from loss of arable land, and growing costs of environmental services such as breathable air and survivable temperatures.

Relevant local sites for nudge-related excursions include the redeveloped Kallang Bishan waterway which transformed a concrete 2.7 km canal (Kallang River) into a 3 km-long sinuous, natural river, with bio-engineered river edges using various plants and bedding materials; Cambridge Road Estate, a low-lying site with a historical record of flooding and limited capacity to increase drain size any further, where several stakeholders such as Government bodies, citizens, and design firms collaborate with a focus on building community resilience and blue-green infrastructure; Pulau Ubin's Chek Jawa Wetlands with its six natural habitats (sandy beach, rocky beach, seagrass lagoon, coral rubble, mangroves, and coastal forest), and our sea-based fish farms.

A weekend stay on a *kelong* to study the impact of shifting climatic patterns on traditional fish farming (the increase in water temperature can lead to more bacteria, viruses, and microbiomes) combined with a boat trip to the new AI-powered Singapore Aquaculture Technologies' (SAT) smart fish farm ("Aquaculture 4.0") or an excursion to Lazarus Island to see how its man-made sea walls with its "rescued corals" can reduce the loss of marine biodiversity seems like an attractive climate education and learning approach. However, the empirical evidence base to come up with the "right" behavioural (nudging) interventions during such site visits is still very weak.

Climate Catastrophe

Other nudging-related challenges faced by climate stakeholders include ethical implications (e.g. "unacceptable paternalism") and lack of understanding of how to design effective technology-mediated nudges.

With regard to digital commitment nudges towards more eco-friendly behaviour (an interesting example is Powerbar developed by Stanford ChangeLabs whose unique behaviour-changing interface design is aimed at reducing residential energy consumption), there is a need to skilfully manage the iterative behavioural design processes and systems testing for optimal behaviour-change purposes. While specialised behavioural design consulting firms and behavioural insights teams (= nudge units) will have the required competencies to alter people's behaviour in predictable ways, an open question is to what extent "non-tech" university instructors command such specialised competencies?

In view of the climate catastrophe (a "hard problem" which requires sacrifices now to reap benefits later according to Professor Meadows), climate-related skill-upgrading measures with emphasis on earth science, behavioural science-informed technology interventions (nudging), human-centric design, climatology, systems thinking-inspired games relevant to climate-change communication, public–private–people partnership (4P) approaches, citizen science, volunteer conservation action, etc. are indispensable so that we can effectively support our youths in adapting to life in a changing climate and to engineer a new sustainable system.

(The Business Times, 25 February 2021)

Index

Printed in the United States
by Baker & Taylor Publisher Services

Printed in the United States
by Baker & Taylor Publisher Services